A NEW SUFFOLK GARLAND

'AMAZING! We've found
two invitations to the
Queen's coronation'

Matt Pritchett, *Coronation Tickets*, 2021.

Matthew Pritchett MBE is a British cartoonist who has worked on the Daily Telegraph *under the pen name Matt since 1988. He lives in Suffolk.*

A New Suffolk Garland

A SUFFOLK ANTHOLOGY

Published for
The Festival of Suffolk
in association with
The Aldeburgh Bookshop

THE BOYDELL PRESS

A New Suffolk Garland
Edited by Elizabeth Burke, Dan Franklin, John and Mary James
Book design: Richard Barber
Layout: Simon Loxley

First published 2022
by The Boydell Press, Woodbridge
for The Festival of Suffolk Ltd
in association with The Aldeburgh Bookshop
ISBN 978-1-78327-693-6

The Boydell Press is an imprint of
Boydell & Brewer Ltd
PO Box 9, Woodbridge,
Suffolk IP12 3DF, UK
and of Boydell & Brewer Inc.
668 Mt Hope Avenue,
Rochester, NY 14620–2731, USA

website: www.boydellandbrewer.com

A CIP catalogue record for this book is available from the British Library

This publication is printed on acid-free paper

This Suffolk anthology
is respectfully dedicated to

Her Majesty the Queen

on the Occasion of
Her Platinum Jubilee

CONTENTS

Contents

Contents

LIST OF ILLUSTRATIONS

———————————

Thank you to all the writers and artists who have given their work so generously and whose love of Suffolk creates this astonishingly rich literary, artistic and musical county.

———————————

A New Suffolk Garland for the Queen

CLARE, COUNTESS OF EUSTON,
LORD-LIEUTENANT OF SUFFOLK

This year we celebrate an awe-inspiring anniversary, Her Majesty the Queen's Platinum Jubilee. Here in Suffolk, we dedicate this book to her, as a humble gift from a county she frequently visits and for which she has a great affection.

We all have a unique reason for loving Suffolk and this glorious book shines a light on everything we treasure. It is completely spellbinding, a magical mosaic of stories, reflections, poems and history pulled together by a golden thread of gentle humour to make us smile.

From the stark beauty of the Breckland wilds in the west across what has been described as the 'breadbasket of England', to the incomparable estuaries and crumbly coastline of the east, Suffolk is, undoubtedly, a county 'on the edge'.

We are the 'South-folk', but who are we? A good, kind and compassionate people. Artistic and creative. Modest and brave. Suffolk people have the courage of lions. I think of Boudicca with her flaming hair fighting invasion, our own Red Lion. Edmund, King and Martyr, slain by the Danes, quite rightly Patron Saint of England for hundreds of years, and should still be. The visionary authors of the Magna Carta, we like to remember them praying at the shrine of the Saint before they put pen to paper. Bartholomew Gosnold, the first explorer from these shores and founder of the first American colony, Jamestown in Virginia, sailed from Ipswich to the New World. The Duke of Wellington's famous tribute after Waterloo: 'If you need a regiment in the heat of battle to hold an impossible position, send for the Suffolks!' *Stabilis*, their motto. The heroism of Suffolk soldiers in the two World Wars, particularly the suffering of the 'forgotten army' in Southeast Asia. One and all, Suffolk has made us. Now we must have the confidence to look forward to a brilliant future.

May I extend a heartfelt thank you to the myriad contributors to this beautiful book for the generosity of their thoughts and words and to the editors for bringing it all together.

This is a tribute from Suffolk to our wonderful and glorious Sovereign.

God Save the Queen.

N O

River Little Ouse

Brandon

Lakenheath

Elveden

Euston

Redgrave

Honington

Rickinghall

Wortham

Mildenhall

Icklingham

River Kennet

Barton Mills

River Lark

Ixworth

Thornham

Kentford

Hengrave

Norton

BURY ST EDMUNDS

Gipping

Barrow

Newmarket

Woolpit

Ickworth

Haughley

Stowmar

CAMBRIDGE-SHIRE

Lidgate

Hawstead

Bradfield

Needham Market

Denston

River Glen

Lavenham

Bildeston

Haverhill

Kedington

Cavendish

Long Melford

River Brett

Clare

River Stour

Kersey

Hintlesham

River Box

Boxford

Hadleigh

Sudbury

Polstead

Stoke by Nayland

Nayland

East Bergh

Bures

0   5 miles

0   8 kilometres

E S S E X

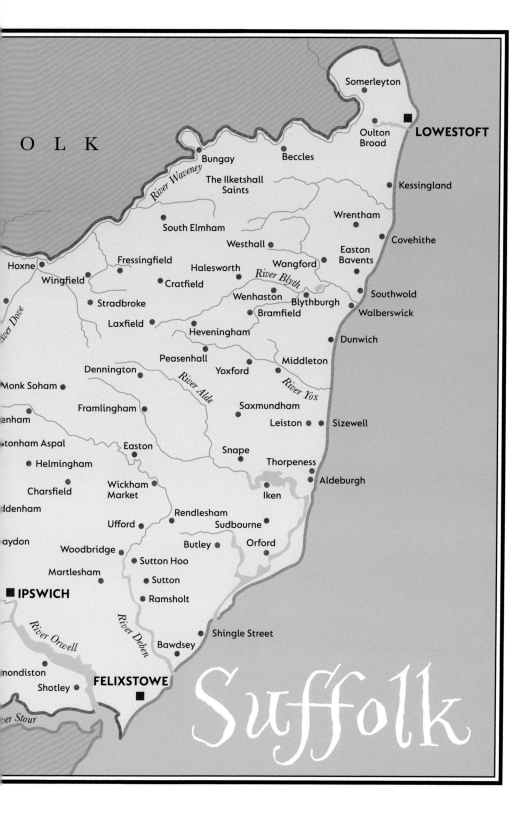

CRAIG BROWN

Introduction

Over the years, the garlands bestowed upon the county of Suffolk have not always smelt quite so sweet.

George Orwell set his dour novel *A Clergyman's Daughter* in Southwold, where he had been brought up. 'If you chose to climb the tower you could see ten miles or so across the surrounding country,' he observed. 'Not that there was anything worth looking at, only the low, barely undulating East Anglian landscape, intolerably dull in summer.'

A more recent Southwold resident, P.D. James, also chose to set her bleakest book there. In her dystopian *The Children of Men*, the town's senior citizens are dressed in white robes, then led into the sea and drowned. As they disappear below the waves, a band plays 'Somewhere Over the Rainbow', 'Abide with Me' and 'Nimrod' while the hero looks on. 'He wanted nothing more than to drive furiously away from this little town which spoke to him only of helplessness, of decay, of emptiness and death ...'

Happy days! I suppose how you view any town, or any county, depends upon your mood. W.G. Sebald could be very up-and-down, though most of the time notably more down than up. Never exactly Little Arthur Askey, his description of a Southwold nightfall in *The Rings of Saturn* plumbs new depths of Germanic despondency: 'The shadow of night is drawn like a black veil across the earth ... one might, in following the setting sun, see on our globe nothing but prone bodies, row upon row ... an endless graveyard for a humanity struck by falling sickness.'

Wisely, the editors of *A New Suffolk Garland* have picked a passage Sebald wrote in a sunnier frame of mind, when paying a visit to the town's Sailors' Reading Room, 'better than anywhere else for reading, writing letters, following one's thoughts, or, in the long winter months simply looking out at the stormy sea as it crashes on the promenade.'

And there are plenty of other writers who are prepared to celebrate Suffolk's joys. Recalling his pre-First World War childhood in Sudbourne, Kenneth Clark declares that his days were 'all pleasure', and says that, later in life: 'I found that the delicate music of the Suffolk coast, with its woods straggling into sandy commons, its lonely marshes and estuaries full of small boats, still had more charm for me than the great brass bands of natural scenery, the Alps or the Dolomites.'

The flatness of Suffolk is, of course, a given, but the responses it prompts— anything from despair to elation, with all stops in-between—are definitely subject to the mood of the observer. Julian Tennyson rejoices in the absence of any sort of view from above; for him, it's what makes Suffolk 'as full of surprises as a Christmas stocking'. Helen Macdonald lists a variety of things she loves about the landscape around Lakenheath, most of them defiantly unpicturesque: 'Forestry blocks, flooded fields, drainage ditches and twisted pines, poplars, reeds, American flags, biker cafés, rabbit-cropped turf and flint-faced cottages.'

The understatement of the landscape has long appealed to artists. We learn from Susan Owens that John Constable listed his favourite aspects of the countryside in 1821. They almost out-drab Helen Macdonald's: 'the sound of water escaping from Mill-dams ... Willows, Old rotten Banks, slimy posts & brickwork. I love such things.' Gainsborough contrived to make his landscapes additionally undramatic by painting them from tabletop models formed of humdrum bits and pieces. 'I have more than once sat by him of an evening, and seen him make models, or rather thoughts, for landscape scenery, on a little old-fashioned folding oak table which stood under his kitchen dresser', recalled one of his friends. 'He would place cork or coal for his foregrounds and make middle grounds of sand and clay, bushes of mosses and lichens, and set up distant woods of broccoli.'

Perhaps the restraint of the Suffolk landscape is what draws us to the sky. In winter, Melissa Harrison watches a kestrel as it hovers over a hedgerow, 'looking for the ultraviolet trails left by the urine of voles passing along their habitual runs'. In May 2020, with the country locked-down by the Covid pandemic, she listens to skylarks and yellowhammers and blackbirds, and delights in 'this sudden new love'. Swimming in the Waveney, Roger Deakin is confronted by a minimalist festival of insect erotica. 'Damselflies of all hues and patterns courted each other madly right in front of my nose, quite unconcerned. They even flew about *in flagrante*, performing the extraordinary feat of flying and copulating at the same time; a kind of insect Mile High Club.'

Bees, too, hover over the Suffolk landscape. George Ewart Evans recalls the courtesy with which they used to be treated: they respond well to good manners. Apparently, an old Debenham villager treated them so politely that he once took a swarm of bees in his hat, then put the hat on and walked home, unstung. Evans was informed by a villager from Stonham Aspal that, whenever there was a death in the family 'our custom was to take a bit of crepe out to the bee skeps and pin it on them. Then you gently tapped the skeps and told the bees who it was who had died. If you didn't do this, they reckoned the bees wouldn't stay, they'd leave the hives—or else they'd pine away and die.'

Is it also the flatness of Suffolk that gives rise to quite so many hallucinations? Or might they be real? We hear of the wild man of Orford, heaved up in the nets of local fishermen in 1200, gobbling raw fish after first squeezing all the moisture out of them with his bare hands. In that same century, two green-skinned children pop up in Woolpit, jabbering in a strange language. And then there is the ghostly hound Black Shuck bursting through the doors of Holy Trinity Church, Blythburgh, running up the nave, killing a man and a boy and causing the steeple to collapse through the roof.

Lucy Hughes-Hallett tells of the sciapod—a man with feet so large they act as a canopy for the rest of his body—carved on a pew-end at the church of St Mary the Virgin at Dennington. Kenneth Clark recalls the sound of ghosts whimpering outside his bedroom door in Sudbourne. More recently, 'a strange glowing object' emitting a pulsing red light on top and a bank of blue lights underneath was seen above Rendlesham Forest, sending the animals on a nearby farm into a frenzy. This is the sort of vengeful apparition M.R. James might well have homed in on— but instead it comes from an official memo of events witnessed by three security patrolmen and signed by Lt Col Charles Halt, the Deputy Base commander of the US Air Force at Woodbridge back in December 1980. Another UFO, whizzing at 90mph down those country lanes around Framlingham, is none other than Suffolk's very own Ed Sheeran, singing 'Tiny Dancer' as his head spins with teenage memories of throwing up. *A New Suffolk Garland* includes the lyrics for his touching love poem to his home town, 'Castle on the Hill'.

Suffolk has a reputation for murder, the more dramatic, the better. Ronald Blythe writes of St Edmund slaughtered by the Danes among the young oaks of Staverton, 'tied naked to one of the trees and made a target for arrows.' Ruth Rendell describes the murder of Maria Martin in the Red Barn at Polstead, which became one of the most popular melodramas of the Victorian era. A Bible bound in the skin of her murderer can still be viewed at the Moyse's Hall Museum in Bury St Edmunds.

The American crime writer Patricia Highsmith lived in Suffolk in the early 1960s. In her novel *A Suspension of Mercy*, she paints an evocative portrait of the worst kind of Suffolk ennui. An American writer, Sydney Bartleby, fantasises about murdering his wife, spurred on by his generalised irritation at his surroundings: the crockety plumbing of their cottage, its low wooden rafters on which he daily bumps his head, and the Suffolk soil that gets under his nails whenever he gardens. Even Suffolk's celebrated birdlife holds little appeal for poor Sydney.

'A huge blackbird pecked in the grass in front of Sydney. Somewhere else, the bird that attempted to sing "Blow the Man Down" was trying again. Sydney wondered what kind of bird it was. The sailorbird, perhaps. He shivered under his sweater as the sun went behind a cloud. He was bored to the point of sleepiness.'

Though *A New Suffolk Garland* is, for the most part, a celebration of the county, quite a few contributors seem to share Sydney's jaded point of view. Having booked into an Ipswich hotel, Charles Dickens's Mr Pickwick is led into 'a large, badly-furnished apartment, with a dirty grate, in which a small fire was making a wretched attempt to be cheerful, but was fast sinking beneath the dispiriting influence of the place'. After a series of misadventures, poor Mr Pickwick spends the night crouched in a corridor, waiting for morning.

Kenneth Clark finds his otherwise cheerful memories of childhood marred by 'servants who naturally despised me and felt in some obscure way that by ill-treating me they were getting their own back on their employers.' Accordingly, they give young Kenneth 'almost uneatable food, rancid butter and cheese so full of weevils that I remember pieces of it hopping about the table.'

It's not only the human population of Suffolk that can sometimes descend to shabby tactics. Paul Heiney details an impressive power struggle between his three Suffolk Punches, the most senior of which sees off its rivals by urinating into their hay.

Beneath the Suffolk skies, things appear and disappear, disappear and appear, like the ship at Sutton Hoo, unearthed after twelve hundred years, 'a giant apparition lying there before us'. Rustling around chunks of cliff that have broken off from a field of carrots, Julia Blackburn stumbles upon 'a human skull, packed tight with soil in which the roots of little plants were growing'. Wilkie Collins's brooding anti-heroine Magdalen stares out at the Aldeburgh sea, counting the ships as they come and go: if the number of vessels passing by during the course of half an hour is uneven, she will drink poison and die; if it is even, she will live.

There are plenty of treasures to find washed ashore in these pages; plenty to make you shiver or smile, delight or wonder. So no more paddling: the time has come to take the plunge.

JULIAN TENNYSON

Everything about Suffolk is Unexpected

From *Suffolk Scene: a Book of Description and Adventure* (1939)

Julian Tennyson (1915–1945), great-grandson of Alfred Tennyson, was only twenty-three when he wrote this captivating love letter of a book to his home county, published on the eve of the Second World War. From his home in Peasenhall, he explored the whole county by bicycle, chronicling a world that was about to be overturned by war. He died aged thirty in Burma and his memorial headstone is in Iken churchyard.

Suffolk in distant days was nicknamed 'Selig', a Saxon word meaning Blessed or Holy. A frivolous and irreverent posterity corrupted 'Selig' into 'Silly', and 'Silly Suffolk' is now a label for all time.

In aspect and outlook Suffolk seems content to amble along at least a century behind the rest of England. Because it has not been visited with the questionable comforts of modernity, it remains shy and unsophisticated. Not only are the people shy, but the spirit of the country itself is independent, capricious and elusive—if you don't treat it properly it will, like an unresponsive tortoise, retire to the seclusion of its own shell and escape you for ever. It is a country for the individualist, for the explorer and the lover of loneliness.

You will have to look for the charm of the Suffolk countryside—it is a charm most carefully hidden. Perhaps this is because we have no downs or high hills from which you can survey the landscape at your leisure—there is just one, 450 feet high, a few miles south-west of Bury St Edmunds, that I have vowed to make the goal of some future pilgrimage. When you can see farms and villages and woods spread out beneath you simply by sitting still and turning your head, then three-quarters of your exploration are already over. But you can't do that in Suffolk; you can never say for certain what is going to confront you round this bend in the lane or past that corner of the hedge, for the very reason that you can't see it. Suffolk is a disconcerting county, as full of surprises as a Christmas stocking, and I find this state of constant speculation one of its greatest delights. But don't think that we have no views at all; John Constable knew where to look for them, and he found in Suffolk some of the most beautiful in the country. And yet, because he knew that the coast did not suit his brush so well as the inland valleys, and because he never painted along that land which shelves down to the sea, there were others that even he did not find.

The views are all the more pleasing because they are unexpected. Everything about Suffolk is unexpected—views, valleys, villages, cottages, farms, the castles and abbeys that have made the county an antiquarian's Utopia. You never suspect their existence until you find them accidentally. An abbey, or what is left of it, may escape you in the guise of a battered cattle-shed, or it may leap at you from the middle of a cornfield, or show you but one coy, crumbled buttress from the protection of a thick wood. As to the castles, I can best show my meaning by telling you that I know one which has been converted into a railway station.

Walk through the county from the high, wide lands of the west, across the thicker, more confined and more sloping country of the centre and the east until you come to the marshes and the sea, and you will be moved by one sensation above all others: the feeling of solitude. Solitude, and all the beauty that goes with it, is the whole essence and character of Suffolk; not the severe, inhuman desolation of the wilderness, but that deep and inherent sense of peace which comes only from an old, wild land, a land too shy and too lonely and too forgotten ever to be tainted by the doubtful benefits of progress. Suffolk was once glorious and wealthy in material things; now it is poor and unkempt; but because no one has tampered with it, because for hundreds of years it has been left to mould its own shape and to decide its own destiny, it has managed to preserve within itself a calm strength and an inward loveliness which are the aftermath of its former power and pride. It is as if a high and noble family were to be stripped of all their worldly possessions. Their fortunes go down and down, but some intrinsic spiritual quality becomes stronger and more apparent in them, by contrast to their material state, with every buffet that adversity deals them. Thus it is with Suffolk; and Suffolk retains not the shell of some vanished glory, but the whole essential spirit of it. It is a spirit that lies deep, that touches the surface from beneath; but it is something so strong and vital that only a little individual sympathy is necessary to coax it from its seclusion.

I have tried to give you some idea of the character of this country as I know it, of the wildness and the loneliness that I love, and of the Suffolk that I would not change for any other county in England.

The Rendlesham Forest Mystery: The Halt Memo (1981)

One of the world's most famous UFO sightings took place in Suffolk. In 1980 an unidentified craft was reported to have landed close to RAF Bentwaters and RAF Woodbridge, where US Air Force personnel were stationed. The memorandum from the Deputy Base commander, Lieutenant Colonel Charles Halt, is the key document in the case.

DEPARTMENT OF THE AIR FORCE
HEADQUARTERS 81ST COMBAT SUPPORT GROUP (USAFE)
APO NEW YORK 09755

REPLY TO
ATTN OF: CD

13 Jan 81

SUBJECT: Unexplained Lights

TO: RAF/CC

1. Early in the morning of 27 Dec 80 (approximately 0300L), two USAF security police patrolmen saw unusual lights outside the back gate at RAF Woodbridge. Thinking an aircraft might have crashed or been forced down, they called for permission to go outside the gate to investigate. The on-duty flight chief responded and allowed three patrolmen to proceed on foot. The individuals reported seeing a strange glowing object in the forest. The object was described as being metalic in appearance and triangular in shape, approximately two to three meters across the base and approximately two meters high. It illuminated the entire forest with a white light. The object itself had a pulsing red light on top and a bank(s) of blue lights underneath. The object was hovering or on legs. As the patrolmen approached the object, it maneuvered through the trees and disappeared. At this time the animals on a nearby farm went into a frenzy. The object was briefly sighted approximately an hour later near the back gate.

2. The next day, three depressions 1 1/2" deep and 7" in diameter were found where the object had been sighted on the ground. The following night (29 Dec 80) the area was checked for radiation. Beta/gamma readings of 0.1 milliroentgens were recorded with peak readings in the three depressions and near the center of the triangle formed by the depressions. A nearby tree had moderate (.05-.07) readings on the side of the tree toward the depressions.

3. Later in the night a red sun-like light was seen through the trees. It moved about and pulsed. At one point it appeared to throw off glowing particles and then broke into five separate white objects and then disappeared. Immediately thereafter, three star-like objects were noticed in the sky, two objects to the north and one to the south, all of which were about 10° off the horizon. The objects moved rapidly in sharp angular movements and displayed red, green and blue lights. The objects to the north appeared to be elliptical through an 8-12 power lens. They then turned to full circles. The objects to the north remained in the sky for an hour or more. The object to the south was visible for two or three hours and beamed down a stream of light from time to time. Numerous individuals, including the undersigned, witnessed the activities in paragraphs 2 and 3.

CHARLES I. HALT, Lt Col, USAF
Deputy Base Commander

ED SHEERAN

Castle on the Hill (2017)

Singer-songwriter Ed Sheeran MBE has sold more than 150 million records worldwide, making him one of the world's best-selling music artists. This song was inspired by his upbringing in Framlingham. Released on the same day as 'Shape of You', 'Castle on the Hill' reached number two in a number of countries, including the UK, Australia and Germany, while 'Shape of You' debuted at number one. It was the first time in the history of the UK, Australian and German charts that an artist has taken the top two chart positions with new songs.

When I was six years old I broke my leg
I was running from my brother and his friends
And tasted the sweet perfume of the mountain grass I rolled down
I was younger then, take me back to when I

Found my heart and broke it here
Made friends and lost them through the years
And I've not seen the roaring fields in so long, I know I've grown
But I can't wait to go home

The Famous Dyed Sheep at the 2019 Latitude Festival at Henham Park, near Southwold.

John Nash, *Framlingham Castle*, 1956. Pen and ink sketch in the collection of
Ed Sheeran's grandfather, Dr Stephen Lock CBE.

I'm on my way
Driving at 90 down those country lanes
Singing to 'Tiny Dancer'
And I miss the way you make me feel, and it's real
We watched the sunset over the castle on the hill

Fifteen years old and smoking hand-rolled cigarettes
Running from the law through the backfields and getting drunk
    with my friends
Had my first kiss on a Friday night, I don't reckon that I did it right
But I was younger then, take me back to when

We found weekend jobs, when we got paid
We'd buy cheap spirits and drink them straight
Me and my friends have not thrown up in so long, oh how we've grown
But I can't wait to go home

I'm on my way
Driving at 90 down those country lanes
Singing to 'Tiny Dancer'
And I miss the way you make me feel, and it's real
We watched the sunset over the castle on the hill
Over the castle on the hill
Over the castle on the hill

One friend left to sell clothes
One works down by the coast
One had two kids but lives alone
One's brother overdosed
One's already on his second wife
One's just barely getting by
But these people raised me
And I can't wait to go home

And I'm on my way, I still remember
These old country lanes
When we did not know the answers
And I miss the way you make me feel, it's real
We watched the sunset over the castle on the hill
Over the castle on the hill
Over the castle on the hill

RICHARD CURTIS

Ed Sheeran Drops Round

From *Yesterday* (2018)

Yesterday is a musical romantic comedy film released by Working Title Films in 2019. It was directed by Danny Boyle, with a screenplay by Richard Curtis, based on a story by Jack Barth. Emma Freud was the script editor. The film is set in Suffolk and was filmed on location in Halesworth, Ramsholt, Shingle Street and the Latitude Festival. The final scene with 5,000 extras takes place on the beach at Gorleston-on-Sea.

Himesh Patel stars as struggling musician Jack Malik, who suddenly finds himself the only person who has ever heard of the Beatles and becomes famous after taking credit for their songs. In this scene Jack, accompanied by his friend and manager Ellie (played by Lily James), has just given a performance on the local TV station. Ed Sheeran played himself.

45 INT. ELLIE'S CAR. NIGHT.

They are in her car, later that night.

>   ELLIE
> That song was really beautiful.

Pause—this is sensitive territory. She senses a mystery.

>   ELLIE (CONT'D)
> When did you write it? … (a little shy)
> Who did you write it about?

He tries to avoid the issue …

>   JACK
> It doesn't matter really, does it—he asked me if I'd
> written any songs about warehouses?

Ellie laughs. Jack can't not.

>   JACK (CONT'D)
> I could have written every song of the Rolling Stones
> or David Bowie I'll always just be Lowestoft's warbling
> warehouseman.

>   ELLIE
> That's not true.

>   JACK
> It so obviously is. And also—actually stop the car. Stop
> here.

She stops it.

> JACK (CONT'D)
> Ellie—these songs—there's something about them that you
> should know …

At which moment his phone goes.

> JACK (CONT'D)
> Hi.

We hear a voice on the other side.

> ED
> Oh, hi - it's Ed Sheeran … The musician.

> JACK
> Beg your pardon?

> ED
> Ed Sheeran—I'm a musician—you may ….

Ellie mimes that she's going to drive on—and does.

> JACK
> No—seriously—who is it?

> ED
> Must be a bad line. I'll call you back.

> ELLIE
> Who was it?

> JACK
> He said it was Ed Sheeran, the musician.

> ELLIE
> That'll be Nick.

His phone goes again.

> JACK
> Nick?

> ED
> No, it's Ed Sheeran.

> JACK
> Can I speak to Carol?

> ED
> No one called Carol here.

> JACK
> Except there is. She's always there.

                    ED
Okay, mate, I'll leave it there. Amazing performance to-
night though, on TV. That song—"In My Life"—it was really beautiful.

He hangs up.

                    ELLIE
What did he say?

                    JACK
He said he liked "In My Life".

                    ELLIE
And what did Carol say?

                    JACK
She wasn't there.

Pause.

                    JACK (CONT'D)
I think it might have been Ed Sheeran.

                    ELLIE
The musician?

                    JACK
Yup.

46 INT. JACK'S BEDROOM. NIGHT.

He goes in to his little bedroom—takes off his t-shirt.
Then hears the doorbell go

                    MUM (V/O)
Jack! It's for you.

                    JACK
Who is it?

                    MUM (V/O)
His name's Ed.

47 INT. JACK'S HOUSE. HALLWAY/KITCHEN. NIGHT.

His Mum stands at the bottom of the stairs as Jack comes
down.

                    MUM
He's got a very friendly face.

Jack looks. It's Ed Sheeran, the musician. In the hallway.
He's very pleasant, very informal.

> ED
> Hi.

> JACK
> Oh. Hi. Come in.

> ED
> Your top's on the wrong way round, by the way.

> JACK
> O—yeah.

> ED
> Easy mistake.

Jack takes it off and puts it the right way round. They head into the kitchen.

> ED (CONT'D)
> So, you may be wondering why I'm here.

> JACK
> Not really—major popstars always dropping round.

> ED
> You're funny.

> JACK
> Well, funny looking at least.

> ED
> I don't know if you know—but I live round here—so I was just watching the TV and saw your song. And I thought it was really … remarkable. So I Googled you and heard the other ones on the Warehouse website. And, if anything, they were even better.

> JACK
> Wow. Thanks.

At that moment his Dad drifts in—in his pyjamas, slightly dishevelled—and starts to make himself a cheese sandwich.

> DAD
> Don't mind me.

Twice in the next minute Dad tries to open a drawer that Ed just happens to be standing in front of—and has to nudge him slightly out of the way.

> ED
> So, we've just lost our support act on the European leg of the tour and I wondered if you'd think about it.

        JACK
Support act for you? Seriously?

        ED
Yes. Why not?

        JACK
Wo! (freaked out …) When would I start?

        ED
Tuesday

        DAD
Do you know where the pickle is?

        ED
No, sorry.

        JACK
Tuesday?! Not like, next July.

        ED
No - Tuesday. Is your hearing okay, Jack?

        JACK
No, my hearing is perfect—it's just you keep saying really strange things. I'll have to get, you know, a passport. But yes, sounds great. How long do you want?

        ED
Thirty minutes max. Any longer than that they might get restless—"bring on the ginger geezer!"

        DAD
Good night …

Through his first messy mouthful of the sandwich.

        ED
Night night—nice meeting you, sir.

        DAD
You look like Ed Sheeran, you know.

        ED
I am Ed Sheeran.

        DAD
O right. Well done.

And leaves.

MILLICENT GARRETT FAWCETT

The Aldeburgh of Long Ago

From *What I Remember* (1924)

Millicent Garrett Fawcett (1847–1929) was a leading Suffragist and campaigner for equal rights for women. She led the biggest suffrage organisation, the non-violent NUWSS, from 1907–1919 and played a key role in gaining women the vote. She was also co-founder of Newnham College, Cambridge. She and her remarkable sister Elizabeth Garrett Anderson, the first female doctor in the UK, were born and brought up in Aldeburgh.

The year of my birth was the year of the Irish Famine and the repeal of the Corn Laws, and the following year saw the downfall of half the old autocratic Governments in Europe. Naturally, I cannot remember anything of these tremendous events; but they may possibly have had an electrifying effect upon the whole atmosphere in which I found myself as a little child. At any rate, I began to hear about public events, and to think, in my childish way, about them at an early age; for instance, I remember walking along the crag path at Aldeburgh (we always resisted with vehemence any Cockney attempt to call it The Esplanade, The Parade, or any such name) when I was young enough to be holding my father's hand and hearing him and listening with all my ears to his arguments, while he was persuading some of the leaders among the beachmen to volunteer for the Navy at the beginning of the Crimean War. I think this must have been in 1853; one man, I can recall perfectly, reiterating again and again that he was as ready as any man to sacrifice himself for his country, 'But wolunteer, sir, I will not.'

There was a very cordial and friendly feeling between my father and the seafaring men at Aldeburgh. He was a merchant and owned a small fleet of trading vessels which plied between our little town and London, and also Newcastle and the North. Later he built vessels for himself at his privileged place of business, Snape, a few miles higher up the river than Aldeburgh. He had some official position which connected him with the beachmen. I remember on his business writing-paper the, to me, mysterious words, 'Agent for Lloyds and Receiver of Droits of Admiralty'. The sound and look of the words *Droits of Admiralty* fascinated me.

In the old days of sailing vessels the coast of Suffolk, and particularly the Aldeburgh bay, were very dangerous, and there was never a wreck without my father being present, and if there were lives to be saved he took an active part in the dangerous and difficult work. The rocket apparatus for sending a cord or rope over a distressed ship had not then been perfected, and lives were often lost in the vain attempt to reach and save mariners in ships which had been storm-driven on one of the shoals off Aldeburgh. The gun, three times fired, which summoned the lifeboat crew for active service was a familiar and none the less an intensely thrilling sound in our ears.

Whenever the lifeboat was launched, even were it only for a practice, every man, woman, and child who heard the gun hurried to the beach, some to lend a hand, and all to see and wish and hope that the departing men would return in safety and bring their rescued comrades with them. It was a deep, angry sea where a tall man would be out of his depth three yards from the shore, and the great breakers in a storm beat with deadly weight upon men and ships alike.

I remember one awful day, 2nd November 1855, when there were seventeen ships driven ashore or broken up on the shoals off Aldeburgh in my father's district. Everything that possibly could be done was done, but there was a terrible loss of life. My father received the official thanks of the Royal National Lifeboat Institution, engrossed on vellum, for his services on this occasion. This document, which now belongs to my nephew Philip Cowell, runs thus: *That the special thanks of the Royal National Lifeboat Institution be presented to Newson Garrett, Esq., in testimony of his highly meritorious conduct in assisting to rescue through the surf nine out of the eleven of the crew of the Swedish brig 'Vesta', which in a gale of wind was wrecked near Orford Low Lighthouse on the 2nd November 1855.*

There was a family of seamen for which we ever after felt a deep bond of gratitude and affection—the Cables. My father and George Cable were taking a leading part in making a human chain along a rope to reach a shipwrecked crew in urgent distress and fetching them off one by one. My father went first, Cable second, and a good number following; after doing this and bringing in his man several times, my father showed signs of exhaustion, and Cable said to him, 'Look here, governor, you have done this often enough,' and he took the leading place on the rope from my father and assumed it himself; he never came ashore again; the rope snapped between my father and Cable, as if it had been pack thread, and Cable was washed away and perished in sight of the gallant men who had undertaken the work of rescue. My father was again, and by his own choice, in the place of the greatest risk, which had just ended fatally before his eyes. We were always taught by my mother to remember that Cable had saved my father's life.

James Cable, the son of George just referred to, was only a boy when all this happened, but as he grew in years he developed into a very fine seaman, much respected and well-known all along the coast and in the Lifeboat Society for combined courage and caution; for many years, indeed until old age compelled him to withdraw, he was coxswain of the Aldeburgh lifeboat. On one occasion this boat, under James Cable's command, had more than usually distinguished itself, so that newspaper men from London came down to learn and retail all the particulars of the brave work. They found Cable the very reverse of communicative; their only chance seemed to be to pump his narrative out of him in fragments, question by question. One of these, and Cable's reply to it, form a sort of epitome of his character.

James Cable, Coxswain of the Aldeburgh Lifeboat, in his cork life jacket, c. 1927.
James Cable (1851–1930) was one of the most celebrated Aldeburgh lifeboatmen. His memoirs,
A Lifeboatman's Days, *tell an astonishing story of courage and service. He received three silver*
medals after fifty years' service.

Newspaper Reporter: 'Now, Mr Cable, you can tell me, I expect, how many lives you have saved at sea.'

James Cable: 'I don't know, I'm sure, sir; I don't keep no count on 'em.'

This was the sort of thing that made everyone in Aldeburgh just love Cable, but he was not a bit spoiled—he was always the same simple, modest, upright man that his father had been before him.

Another incident of my childhood in connection with the lifeboat was an intense joy to me. The lifeboat gun had been fired, but only for a practice. The crew received three shillings a head for practice on a smooth day and five shillings on a rough day; this was a five-shilling day. We all ran off to the beach as usual, I, again, holding my father's hand. While the boat was still on the rollers one of her crew said to my father, 'Come along with us, governor,' he replied, 'I should like it, my lad, but you see I can't, I've got the child with me.' Looking down on me, the sailor rejoined, 'Little missie would like to come too, sir.' There was no need for me to say anything. I was too enchanted at this unexpected adventure. The smallest cork jacket in the collection was found and slipped over my head, and we embarked.

The seas broke over the boat as we crossed the shoal, and drenched my head and shoulders; one of the kind sailors produced a pink cotton handkerchief from his pocket and said, 'Here, missie, wrop this round your neck.' Of course, I did so, and of course, the pink handkerchief was soon as wet as the rest of my clothing. I was intensely happy, and never dreamed of being sea-sick.

My father was a very good sailor himself, and he never quite succeeded in ridding himself of the notion that to be sea-sick was affectation. One day, however, a little party of us, headed by my father and completed by a dog, embarked in a small boat for a sail. Before long the dog was sea-sick. My father was immensely astonished; he said several times, 'God bless my soul, look at that poor thing; then it is not affectation, after all.'

The Aldeburgh of my earliest recollections was very different from the Aldeburgh of today. It is true that its two ancient buildings, the church and the Moot Hall, still remain unchanged in essentials, but its ancient corporation has been re-formed. The two Bailiffs have been converted into one Mayor; and the Council is elected by the vote of the ratepayers; the dignified robes of office are retained, and so are the old silver maces dating from the reign of Queen Elizabeth, decorated by a large 'E' with a crown.

Crabbe's house has entirely vanished, but in lieu of it a bust of our one poet has been put up in the church. He is still our one poet …

At the time of my first visit to London, January 1858, the nearest railway station was at Ipswich, twenty-six miles away. The journey to London, the first I had ever taken, was one prolonged delight—first the drive of twenty-six miles in my father's carriage, himself, I think, driving, and then the railway train and all its wonders. I remember an old gentleman who travelled in our carriage and took a great deal of notice of us children, but whom we suspected of not being quite right in his mind, as he vehemently protested against the guard locking the carriage door, shouting out that he was a free-born Englishman and would not submit to being locked up.

NEIL MACGREGOR

Sutton Hoo Helmet

Anglo-Saxon Helmet, found at Sutton Hoo, Suffolk 600–650 AD
From *A History of the World in 100 Objects* (2010)

*Art historian Neil MacGregor was Director of the British Museum from 2002–2015.
This innovative history of human civilization through a selection of artefacts in the museum
was ground-breaking and has been much imitated.*

From the heat of Arabia, the rise of the Islamic empire and the reshaping of Middle Eastern politics after the death of the Prophet Muhammad, the next object takes us to the chill of East Anglia and a place where just over seventy years ago, poetry and archaeology unexpectedly intersected and transformed our understanding of British national identity. The discovery of this object—a helmet—was part of one of the great archaeological finds of modern times. It speaks to us across the centuries, of poetry and battle and of a world centred on the North Sea.

At Sutton Hoo, a few miles from the Suffolk coast, one of the most exciting discoveries in British archaeology was made in the summer of 1939. Uncovering the tomb of an Anglo-Saxon who had been buried there in the early 600s, it profoundly changed the way people thought about what had been called the 'Dark Ages'—those centuries that followed the collapse of Roman rule in Britain. Angus Wainwright, the National Trust archaeologist for the East of England, sets the scene:

> There are a number of large mounds, high up on an exposed ridge—about 100 feet up—looking down towards the River Deben. One of the biggest mounds, which we call Mound 1, is where the great ship grave was discovered in 1939, and we've got about eighteen or twenty other mounds around.

It was in this grave ship that the famous Sutton Hoo helmet was found, together with an astonishing range of valuable goods drawn from all over Europe: weapons and armour, elaborate gold jewellery, silver vessels for feasting, and many coins. Nothing like this had ever been found before from Anglo-Saxon England. The big puzzle, when the excavation took place, was that there was no body in the grave. But Angus Wainwright has an explanation:

> People wondered whether this could be a cenotaph, a burial where the body had been lost—a sort of symbolic burial. But nowadays we think a body was buried in the grave but because of the special acidic conditions of this soil it just dissolved away. What you have to remember is that a ship is a watertight vessel, and when you put it in the ground the water percolating through the soil builds up in it and it

basically forms an acid bath, in which all these organic things like the body and the leatherwork and the wood dissolve away, leaving nothing.

The discovery of this ship burial captured the British public's imagination—it was hailed as the 'British Tutankhamen'. But the politics of 1939 lent a disturbing dimension to the find: not only did the excavation have to be hurried because of the approaching war, but the burial itself spoke of an earlier, and successful, invasion of England by a Germanic-speaking people. Angus Wainwright describes what his team found:

> Very early on in the excavation they discovered ship rivets—the iron rivets that hold together the planks of a ship. They also discovered that the wood that had made up the ship had rotted completely away, but by a rather mysterious process the shape of the wood was preserved in a kind of crusted blackened sand. So by careful excavation they gradually uncovered the whole ship. The ship is 27 metres long; it's the biggest, most complete Anglo-Saxon ship ever found.
>
> Ships were very important to these people. The rivers and the sea were their means of communication. It was much easier to go by water than it was by land at this time, so that people in, say, modern Swindon would have been on the edge of the world to these people, whereas people in Denmark and Holland would have been close neighbours.

We still don't know who the owner of the boat was, but the Sutton Hoo helmet put a face on an elusive past, a face that has ever since gazed sternly out from books, magazines and newspapers. It has become one of the iconic objects of Britain's history.

It is the helmet of a hero, and when it was found, people were at once reminded of the great Anglo-Saxon epic poem *Beowulf*. Until 1939, it had been taken for granted that *Beowulf* was essentially fantasy, set in an imaginary world of warrior splendour and great feasts. The Sutton Hoo grave ship, with its cauldrons, drinking horns and musical instruments, its highly-wrought weapons and lavish skins and furs, and not least its hoard of gold and silver, was evidence that *Beowulf*, far from being just poetic invention, was a surprisingly accurate memory of a splendid, lost, preliterate world.

Look at the helmet, decorated with animal motifs made out of gilded bronze and silver wire and bearing the marks of battle. Then see what *Beowulf* has to say:

> To guard his head he had a glittering helmet
> that was due to be muddied on the mere-bottom
> and blurred in the upswirl. It was of beaten gold,
> princely headgear hooped hasped
> by a weapon-smith who had worked wonders
> in days gone by and embellished it with boar-shapes;
> since then it had resisted every sword.

Clearly the Anglo-Saxon poet must have looked closely at something very like the Sutton Hoo helmet.

I asked the Nobel laureate and poet Seamus Heaney, who made that translation of *Beowulf*, what the Sutton Hoo helmet means to him:

> I never thought of the helmet in relation to any historical character. In my own imagination it arrives out of the world of Beowulf and gleams at the centre of the poem and disappears back into the mound. The way to imagine it best is when it goes into the ground with the historical king or whoever it was buried with, then its gleam under the earth gradually disappearing. There's a marvellous section in the *Beowulf* poem itself, 'The Last Veteran', the last person of his tribe burying treasure in the hoard and saying, lie there, treasure, you belong to earls—the world has changed. And he takes farewell of the treasure and buries it in the ground. That sense of elegy, a farewell to beauty and farewell to the treasured objects, hangs round the helmet, I think. So it belongs in the poem but obviously it belonged in the burial chamber in Sutton Hoo. But it has entered imagination, it has left the tomb and entered the entrancement of the readers of the poem, and the viewers of the object in the British Museum.

The Sutton Hoo helmet belonged of course not to an imagined poetic hero but to an actual historical ruler. The problem is, we don't know which one. It is generally supposed that the man buried with such style must have been a great warrior chieftain. Because all of us want to link finds in the ground with names in the texts, for a long time the favoured candidate was Raedwald, King of the East Angles, mentioned by the Venerable Bede in his *Ecclesiastical History of the English People* and probably the most powerful king in all England around 620.

But we can't be sure, and it's quite possible that we may be looking at one of Raedwald's successors or, indeed, at a leader who's left no record at all. So the helmet still floats intriguingly in an uncertain realm on the margins of history and imagination. Seamus Heaney says:

> Especially after 11 September 2001, when the firemen were so involved in New York, the helmet attained new significance for me personally because I had been given a fireman's helmet way back in the 1980s by a Boston fireman which was heavy, which was classically made, made of leather with copper and a metal spine on it and so on. I was given this and I had a great sense of receiving a ritual gift, not unlike the way Beowulf receives the gift from Hrothgar after he kills Grendel.

In a sense, the whole Sutton Hoo burial ship is a great ritual gift, a spectacular assertion of wealth and power on behalf of two people—the man who was buried there and commanded huge respect, and the man who organized this lavish farewell and commanded huge resources.

The Sutton Hoo grave ship brought the poetry of *Beowulf* unexpectedly close to historical fact. In the process it profoundly changed our understanding of this whole chapter of British history. Long dismissed as the Dark Ages, this period, the centuries after the Romans withdrew, could now be seen as a time of high sophistication and extensive international contacts that linked East Anglia not

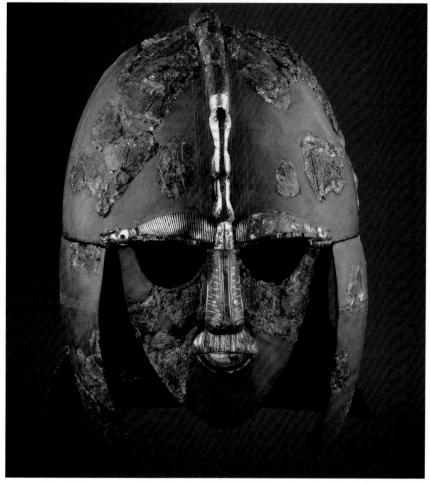

The Sutton Hoo Helmet.

just to Scandinavia and the Atlantic but ultimately to the eastern Mediterranean and beyond.

The very idea of ship burial is Scandinavian, and the Sutton Hoo ship was of a kind that easily crossed the North Sea, so making East Anglia an integral part of a world that included modern Denmark, Norway and Sweden. The helmet is, as you might expect, of Scandinavian design. But the ship also contained gold coins from France, Celtic hanging bowls from the west of Britain, imperial table silver from Byzantium and garnets which may have come from India or Sri Lanka. And while ship burial is essentially pagan, two silver spoons clearly show contact—direct or indirect—with the Christian world. These discoveries force us to think differently, not just about the Anglo-Saxons, but about Britain, for, whatever may be the case for the Atlantic side of the country, on the East Anglian side the

British have always been part of the wider European story, with contacts, trade and migrations going back thousands of years.

As Seamus Heaney reminds us, the Anglo-Saxon ship burial here takes us at once to the world of *Beowulf*, the foundation stone of English poetry. Yet not a single one of the characters in *Beowulf* is actually English. They are Swedes and Danes, warriors from the whole of northern Europe, while the ship burial at Sutton Hoo contains treasures from the eastern Mediterranean and from India. The history of Britain that these objects tell is a history of the sea as much as of the land, of an island long connected to Europe and to Asia, which even in AD 600 was being shaped and reshaped by the world beyond its shores.

JOHN PRESTON

Major Find in Suffolk

From *The Dig* (2007)

This novel about the excavation of the Anglo-Saxon burial ship at Sutton Hoo in 1939 is told from the perspectives of different characters involved in the dig. Here professional archaeologists Stuart and his wife Peggy Piggott (who was in fact the author's aunt) are summoned by Cambridge academic Charles Phillips to take over the work from the local amateur Basil Brown. Peggy describes the scene as they arrive at Mrs Pretty's estate.

Telegram to Stuart Piggott:

MAJOR FIND IN SUFFOLK STOP SHIP-BURIAL
EVEN BIGGER THAN OSEBERG STOP COME AT ONCE STOP BRING
WIFE STOP REGARDS PHILLIPS STOP

The next morning we drove out to the dig. It was only a couple of miles away, on the other side of the estuary to Woodbridge. The driveway passed through a tunnel of beech trees. Sunlight flickered between the leaves, casting patterns on the gravel below. The house itself was a large white Edwardian building, set up on a bluff above the river, complete with squash court and garages.

Despite my having tried to envisage the site beforehand, I was still astonished by what I saw. There was a majesty about the sweep and scale of the ship that far exceeded any expectations. There was also something intensely moving about its tenacious hold on survival. About the way in which it had resisted obliteration by transforming itself from one substance into another. From wood into sand. It was like a giant apparition lying there before us. I looked at Stuart and saw that he was just as affected.

Three men were lined up on one side of the trench, apparently waiting for us. Phillips introduced them. 'Mr Spooner and Mr Jacobs, and this is Mr Brown, who did such sterling work on the earlier stages of the dig.'

Mr Brown was a small, ferrety-faced man wearing an ancient tweed jacket and what might once have been a matching tweed cap. After we had shaken hands, Stuart and I began by dividing the centre of the ship into a grid. We then laid down a planning frame and marked off the squares with lengths of string. The men, meanwhile, were put to work shifting the spoil heaps—Phillips had decided these were too near the ship and should be moved further away. With only one wheelbarrow between them, this proved to be a lengthy business.

Stuart and I, however, made rapid progress. Once we had divided the ship into squares, we started cleaning down the south side of the burial area. During the morning Mrs Pretty and her son, Robert, came out to see how we were getting along. Once again, Phillips performed the introductions. Mrs Pretty seemed much too old to be the mother of such a young son. The boy, Robert, twisted shyly away while he was being introduced and then ran off towards the spoil heaps as soon as Phillips had finished.

[The next day] Stuart and I started where we had left off. He carried on making a map of the site, while I continued trowelling and sieving in the southern corner of the burial chamber. The clouds soon parted and lifted. By the time Mrs Pretty and Robert came out, the sun was shining more fiercely than it had done all summer. I wished I had packed a hat—my skin turns an off-puttingly dark shade of brown in the sun.

At eleven o'clock, Mrs Pretty's butler brought out a tray with two jugs of lemon barley water on it and some glasses. We all broke off and drank our fill. No one said very much. I know that I am apt to misread people's moods, but it seemed to me to be an eager, expectant sort of silence. A sense of anticipation that everyone shared, but no one wished to acknowledge out loud.

When we had finished, I set off again. The crust of earth felt quite solid beneath my feet. Dust rose all round, caking my hands and stiffening my hair. Normally, there is something not simply absorbing about narrowing one's focus to such a small area, but also soothing. Your world has shrunk to a few square inches of earth and nothing else matters. Nothing else can be allowed to matter.

As my hands kept on trowelling, my eyes started to mist over. Angrily, I wiped the moisture away. It was only then that I saw what was lying in front of me. My first thought was that I must have dropped something. Or that someone else must have done. It looked so bright, so raw. So absurdly new.

I reached out and my fingers touched a small, hard object. At the same time I heard myself saying, 'Oh,' in a faraway voice. Then I picked it up. Lying in the palm of my hand was a gold pyramid. It was flattened on top and decorated with what appeared to be tiny pieces of garnet and lapis lazuli. In the centre of the flattened top was a square made up of even tinier blue and white chequered glass.

CHARLIE HAYLOCK

A Suffolk Glossary

From *Sloightly on th' Huh! An affectionate look at the Suffolk Dialect* (2004)

Charlie Haylock is an historian of spoken English, a dialect specialist, and an authority on his native Suffolk. His favourite Suffolk term is Hobbly Dobbles for molehills. He was Ralph Fiennes's dialect coach for the film of The Dig.

Suffolk is where the English (the Angles) first settled and gave England, English and East Anglia their names. It is where the Angles and Saxons first mixed and formed the basis for our rich language. So Suffolk is where the English language began and by simple deduction, Suffolk is the oldest English dialect.

Suffolk is a complete mix of all our uninvited guests, from the Romans to the Normans, plus those that were invited, like the Dutch. Only in Suffolk do you find this particular rich mix. Up till about fifty years ago, East Anglia was very insular; it was that large lump on the side of England. No one passed through to get somewhere else. You actually had to visit the place. This meant the dialect was largely unspoiled by outside influences, especially inland, away from the coast and the limited number of resorts.

Generally, with films, TV, travel, so-called education and a host more influences, the English dialects appear to be changing into accents, which are changing into brogues, which are changing into lilts, which are changing into a sameness. Fortunately there are still enough people living to keep the Suffolk dialect alive for a while longer yet.

This is a glossary of Suffolk words. A few are ordinary English words with a different Suffolk meaning. Some just plain Suffolk.

Abroad —Outside the local vicinity

Airy-wiggle —the earwig (from Old English earwicga, a compound of 'eare' ear + *wicga*, probably related to *wiggle*, so named because it was thought to crawl into people's ears)

Bang—a type of cheese made in Suffolk from milk skimmed several times; as a consequence it is very hard. Also known as *Suff'k thump*. It has poetically been described as 'too large to swallow and too hard to bite'.

Barley Bird—the nightingale

Chates—scraps; leftover food

Dungy—not very good

Ebble—the aspen tree

Furrener—anyone born outside the local area, especially someone from outside Suffolk

Gussock—a strong and sudden force of wind; a gust

Haggy—newly ploughed soil

Jammock—to beat to a pulp

Kedgy—alive, alert. *'How dew yew fare? Kedgy 'n' well, bor.'*

Lorker—a seagull

Maggoty—pernickety, fastidious. 'She be too maggoty t'eat stoo 'n' dumpl'ns'

Nannocking—to idle about, play the fool

Ought—nought, zero

Quackle—to choke

Rokey—misty, foggy

Sally—the hare (via Norman French from Latin *salire*, 'to leap')

Sloightly on th' huh—lop-sided or wonky

Twizzling stick—a stick used to flatten beer/ale that is too gassy or lively by giving it a twizzle or stir

Wet bird—the green woodpecker

Yip—to chirp and sing like a newly hatched bird

DAVID SHEEPSHANKS

The Tractor Boys: Ipswich Town
2000–2001

David Sheepshanks CBE was chairman of Ipswich Town Football Club from 1995 to 2009. During this time he oversaw a complete reorganisation of the club which led to the club's promotion back to the Premier League in 2000 and qualification for the UEFA Cup. Here he describes the moment remembered by all ITFC fans. This extract is from his forthcoming memoir.

'Naylor to Reuser, he's stabbed it through, Reuser is onside … Reuser … PREMIERSHIP!'

For every Ipswich Town fan of that era, these are the immortal words of ITV commentator, Peter Drury. Many of us were, of course, there at Wembley, so we only saw or heard this commentary afterwards and still, whenever I hear it twenty years on, the spine shivers and the hairs stand on the back of my neck.

And when interviewed in the heat of excitement afterwards, the words, 'the best day of my life' came tumbling out of my mouth, emotionally and perhaps ill-considered. When seeing the interview the next day on television, my wife, Mona, said with incredulity, 'The best day of your life?' 'Of my football life,' I quickly corrected. Wedding-day bliss was not in doubt, however; Ipswich back in the Premiership was an exhilarating close second.

Against all the odds and after being repeatedly frustrated and thwarted at many a turn in the preceding five years, we had to endure the 'so near yet so far' Bridesmaid tag. In repeated play-off defeats, journalists would say, 'Well, David, let's face it, this is the end of the Premier League dream, isn't it, you'll have to sell your best players, won't you?' 'No, this is not the end, it is incredibly disappointing, heart-breaking even, to come so close. Selling players is for another day, but we will learn from this, take stock and come again even stronger next season.'

For all of us who persevered throughout those five years, it was, as ever, a gigantic team effort by players, staff, directors and fans united, this was indeed a TRIUMPH TO TREASURE. Ipswich Town back in the Premier League in 2000, in what was the last competitive club game at the old Wembley, it was a dream come true.

Back in the Premiership, we were on the crest of a wave. Looking back, I only wish we could have bottled the extraordinary spirit and togetherness we had as a club that year both on and off the field.

We rode it all summer, signing only one player, the lion-hearted Hermann Hreidarsson, to complement the terrific team that manager George Burley and captain Matt Holland had moulded. Now, in our first home match of the season, we were welcoming Manchester United, Sir Alex Ferguson, David Beckham and all to a fever-pitched capacity crowd at Portman Road as Fabian Wilnis blew the roof off with his early opening goal and, as the season progressed, we were beating both Liverpool and Leeds away.

Unbelievably, we qualified for Europe in fifth place (and, but for the last-day results) might have even qualified for the Champions League.

It was dizzy stuff. George Burley deservedly scooped the Manager of the Year Award and, as the Pride of Anglia that year, our fans memorably christened us 'The Tractor Boys'.

Into Europe we strode, the following year defeating Torpedo Moscow and Helsingborg in memorable trips away for the fans. None more so than our visit to the San Siro for the third round, second leg versus Inter Milan. We had quite wonderfully beaten them 1-0 at Portman Road: however, the visit to Milan proved one step too far as the mighty Brazilian, Ronaldo, and his teammates came out 4-1 winners.

Over 9,000 fans travelled from Suffolk to support the team. Witnessing the sea of blue and white in Piazza Duomo (outside Milan Cathedral) is a sight that will stay with me and many others for ever. A chorus of thousands of wonderful Suffolk voices made us all so proud to be Tractor Boys.

Not least one senior supporter who epitomized the practical sense of humour of our county: *'Daievid, you see that there spoire on Cathedral and the loit on top, how do yer reckon they chainge the loit bulb, bor?'* Oh! So happy memories!

A More Gentle Country (2021)

Josephine left Rwanda in 2013 with her two young sons; her husband had left three years earlier, and had studied and settled in Suffolk. Josephine is a home carer for the elderly. They now have three boys and live in the county.

I was born into a big family but when the fighting started, my family was killed, apart from my aunt. I came to England in November 2013; when I got off the plane, I thought I was going to a beach—I was wearing a summer dress and sandals. I had never worn trousers or jeans in my life, only dresses. So the cold was a great shock to me. In my country we have only two seasons and it's never as cold as here. My husband had bought me a jacket but when I arrived in Suffolk I was very, very cold.

We went to our local church and another woman looked at me and could see I was only wearing a cotton dress. She took me aside and showed me what she was wearing, several T-shirts on top of each other, and she showed me how to wear layers to get warm. So I went to the shops and bought winter things.

When I first came, I used to see people wearing hats and gloves and boots. And I wondered 'Are they real?' I thought they might be mannequins like in shop windows, or statues. I was surrounded by all these unreal people. But as soon as I worked out how to wear winter stuff I thought, 'I am going to be a statue too!' Another strange thing was to see trees without leaves, and leaves all over the ground. I thought, 'Why in this country are there dead trees everywhere?' When I travelled to work by bus everyone waited in a queue—that's not normal in my country. I thought 'Wow, this is a more gentle country.'

I was struggling with English and people were trying to be kind and to teach me. Friends from the church used to come to my house to chat with a cup of tea every week. I went to a class for refugees. So when I came to Suffolk my first family was the church, and my second family was the Suffolk Refugee Support organisation. I've found a lot of friends through them, it's an amazing place.

I love Suffolk. If you go out to the shops everything closes at about four, and there aren't lots of bars open in the evening like in London. It's a quiet place, a lovely place to live. We're lucky that we have our own garden now and also a park where my boys can ride bikes and play with friends. When I go to the park with my children some white people don't like their children to play with my children. But others are happy. I don't mind, most people are friendly and they ask where you come from, and they want to know about your country.

I miss my family and friends in Rwanda but now with technology we can talk on WhatsApp (before, it used to be so expensive to top up the mobile card). We have a group which reads the Bible together; we all read the Bible every day and we post comments and questions.

I love my job as a carer. I'm looking after old people and they're nice to me. But I really, really want to go to university and train to be a nurse. At the moment my English is not good enough. My husband is studying for his Masters, so we are all students in my house. I struggle with English spelling and work as hard as I can. We speak our own language at home, but the younger boys now know more English.

The people here have everything, they don't know suffering. If you don't have money people will help you; if you want to be educated they will help you. At home I had to walk two hours to school. Here everything is easy. But I know what it's like to live with nothing. And I'm used to wearing trousers now. I enjoy it. It's much more practical. Because I wear trousers, I am even learning how to ride a bike!

ESTHER FREUD

A Summer Fête

From *The Sea House* (2003)

Inspired by the letters of Esther Freud's grandfather, the architect Ernst Freud, her evocative novel is set in the coastal village of Steerborough (Walberswick). The story alternates between two time-frames: in the present, Lily is spending her summer in Steerborough reading the letters between architect Klaus Lehman and his wife Elsa; in the past, the story follows a group of German-Jewish émigrés in the summer of 1953.

Lily was still sitting outside the beach hut when she heard music drifting to-wards her from the Green. She stood up and stretched, and trudged off through the dunes.

The Green had transformed into a fair. Children, their faces painted—butter-flies, leopards, cats and clowns, monsters, bumblebees and princesses—ran from game to game. Some tried their luck at bowling, throwing quoits, while others knocked coconuts from posts which actually fell when they were hit. The littlest ones dug for parcels in the lucky dip or bought tenpence tickets for the tom-bola. Behind a table two women and a man stood guarding a bowl of fruit. Lily watched as a boy paid his money and picked up a bell. As soon as it rang, the adults pulled blindfolds down over their eyes and began to spin their arms. They spun them fast until the bell rang again, and then they stopped and plunged their hands into the bowl.

'Bad luck.' The man smiled, pushing up his blindfold. 'Two bananas and a pear.' And as a consolation prize for failing to win on the human fruit machine the unlucky gambler was offered a boiled sweet.

There was a cake to guess the weight of. A doll that needed you to guess her name. And then the music that had led her here started up again. A band was playing right outside Lily's house. It was the girl from the ferry, singing into a microphone still in her rowing clothes, her heavy boots, her jeans, a short-sleeved T-shirt showing the smooth brown ripple of her arms. There was a boy on key-boards with bright white hair, and another, darker boy who played the sax.

Lily hummed along to the music as she sifted through a stall of clothes. She pulled out polka-dot aprons, rose-patterned dresses in size 20 and up, candy-striped shirts, their cuffs scorched by irons, and a green velvet jacket with '70s lapels.

'One pound the lot,' Ethel called to her, hardly visible over the mountain of remaining clothes, and Lily, rather than throw them back, rummaged for her change.

A little further on, two tables had been pushed together. They were piled with

The Human Fruit Machine at the Orford Flower Show and Fête, 2021.

lampshades, napkin rings, dishcloths and bowls. Scattered on the grass around were deckchairs and an old bicycle with rusty wheels. Lily picked up a small tin saucepan with a compartment inside dented like the petals of a flower. What it was she didn't know, but it was irresistibly pretty. 35p the label said and Lily held out her money.

'Oh,' the stall-holder protested. 'The egg poaching pan. That was from a previous fête. It's 25p now.'

The window of Fern Cottage was latched open, and Lily pushed her purchases through. What on earth am I going to do with them? she wondered, but she couldn't help herself, she went out to search for more.

At the far end of the Green the raffle was being drawn, the numbers and prizes ringing out from a loudspeaker—a hamper from Stoffer's, a bottle of whisky, dinner for two at The Ship! And then a whistle blew and the children flew from every corner of the Green to where the Punch and Judy show had been set up. They arranged themselves in rows, cross-legged, gazing up, and then the Punch and Judy man appeared from behind his booth. He was tall and thin with a striped blazer, and his nose was miraculously hooked to fit his job. The children tensed towards him, their faces alight, and when he had them enchanted, he stepped back inside. Lily moved closer to watch. Bash went Punch. Waaa went Judy. Grrr went the dog. Hurrah shouted the children when the policeman appeared. Bash went Punch. Waa went the baby.

BROUGH SCOTT

Suffolk's Greatest Treasure (2021)

Brough Scott is a British horse racing journalist, radio and television presenter, and a former jockey.

Never undersell your heritage even if you only have the right to half of it. Suffolk, through the virtues of Newmarket, can claim to be the cradle of Britain's greatest gift to the animal kingdom, the thoroughbred racehorse, the fastest weight-carrying creature the world has ever seen. The snag is that a good bit of that cradle is in Cambridgeshire.

The 'greatest gift' is no small claim even if it's hard to weigh the merits of the opposition. If Hereford Cattle or Yorkshire Pig might be the most numerous, the Suffolk Punch the most local, and the King Charles Spaniel the most historically relevant, none of them are a patch on the ubiquity or the wonder of the thoroughbred. Back in the early eighties I even wrote a book about it.

From Sha Tin to Saratoga, San Isidro to Sydney, New York to Newmarket, photographer Gerry Cranham and I logged the people, places, and above all the horses, that populate our racing world. Amidst all the intoxicating differences it was easy to forget that all of the equine athletes involved were of the same breed and all of them traced back to three stallions imported from the Middle East in the late seventeenth and early eighteenth century and then developed in races which centred on Newmarket.

It was at Newmarket that racing was first called 'The Sport of Kings' for the simple reason that it was at Newmarket that Charles I, and more importantly his 'Merrie Monarch' son Charles II, found their sport by racing horses across the Heath. James I did a bit of it too but he was more involved with his unattractive hunting obsessions which included the perceived health benefits of dabbing his feet in the hot blood of stricken deer. Ugh!

Charles II's evening diversions are rather better known and his mistress Nell Gwyn was installed in a house right next to the Palace he had built just off the High Street. On that site the National Horseracing Museum is now an essential stop. Opened in 2016, it tells one of Britain's proudest stories using everything from ancient prints to ultra-modern video footage of the heart rate and air intake of the galloping horse.

The human heart rate can be as slow as 40 beats a minute and go up to 180, but a racehorse's heart goes from 25 to 240 beats a minute—that's 4 beats a second. A racehorse takes in 18 to 20 litres of air per breath so would take in 10,000 litres of air during a two-and-a-half-mile race. A human athlete takes 60 breaths,

John Wootton, *The Warren Hill, Newmarket*, c. 1715.

This picture is one of the most celebrated images of eighteenth-century racing. George Vertue recounted how John Wootton (1685–1764) 'by his assiduous application & the prudent management of his affairs rais'd his reputation & fortune to a great height being well esteemed for his skill in landskip … & in great vogue & favour with many persons of ye greatest quality, his often visiting of Newmarket in the seasons produced him much imployment in painting of race horses, for which he had good prices, 40 gns for a horse.' The artist himself can be seen standing in the foreground sketching the grey.

that's 300 litres of air a minute so would take 10 hours to move the amount of air a horse does in two-and-a-half mile race. Purists may claim that the title of fastest weight-carrying creature belongs to the American 'Quarter Horse' but its speed, a slightly quicker pace, only lasts for a quarter mile. It would be well beaten at five-eighths of a mile, the shortest thoroughbred distance, and probably lapped if they attempted two and a half.

But, revel in the history as you should, the true pleasure of the thoroughbred at Newmarket is to see them on the hoof—and there are literally thousands of them. Forty years ago I recorded 1700 horses on the gallops and forty trainers.

Today, despite perennial problems with staff recruitment and uncompetitive prize money, there are seventy trainers, 3000 active racehorses and as many again in mares and foals and youngstock in the studs and preparatory yards that ring Suffolk's, or is it Cambridgeshire's, unique equine city.

The riders in John Wootton's famous picture of horses galloping up Warren Hill 300 years ago may have rather different kit, and the idler trainers use a carriage rather than a Cadillac, but what they are doing is essentially the same. Conditions may have changed radically since I wrote that book in the eighties when few of the fifty miles of gallops were railed off, women hardly featured as stable staff let alone as jockeys, and Asian stable lads were a distinct oddity. In early June 2021, Hollie Doyle had ridden more winners in the year than any other jockey, a large percentage of stable staff were either female or Asian and white rails with advanced fibre-sand surfaces adorn the 2,500 acres of what must be the world's largest area of tended grassland. Go out and watch early of a morning. Better still, at least in mind if not in body, put yourself on a horse and point up Warren Hill.

To saddle up an old line it is among 'the most fun you can have with your clothes on.' In the first half of 2005 I was involved in the happiest of projects, to record the progress of Motivator, the Derby favourite, on his road to Epsom. Every month from January, snowfall to summer sunshine, I had a galloping observation post as I spun up Warren Hill in the wake of the sparky three-year-old who on the 4th of June would leave his rivals floundering as he scorched to Classic glory.

Up beyond the gallops the eyesore that is Warren Towers is one of the less pleasing evidence of the unprecedented Middle Eastern investment by Sheikh Mohammed and his brothers and by other big owners from the region most notably the late Prince Khalid Abdullah from Saudi Arabia. All around stud buildings have been refurbished, paddocks revitalised and in 2012 it was Prince Khalid's Frankel who lit up Warren Hill as the most exciting horse of modern times.

Today Frankel has just fathered his first Derby winner and holds court as the world's most sought-after young stallion a couple of miles south at Banstead Manor, the heart of Prince Khalid's magnificent Juddmonte bloodstock empire. It is not the least treasured of Newmarket memories to wind the clock back to 1890 and picture a fifteen-year-old Winston Churchill riding up from that same Banstead Manor alongside his father to watch Lord Randolph's 1889 Oaks winner L'Abbesse de Jouarre do her own spin up Warren Hill.

Forget about Cambridgeshire's slice, what Suffolk has at Newmarket is something beyond exaggeration. It houses one of the most wonderful parts of living, galloping history.

BILL OPPENHEIM

The Newmarket Sales

From *Tattersalls 250 Years* (2016)

Tattersalls is the oldest bloodstock auctioneer in the world and the largest in Europe. It was founded in 1766 by Richard Tattersall, who had been stud groom to the second Duke of Kingston. It sells over 10,000 thoroughbreds each year. Auctions for horses can be as exciting as the races that will be run. Kings, sheikhs and celebrities flock to find their own Frankel. Journalist and pedigree consultant Bill Oppenheim describes an auction.

The real action is inside, in the Ring. Much of the time it's just humdrum, every-day stuff, horses selling for a few thousand, tens of thousands, hundreds of thousands of that quaint currency known as 'guineas'. But as the appearance of a top lot nears—especially after nightfall—the crowds rush in, the place is packed—but quiet. Hushed. The teams find their spots, some hidden, some not. John Magnier and the Coolmore team are in their customary spot at the top of the stairs above the so-called Bidders Only enclosure. Sheikh Mohammed and his team might be on the wall directly below them. Might not.

If the Sales grounds are a campus, then this is the campus theatre, you bet. As an American who's been attending Sales at Tattersalls for more than thirty years—well, as any American who's only been here once can tell you—the pace of the Sales is completely different here. It has a calmer, more gentlemanly feel. In Kentucky they're yipping and challenging you; at Tattersalls it's quieter, less frantic, more dramatic and less brusque and businesslike—takes longer, too, though at the end of the proceedings those gentlemanly types are just as deadly at extracting that last guinea as their American counterparts are at squeezing out that last dollar. There's a big difference in the presentation, too: in Kentucky, the horses stand in the Ring; at Tattersalls they're walking around the Ring the whole time.

So when the crowds gather and hush falls, it's magic. The bidding starts, sometimes very slowly. 'C'mon, the horse is going to make a million, you don't need to think about bidding fifty thousand.' It's hushed; it's tense. It's like watching tennis in slow motion: a nod; a twitch. You're trying to look inconspicuous. Then the auctioneer calls out something more helpful like, 'The bid is against the wall, with the light green sweater and baseball cap.'

Then, when the serious bidders step out of their hiding places against walls, hidden on the stairs, behind doors, in 'the Gods'—well, it's very dramatic; you can imagine. Hushed. Eyes are trained at the top of the stairs by the 'Bidders', at the Coolmore team. Or eyes are trained somewhere else, around a corner. A nod; a twitch. Are you bidding? Is that a bid? Big money. Great theatre.

Sir Alfred Munnings, *Moving up for the Start: Under Starter's Orders*, Newmarket, c.1937.

Sir Alfred Munnings (1878–1959) was known as one of the finest British Impressionist painters of the twentieth century. He was born in Mendham on the Suffolk-Norfolk border and spent most of his life on the Suffolk-Essex border in Constable Country in the village of Dedham at Castle House (now the Munnings Art Museum). During the First World War he was posted to the Western Front, where he worked at a horse remounting depot, before being commissioned as an official war artist to the Canadian Cavalry Brigade.

A prolific painter, he left a body of work that largely depicts rural scenes, racing and hunting, and most commonly his favourite animal, the horse. Munnings' equine portraits attracted the attention of patrons on both sides of the Atlantic, including a portrait of Queen Elizabeth II with her champion racehorse, Aureole, at the Epsom Derby.

FRANKEL

A Champion Pedigree

Frankel (b. 2008) is a bay horse with a large white star, a white snip just above his nose, and four white feet. He was bred by Juddmonte Farms and trained by Henry Cecil, and is owned by the late Khalid bin Abdullah. He was unbeaten in his fourteen-race career and was the highest-rated racehorse in the world from May 2011. The World Thoroughbred Racehorse Rankings Committee rank Frankel as the best racehorse they have assessed since their ratings were introduced. Frankel's performance in the 2000 Guineas in 2011 has been described as 'one of the greatest displays on a British racecourse'.

Frankel is now retired and standing at stud at Banstead Manor Stud at Cheveley in Suffolk, where he was born. He covered his first mares on Valentine's Day, February 2013. His current stud fee is set at £175,000.

Galileo b 1998	Sadlers Wells b 1981	Northern Dancer b 1961	Nearctic br 1954	Nearco
				Lady Angela
			Natalma b 1957	Native Dancer
				Almahmoud
		Fairy Bridge b 1975	Bold Reason b 1968	Hail to Reason
				Lalun
			Special b 1969	Forli
				Thong
	Urban Sea ch.1989	Miswaki ch 1978	Mr Prospector b 1970	Raise a Native
				Gold Digger
			Hopespringseternal ch 1971	Buckpasser
				Rose Bower
		Allegretta ch 1978	Lombard ch 1967	Agio
				Promised Lady
			Anatevka ch 1969	Espresso
				Almyra
Kind b 2001	Danehill b 1986	Danzig b 1977	Northern Dancer b 1961	Nearctic
				Natalma
			Pas de Nom br 1968	Admirals Voyage
				Petitioner
		Razyana B 1981	His Majesty b 1968	Ribot
				Flower Bowl
			Spring Adieu b 1974	Buckpasser
				Natalma
	Rainbow Lake b 1990	Rainbow Quest b 1981	Blushing Groom ch 1974	Red God
				Runaway Bride
			I Will Follow b 1975	Herbager
				Where You Lead
		Rockfest ch 1979	Stage Door Johnny ch 1965	Prince John
				Peroxide Blonde
			Rock Garden	Roan Rocket
				Nasira

RONALD BLYTHE

Staverton Thicks

From *The Time by the Sea* (2013)

The Time by the Sea is about Ronald Blythe's life in Aldeburgh during the 1950s. He had originally come to the Suffolk coast as an aspiring young writer, but found himself drawn into Benjamin Britten's circle and began working for the Aldeburgh Festival. Blythe is famous for his intimate portrait of a Suffolk village, Akenfield, *which was made into a film by Peter Hall in 1974.*

One April morning in 1956 I made one of my planless walks from Slaughden towards Orford and with the usual elated feeling. There would be a wonder midway although I knew nothing of its existence. All I experienced at this moment was a tossing about of freedom. The sea was glorious and near at hand, the gulls screamed and the air was intoxicating. At Slaughden the Alde turned into the Ore, and the Aldeburgh Marshes became the Sudbourne Marshes. On the left were the Lantern and King's Marshes. Orford Castle was the obvious destination but like a boy leaving the biggest sweet in the bag until last, I turned right towards Butley. Somebody had told me that Chillesford Church tower was pink because it contained lots of coralline crag. But what drew me would be the stunted oaks and the limited nature of things. And yet at the same time the grandeur of things, for Victorian aristocrats had shot over these acres. So I saw Hansel and Gretel Lodge, and dark entrances to country houses, and signposts to Hollesley where Brendan Behan would be a Borstal Boy. This walk would become a preface to a guidebook as yet unwritten. The poor soil of the Suffolk sandlings had made for skimpy farming but had provided the next best thing for shoots.

Just below it there existed something else. Butley loomed large on my 'Geographical' two-miles-to-the inch map. A rivulet wriggled in its direction. And so I came to the Thicks a little way on the right of the Woodbridge road. It would play a large part in my imagination. I took all my friends there, the poet James Turner, John Nash, the Garretts, Richard Mabey. 'Yes,' said Benjamin Britten, 'I know it well.' John Nash had told me that when he was painting he 'liked to have a dead tree in the landscape'. Except that Staverton Thicks was not dead, only perpetually dying. And thus everlastingly alive. Although with no apparent struggle. It showed its great age and exposed its ageing, and one flinched from such candour. But why had no one cleared it and replanted it? What had happened? What was happening?

According to his youthful armour-bearer it was among the young oaks of Staverton that St Edmund was murdered by the Danes, tied naked to one of the

Derek Chambers. *Staverton Oaks.* 2021.

Derek Chambers worked as a graphic designer from 1953 until 1993. He moved to Suffolk in 1994, after which he gradually withdrew from the commercial world in order to follow his own interests in drawing and painting. He now creates images using every available medium, and has a special fondness for all the techniques of printmaking, including lithography, etching, monotype and woodcut.

trees and made a target for arrows. This armour-bearer lived, like the trees, to be very old and thus he was able to tell this execution to Athelstan, who told it to Dunstan, who told it to his friend Abbot of Fleury, who sensibly wrote it down.

The Thicks was also the scene of a Tudor picnic, when Charles Brandon, Duke of Suffolk, and his wife, Henry VIII's sister, spread linen in its shade, drank wine, sang songs and ate—what? This story delighted me as a kind of alfresco masque; when I imagined a pretty site a mile or so from the shield-bedecked Augustinian Priory, and some spontaneous desire to make merry out of doors. But then I looked up the Duke—and what a monster! But a good-looking monster, one of the 'new men' of the Reformation who had gone from strength to strength without losing his head. I see him lying full length on the then summer grass, the oaks above as young as he is, and by his side his wife Mary who was once Queen of France. Henry was furious when they married in Paris without his permission, but calmed down when her enormous dowry for the first husband was returned in instalments. In Suffolk they call her 'the French Queen', not the Duchess. She would have been buried in St Edmundsbury Abbey had not her brother pulled it down. But she can be found in a corner of St Mary's Church nearby, the woman who ate—what?—in Staverton Thicks.

Hugh Farmer, into whose little wood I stole so long ago, himself describes it in a [Aldeburgh] Festival Programme Book. He lived there and his account of it is incomparable. He tells of his life there in *A Cottage in the Forest*. But it has never been the adjunct of a great house.

> The trees consist chiefly of oaks of every conceivable shape, although none is of very great height, and of an age estimated at between seven and eight centuries. Many are stag-headed because, until its abolition a century and a half ago, there was a right for local people to top and lop the trees for fuel.
>
> Many of them are hollow and hollies and elder seeds brought by birds have rooted and grown up from the crowns, so that sometimes a tree grows out of a tree … There is a tradition that this is a Druidic grove and at night, when the owls are crying and the gaunt arms of the ancient trees seem outstretched to clutch, this is an eerie place … A remnant of primeval forest. A very ancient plantation to provide the Priory with fuel and timber for building … What does it matter? Staverton Thicks is probably the oldest living survival in East Anglia, a strange place, history and tradition apart, with a character all its own. On a still midsummer night when the nightjars churn, and the roding woodcock croak overhead, in deep winter when the snow under the hollies is crimsoned by the berries dropped by ravenous birds, or at autumn dusk when the mist rises wraithlike from the stream and the rusty wailing of the stone curlew sounds across the trees, it has a magical beauty.

I thought of the Saxon and Viking princelings. The Thicks has a partly thwarted Phoenix ambition, to die and yet live. But the thing is itself a form of dying. The long-settled condition of these botanic infirmaries, for they exist here and there where a tidying hand has not invaded them, are a requiem. The rich deep mould of their floor, the feeble barriers of guelder and hazel which let through the north-coast wind, the close canopy of undernourished branches which check full leafage, all these 'disadvantages' are time-protracting. For an oak, a holly, the chief enemies of existence are parasitic fungi, canker caused by sunburn, frost aphis of one kind or another—and lightning. They say that it strikes an oak more than any other tree. Once, cycling from Framlingham on a storm-black afternoon, I saw lightning fire an old oak in a park. It blazed up only a few yards away with a mighty crackle of dead and living wood.

Most of the Staverton oaks are so near death that they seem to be nothing more than gnarled drums for the gales to beat. Yet so tenacious is their hold on life that the twigs sprouting from them are still April green. And come August 'Lammas' growth will hide some shrivelled bole.

The mood of the Thicks depends on that of its visitor. I found it a contemplative, loving silence. Little or no birdsong. An absence of that rustling busyness created by small unseen animals. A carpet-soft humus deadened my every step. So soft was it that sparse forest flowers—sanicle shoots, wild strawberry, speedwell— can be trodden into it without injury. A sequence of glades has its own special senescence. It is like walking through an ill-lit gallery of sculpted last days. Except that here there is an endless putting off of last days.

As Staverton means a staked enclosure, what was it that was enclosed? And why were its 'thicks' left to degenerate when the remainder of the forest was not allowed to? Why was it allowed to do what it liked? Yet it feels neither cursed nor abandoned. It is like a woodland mortuary, yet not tragic. Its enigma lies in some destiny which we know nothing of. For some reason it was intentionally untouched—and staved in. It is grotesque, part of a wood from Gormenghast, part a lecture on death, part a ruin of miscegenation. Holly props up oak; ivy alone flourishes. Wild creatures for the most part avoid it. It is botany as departure—yet neither root nor leaf ever goes.

St Edmund

St Edmund, or Edmund the Martyr, King of East Anglia, was the first patron saint of England, until replaced by St George. Edmund is still the patron saint of Kings, pandemics, the Roman Catholic diocese of East Anglia, Douai Abbey, wolves, torture victims and protection from the plague. There is a theory that he is buried under the tennis courts in the grounds of the ruined abbey at Bury St Edmunds.

Born on Christmas Day 841 AD, Edmund succeeded to the throne of East Anglia in 856. Brought up as a Christian, he fought alongside King Alfred of Wessex against the pagan Viking and Norse invaders (the Great Heathen Army) until 869 when his forces were defeated and Edmund was captured by the Vikings. He was ordered to renounce his faith and share power with the pagan Vikings, but he refused. According to the tenth-century account of the saint's life by Abbo of Fleury, who quotes St Dunstan as his source, Edmund was then bound to a tree, shot through by arrows and beheaded. His decapitated head is said to have been reunited with its body with the help of a talking wolf who protected the head and then called out *'Hic, Hic, Hic'* ('Here, Here, Here') to alert Edmund's followers.

There have been several campaigns to reinstate St Edmund as patron saint, most recently the 'St Edmund for England' e-petition in 2013. It questioned whether St George, patron saint of sixteen other countries, ever even visited England, and suggested he should be replaced by an Englishman, and who better than the Anglo-Saxon martyr-king St Edmund.

The Martyrdom of St Edmund from *Life, Passion, and Miracles of St Edmund, King and Martyr*, c.1130.

ROBIN ROBERTSON

Robin Robertson is originally from the north-east coast of Scotland, but has recently taken a cottage in Suffolk. His work has received many awards, and The Long Take, *his narrative poem set in post-war America, won the Walter Scott Prize for Historical Fiction, the Goldsmiths Prize for innovative fiction and the Roehampton Poetry Prize. It was the first poem to be shortlisted for the Booker Prize.*

SPRING

Unlike the world that greens
around us, greens and dies
and greens again,
we only have a single turn at this:
one day's tide,
one year's worth of seasons;
we make these children – re-make
ourselves, our own beginnings –
because we only have
one spring, one flood,
one chance at life, at love,
before it closes over us, in the dark
on frozen shingle.

RALPH FIENNES

My Father's Arms (2021)

Ralph Fiennes is an actor and director.

My father's arms, his chest, his neck, his presence. He takes up the space in the room. It might be intimidating. It might be threatening, but there is a centre of gravity that makes you feel safe.

I must have been aware of this from a very early age. In the kitchen, with my mother, I can see him organising, assisting, helping. My father's hands, as he teased and stroked his favourite Labrador—Sinner. I remember the pattern of tiny creases of skin in his index fingers seamed with dirt. I can see him manoeuvring those hands in the uterus of a cow—and then dipping them into some lubricating oil to help ease the passage of a struggling calf. I'm fascinated; I'm not horrified.

My father mowing the large lawn behind the house called Elm Farm, or The Elms. He sat on a metal seat driving the mower. Sometimes I would sit on his lap and he would allow me to steer the mower holding its steering mechanism—was it a wheel? The memory is one of assurance, feeling safe.

The stripes of grass shaded alternately due to the opposing directions of the mower gave me pleasure: the ordered lines.

A big event was the aeroplane arriving to spray the crops. Standing between my mother and father as the plane swooped low over the field. My parents seemed to want to maximise a sense of occasion and excitement. But I remember their wish for it to be an event more than I remember the aircraft itself—which seemed to come and go so quickly.

The fields of Suffolk—dark green hedges, the oaks, the broken elms—diseased and ivy-choked and, in the summer, the pale coloured crops: wheat and barley. A landscape that might be dull for many people but its rhythm is hypnotic, compelling. Small churches pricking the horizon line under skies that dominate.

In my adolescence—16 or 17 years old—over two summer holidays, I worked on the farms of my father's friends. I pulled wild oats, painted metal roofs, shovelled grain in silos, stacked hay-bales. Summer heat. Summer sweat. A delicious tiredness—no responsibilities.

I worked alongside Ron, teasing me with his dry, laconic Suffolk wit. 'Yeah, a blind man would like to see that'—if something was done badly. Or: 'It's the early bird what catches the worm, but it's the second mouse what gets the cheese.' Or, asking him: 'Have you lived in Suffolk all your life?' 'Not yet.'

At this time my father was no longer farming but I worked somehow in his shadow—some attempt at emulation or whatever my memory of his farming life thought I ought to emulate.

Perhaps in some way it lay in the emulation of his hands—what they carried. Even after he gave up farming to become a photographer, his hands still carried their firm sensitivity—in the darkroom, gently rocking the developing chemical in its tray, in the garden: digging, planting, weeding. His hands on a spade, a pitchfork or a shovel, building shelves, laying a wooden floor, putting up wallpaper.

I helped him repaint old sash windows: sanding, filling, sanding again. One coat of primer, two of undercoat, one coat of gloss.

I felt I could never match my father's easy dexterity with things, although sometimes he seemed over-assertive: handing you an object with too much physical pressure, as if to say 'Here. I'm giving you this: take it firmly, don't drop it.' And, by implication, 'use it efficiently'. This force-field of intent could be pressurising—and I could breathe more easily away from it. Daydreaming, mooching, were antithetical to my father but I found that they could be havens of no planning, no order, personal arenas of imagination.

Is the landscape of childhood an anchor? Do we want to return to it? Is it even good to return to it?

The lanes and small roads around Elm Farm connect the small villages of Wangford and Frostenden. They seem unchanged. If you break out of them heading east towards the sea you can reach Southwold or, a little further north, the beach of Covehithe. Southwold is a magnet for summer visitors. Small picturesque houses sit above a concrete esplanade facing the North Sea. Coloured beach huts parade along the sea-front. These too seem unchanged since the 1960s. Perhaps there are more of them, perhaps they are more brightly painted or more fastidiously well-kept. My parents rented a beach hut there in the summer months—perhaps two or three years running—in the late 60s. It was exhilarating to be able to challenge the waves or 'dig to Australia' in the sand and then be given tea or an ice-cream in the sheltered confines of the hut. Always the sense of salt, sand, post-swim fatigue, appetite, the flirtation of the ebbing wave.

I went to a nursery school in Southwold—a small room in a Victorian house, walking distance from the cannons that squat on the edge of the green, pointing stubbily over Sole Bay. After school we might climb on them—their weight and threat carrying some intuitive attraction for me.

Mark Fiennes, *The Weighing of Souls, St Michael and the Devil*, Wenhaston Doom, St Peter's Church, c. 1500–1520.

Ralph Fiennes' father, Mark, took a series of photographs of interior features of Suffolk churches. The Wenhaston Doom is a sixteenth-century panel painting depicting the Last Day of Judgment. This rare work of art was discovered during restoration work in 1892, hidden under whitewash on the wooden tympanum taken down from above the chancel arch. The story goes that in refitting the church, the architect removed the plank and left it outside on the bonfire. Overnight the rain washed the paint off and the painting underneath was revealed.

Recently I have driven past Elm Farm and seen how the old farm-buildings on either side have been obliterated and new residential buildings have appeared. But the farmhouse itself seems unchanged. The white-painted kennels to the side are still there. A small terrace of dog houses.

Dogs were part of childhood too. The hot, sour breath of Labrador stinking up the car. Dog heat. The comfort of it—dog spirit. Tongue-hanging appetite— tails frenetic, eyes looking for assurance, guidance and approval. My heart goes out to our dogs. Their loyalty moves me. Their loyalty to my parents. Loyalty to our family. Dog spirit.

This summer I visited my father's grave in a small cemetery in Oxfordshire. His life, his whole big expansive essence distilled into dates, engraved in clear script: *November 11th 1933–December 30th 2004.* Within these simple dates the whole man, the whole spirit.

ELS BOTTEMA AND LIDA KINDERSLEY

One Shell Wide

From *The Shingle Street Shell Line* (2018)

In 2005 two childhood friends, Els and Lida, spent a week in Suffolk after each had been through a year of cancer. On their first long walk along the beach, they picked up some white shells and, sitting down to rest, arranged them around a plant. From that day on, every walk added more shells to a growing line, symbolic of their slow day by day, shell by shell recovery. Twice a year they spend a week repairing and relaying the line and find many people have added to it. Frail and transitory, like us and those who come and wonder at it, the line is a signal of courage and survival.

the sea was our aim
the flag-pole our focus
day in day out
that first week
we gathered shells, white whelks only
and laid them one by one
on our knees on the shingle
hard pebbles, unpleasant large ones
and gentle pea-shingle
that first week we laid
some twenty yards
whilst we were raw with abuse
…
nothing new was brought to the beach
the shells were there, thrown from the sea.
beautifully white and tempting shapes
we had to pick them up, the best
the least battered ones
they are all a little broken
we are all a little broken
none are perfect here in this wild corner
wind blowing, howling and rain beating
and we brave the elements
as we conquered our misfortunes
together
…

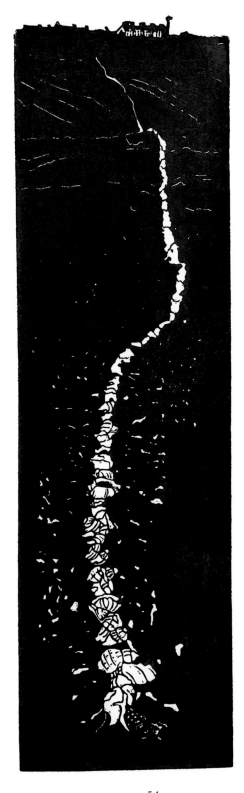

Janet Watson, linocut,
*The Shingle Street Shell
Line*, 2021.

it is a white line of dog-whelks
small ones and big ones
contrasting with small, big and bigger pebbles
they lie easiest on pea-shingle
but whatever the size of the stones
the line continues undisturbed
one shell wide

JULIET BLAXLAND

The Cricket Match

From *The Easternmost House* (2019)

Juliet Blaxland's book describes a year in her cottage on the easternmost edge of England just north of Southwold, where the crumbling cliff is bringing the sea ever closer. The cottage has now gone. She recounts, too, her fight to maintain the rural ways she grew up with, here describing a village cricket match.

Picture the cricket match scene: the little grey flint church in the background, the pitch, the field in the foreground normally grazed by my mother's Jacob (spotty) sheep, mown so closely that it now pulls off a bucolic impersonation of the Centre Court at Wimbledon, but with a few molehills. The sheep, who have been helping to prepare this cricket pitch for months, are moved off the scene of their duty, so they watch with ovine interest from the other side of the old post-and-rails fence.

A green pony trailer, of the sort normally used for transporting Thelwell ponies, serves as the cricket-kit storing pavilion. Little wonkily-painted number boards are strewn about on the grass beside it. The scoreboard is propped up on the nursery blackboard. The scorer arranges his trestle table and the book. Soon, he will ask for a pencil sharpener, as he always does. Somehow the pencil sharpener is never provided until he asks for it.

The players and spectators may include farmers, fishermen, shepherds, gunsmiths, gamekeepers, wildfowlers, livery yard owners and possibly a few poachers, alongside estate agents, accountants and solicitors. It is a broad church and broadly assembled in support of the church. If it wasn't right there in front of us all for six days a year, it might seem from another age. Wikipedia, and an article in the *Guardian*, refers to this kind of thing as 'deep England', as if it were imagined and not real.

The umpire is flailing about like a drowning man in a Jacques Tati film, as he tries to put on his white coat. The white coat is provided by Mr Clevely, the poultry farmer, to lend gravitas to the umpire's decisions. A rugged open-sided tent and two flimsy garden-centre-ish 'gazebos' are assembled along the hedge-line, housing the commercial heart of the operation: the tea tent, barbecue and bar.

If you could now imagine retuning your ear to 'eavesdropping mode', you will pick up fragments of utterances along the lines of, 'What a lovely setting', 'This is so English', 'I can't believe this is real', 'It's lovely that this sort of thing still actually happens', 'Sorry, I'm so late. I got completely lost...' and so on. The regulars say no such things, as it happens every year, but we usually try to pull in some new blood, hence the commentary. You are now as good as there in person.

So here we all are again. We are hosting the cricket match as one of many in the Saints' Festival of Cricket. The title is not an indication of the characters of the assembled people, but of the names of the scattered collection of villages taking part, all named after saints and collectively known as The Saints. On one map, which explained Suffolk in relation to farming, tourism and second homers, The Saints area was marked, 'They shoot burglars here'. Here be dragons, bow and arrow country, or Bermuda Triangle, would also give a sense of the *genius loci*. In the war, it was a vital zone of airfields and land girls, still utterly confusing to outsiders. Tonight, none of The Saints is playing in the Saints' Festival of Cricket, and the postal address says we are in Norfolk even though we are physically in Suffolk. Typical Suffolk.

The Cricket Festival is an annual event, but not an ancient one. It started about twenty-five years ago when the dreary village fêtes of our childhood finally dissolved through a combination of natural forces, diminishing public desire to throw horseshoes at a stick and not raising enough money to pay the church quota (officially the 'parish share'). Health and Safety bods also frightened us by describing the liabilities which could occur if we offered pony rides. Some might see the disappearance of those traditional village fêtes as a tragic loss, another vital chunk of our 'cultural cliff' metaphorically falling into the sea. But in reality, they were dire.

The cricket-pitch church's saint, St Margaret of Antioch, is the patron saint of peasants. How appropriate. As the population was decimated by the Black Death and somehow never replenished itself, each church must now be maintained by twenty-odd (or twenty odd) people. None of us wants to be part of the generation that allows any of the cornerstones of rural England to fall off the cliff, so we truck on, until it's not our turn any more.

The church and these cricket matches are far removed from any notions of religion itself. At the cricket, Belief, or genuine Faith, would be far too serious a subject to bring up in a tea tent conversation. Belief is of the utmost irrelevance in this context. We have a duty to support the church regardless. 'To everything there is a season, a time to reap and a time to sow.' 'That peace which the world cannot give.' 'Lighten our darkness.' 'We have erred and strayed from thy ways like lost sheep.' The language alone is worth saving. Words like 'Rogation' still have meaning here, surrounded by crops, in what is still referred to as a parish.

There is a long collective memory involved in this ritual: seven years of bumper crops; plagues of locusts; loaves and fishes; water into wine; a last supper. Lent, Ramadan, Diwali. Feast and famine. Food is central to all religions, so the tea tent with its expert cake exhibitions seems an appropriate way to raise the necessary funds. We also run a bar and a barbecue all day, the cooking kit itself having evolved from a recycled tractor in the old days, to a proper modern barbecue made out of an oil drum. On the raffle-prize table, there are a few jars of home-made jam, with a sign saying, 'Better than Bon Mammon', in Suffolk Franglais. 'Bun Mammon' would accurately describe the cricket economy.

Realistically, unless all these tiny rural churches can become something useful, they will soon become romantic ruins, as surely as our vanished clifftop church of St Nicholas at Easton Bavents has fallen into the sea.

MICHAEL ONDAATJE

The Saints

From *Warlight* (2018)

Michael Ondaatje is the author of seven novels, a memoir, a non-fiction book on film, and several books of poetry. The English Patient *won the Booker Prize in 1992 and the Golden Man Booker in 2018. This novel, a story of veiled memory and intrigue, is set in the shadowy world of London in 1945 in the aftermath of the Second World War. A dozen years later the narrator returns to Suffolk to investigate what happened to his mysterious mother and uncover what happened in her—and his own childhood—past.*

I bought the house from Mrs Malakite, and on my first day as its owner walked across the fields towards White Paint, where my mother had been raised and which had now been sold to strangers. I stood on a rise on the perimeter of what had once been her land, with the slow meander of a river in the distance. And I decided to write down what little I knew of her time in this place, even if the house and the landscape that once belonged to her family had never been the true map of her life. The girl who had grown up beside a small Suffolk village was in fact well travelled.

My grandfather, being born within a family of older sisters, was content to be surrounded by the company of women. Even when he eventually reached the rank of admiral, with no doubt draconian control of the men who obeyed his rigorous demands at sea, he relished his time in Suffolk and was at ease in the domestic habits of his wife and daughter.

Knowing he would spend most of his active life with the navy, my grandfather had intentionally bought a house in Suffolk that was not beside an 'active river'. So where my mother was taught to fish as a teenager was a wide but quiet stream. There was no rush to it. Water meadows sloped down towards it from the house. Now and then in the distance one heard a bell from one of the Norman churches, the same toll earlier generations had heard across those fields.

The region was made up of a cluster of small villages, a few miles from one another. The roads between them were often unnamed, causing confusion to travellers, not helped by the fact that the villages were similarly named—St John, St Margaret, St Cross. There were in fact two communities of Saints—the South Elmham Saints, made up of eight villages, and the Ilketshall Saints, which had half that number. A further problem was that the mileage on any signpost in the region was guesswork. A sign announced the journey between one Saint and another as two miles, so after three and a half miles a traveller would turn back assuming he had missed a turn, when in fact he need to continue another half mile to reach the slyly hidden Saint. The miles felt long in The Saints. There was no assurance in the landscape. And for those growing up there, assurance felt similarly hidden. Since I spent some of my early years there, it might explain why as a boy in London I was obsessively drawing maps of our neighbourhood in order to feel secure. I thought that what I could not see or record would cease to exist, just as it often felt I'd misplaced my mother and father in one of those small villages flung down randomly onto the ground with too similar a name and with no reliable mileage towards it.

During the war, The Saints, being near to the coast, had taken on an even greater secretiveness. All signposts, however inaccurate, were removed in preparation for a possible German invasion. The region became signless overnight. There would in fact be no invasion, but American airmen assigned to the recently built RAF airfields were as a result constantly getting lost when they tried to get back from the pubs at night and were often found searching frantically for the correct aerodrome the next morning. Pilots crossing the Big Dog Ferry travelled unnamed lanes and found themselves crossing the Big Dog Ferry again going the other way, still attempting to stumble on their airfield. At Thetford the army created a life-sized model of a German town, which Allied troops were trained to surround and attack before their invasion of Germany. It was a strange contrast: English soldiers carefully memorising the structure of a German town, while German troops were preparing to enter a bewildering Suffolk landscape where not one road sign existed. Coastal towns were secretly removed from maps. Military zones officially disappeared.

Much of that war work in which my mother and others participated was carried out, it is now clear, with a similar invisibility, the real motives camouflaged, the way childhood is. Thirty-two aerodromes, along with decoy airfields to confuse the enemy, were built almost overnight in Suffolk. Most of those flesh-and-blood airfields would never exist on a map, even if they appeared in several short-lived bar-room songs. And eventually by war's end, the aerodromes disappeared, in much the same way four thousand air force servicemen would leave the region as if nothing untoward had happened there. The Saints slipped back into everyday life.

JON CANTER

New Neighbours

From *Worth* (2011)

Jon Canter is a comedy scriptwriter, dramatist and the author of three satirical comic novels. In this novel set in the imaginary village of Worth just inland from the Suffolk coast, the protagonist and his wife have just left the rat-race of London for the sleepy village of Worth. It feels like a dream come true. But their new life isn't quite as idyllic as it first seems.

Worth had a population of a hundred and fifty, which didn't include second-home owners. On the first morning we woke up there, seared by damp, we were warmed by our superiority to those glorified visitors. We lived in Worth. We lived nowhere but Worth. What, though, was Worth? Without a pub (the Bell had closed down, though the sign remained), a shop (converted and sold, as a modest third home, to a man who worked for Goldman Sachs), a church or a school, Worth was a place that existed more in the minds of its inhabitants than on a map. When asked where I lived, I never said Worth. To foreigners, I'd say I lived about eighty miles from London; to Londoners, I'd say I lived about forty minutes from Ipswich; in Ipswich, I'd say I lived near Orford, famous for its castle and church and quay and lighthouse and shingle spit and general shop. Famous to me for its general shop, which was the nearest to our cottage. There, on day three, I had my first conversation with a Worthian. She was at the till, ahead of me, a mannish woman in her late sixties. To judge from her basket, she lived on chocolate cake and budget, sub-drinkable red wine. She told me I'd just moved into Hay Cottage. I agreed. Hers was the cottage 'next to Keith and Margaret'. I looked blank, which was fair enough. I couldn't be expected, after three days, to know Keith and Margaret. She said hers was the pink cottage with the quince tree. That only made me look, if it were possible, blanker. She stared at me as if I didn't know what 'pink' meant whereas, of course, I was trying to remember what a quince tree looked like. I was fooling myself. I had never known.

'Where's your cottage in relation to the?' I asked. And then I ran out of words. What were the landmarks of Worth, in relation to which she could place her cottage? In London, I could have said 'station' or 'bank' or 'Tesco Metro' or 'Pizza Hut'—there were so many easily remembered, man-made marks on the land. Here, the landmarks were natural: were bushes, were trees, were fields. I couldn't name any of them, not yet. I was still in a rural daze. No matter, though. Something else was now on her mind.

She'd paid for her goods, so our time together at the till, as two shoppers, had passed. At this point, she was asking a question in her own time.

'Where will you pray? I go to Sudbourne, but there's Iken. And Orford. If you want to go to Sudbourne, we can share a car. What do you think?'

She had a reddish face, the colour of a cherry boiled sweet. We had nothing in common but Worth, yet that meant everything to me now. It was my new home, a place of love and goodness and marriage. Had I met this woman in a shop in London, round the corner from some new flat we'd bought, I'd have said we weren't believers or, to lessen the blow, we weren't churchgoers. Either way, I'd have delivered a blow with the London subtext: Don't talk to me ever again because you are mad. But here I felt a duty to her, because of our shared landscape. I wanted to make her happy, or not unhappy, as a tribute to our countryside.

'Nineteen pounds eighty-five,' said the shopkeeper, who was our witness. Where did he pray, this Orford shopkeeper? I couldn't choose Orford as my pretend-church, for fear he'd expect to see me there on Sunday.

'I'll discuss it with my wife,' I told her. I'd been married no more than a few months. 'My wife' still felt like a bogus claim, much as a con man might refer to 'my three-hundred-acre estate', the faster to induce you to give him your trust and your money. 'My wife' didn't belong to me, as the estate didn't belong to him. But this woman heard the opposite: she understood immediately that I belonged to my wife. Without my wife I couldn't make the churchgoing decision, though my wife could make that decision, and many more, without me. This was marriage at its most protective. She, my wife, was the shield—was the marriage—and all I had to do was hide behind her, even when she was absent. 'My wife' terminated the conversation. It repelled the outsider, who told me to drop in the next time I was passing. Then she left the shop.

'She should mind her own business,' said the woman rearranging the meat in the freezer. I thought she must be the wife of the man behind the till, which he confirmed, in his embarrassment, by trying and failing to look as if he'd never met her.

You might think this was what I wanted to hear; you might think I'd find it liberating to hear someone say it. But I didn't. I thought it was mean to talk about a person as soon as they left a shop. Leaving a shop, or any kind of room, was a social death. Those who were left behind should observe a decent silence, before they spoke ill of the departed. Was it pious of me to think like that? Was I trying to be a better person? Yes. What was wrong with that? It was a worthwhile aspiration.

I left the shop, without comment. Fifteen minutes later, I saw, up ahead, a pink cottage with what had to be a quince tree, for there was the boiled-sweet-faced woman getting out of her freshly parked car, with her shopping. This was it: this was the next time I was passing. I had no intention of dropping in. Nevertheless, I braked, as if a slow drive-by were an excellent compromise between dropping in and not.

I pulled up, about twenty feet beyond her cottage. I sat there for a minute, to give her time to enter her cottage and put down her shopping. I imagined a cat. Then, to give both of us more time, I imagined a dog. The set of her features strongly resembled a bulldog's, which made it more likely she'd choose one as a pet. I carried on sitting. This dropping-in: it was like the putting-in of the garden fence posts we'd bought to replace the ones that had rotted. I didn't want to do it. I wanted to *have done it*.

Full Circle to Walberswick (2021)

Libby Purves is a journalist and author who has been writing for The Times *since 1982. A previous Columnist of the Year and author of twelve novels and non-fiction books, she was for forty years a BBC Radio 4 broadcaster after becoming the* Today *programme's first woman and youngest-ever presenter.*

In 1956, my father Grant Purves was posted to the British Embassy in Angola. Foreign Office advice was against taking families: a previous incumbent lost a child to yellow fever, and the old Empire assumptions about family separation still ruled. So my eldest brother was to be enrolled in a distant prep school and my mother, with the other three of us aged two to six, would be found some suitable house.

Dad favoured Suffolk because the low, sandy coast and wide skies reminded him of his own childhood in Cupar, Fife. We had a year renting in Thorpeness. We two eldest were put in a parent-run village school which existed mainly for the sake of the Ogilvie clan who built the Meare and the fairytale holiday village. Then we found Longroof in Leverett's Lane, Walberswick, and I was enrolled in the proper village school. It had two classes: the Big Ones (over eight) with Mrs Hargreaves, and the Little Ones under Mrs Brown. Big boys pushed the tables together and helped serve school dinners of hot stew and treacle pudding. One was Keith Webb, later the legendary Wally Webb the builder and village leader whose plaques adorn many houses to this day. My mother's single-parent sanity was preserved by the active and welcoming Women's Institute and an ex-WRAC mother's help full of soldierly songs and disciplinarian instincts.

The memories of those three years stay sharp. There was Ginger Winyard's shop round the corner for penny-bars of chocolate and proud errands (usually for my grandmother's Wild Woodbine fags). There was a first bike to ride across the Bailey Bridge to Southwold, and being sent to the Anchor's off-licence on Sunday for a bottle of beer and a bottle of ginger-beer, ensuring shandy for the grownups and a treat for us. We village children ran around free, raced scooters and wheeled a barrow doing penny-for-the-guy before building the November bonfire. We swam off the pebbled beach and, when my brother was home, borrowed old Mr Cleminson's Indian canoe to explore the creek. In summer an exotic tribe we reverently called 'The Holidaymakers' would appear, and we would look wonderingly at their expensive beach gear and picnic baskets. We used to beg, 'Mum, can we play at holidaymakers?'

Another summer delight was the arrival of Major Bugg's Riding Stables to the Anchor yard. Lessons and hacks cost seven and sixpence, disgorged only once

Sarah Muir Poland, *Walberswick Marshes*, 2016.

Sarah Muir Poland is a contemporary painter living in London and Suffolk. She paints in oils and her increasingly popular work is in the colourist tradition, inspired by the colours of the East Anglian landscape.

a week by Mum. But once you got to know them you could help out. The best trick was to turn up at six in the morning to bring the horses in from the marsh. The chosen few would grab the appropriate bridle and pile into the 'rumble seat' opening at the boot of Major Bugg's car. We'd catch the horses and ride them across the Common to the stables to be groomed. I was never really confident bareback, especially on the wilder horses, but usually stayed aboard. It was worth it for the free ride, the comradeship of the cavalcade, the birds' morning cries and the pale early light on the flowering gorse. Later, a less romantic bonus of the Bugg summer months was taking a bucket and shovel out to collect dung to sell to gardeners, thus earning another proper riding lesson.

Idylls end. Dad got a new post and after some hasty lessons with the Madame Souris lesson book I was pitched into a serene and decorous French convent school in Lille. Walberswick remained our UK home for years between posts and in Dad's retirement, but the thread was broken by his more distant postings and the boarding-school destiny of 1960s diplo-brats. They moved to Southwold when they grew older and the house harder to keep going (my mother used to say airily to prospective buyers 'We haven't had any trouble with the rats since the chimney fire'). The village had by then become expensive as family houses were snapped up as second homes by Londoners. In my childhood there were of course Freuds here (Ernst and Mutti down at Hidden House and the Clement Freud family at Westons), and some showbiz lustre was spread by the presence of the early newsreader Robert Dougall. But later it got—well, a bit chic. So that was it for me and Walberswick, or so it seemed.

Yet when my own children were born we moved from London to Knodishall, and another village school for the new generation. Then there was a decade farming with Suffolk Punches near Middleton, and then a lonely house on Dunwich Heath. It felt as if we were oddly creeping closer to my roots. I kept finding myself cycling across to Walberswick and re-living every lane and track of childhood. When a little house up Church Lane came on the market we sold up and pounced.

And dammit, when we moved in we discovered that on either side of us, by mere chance, lived fellow-pupils from Walberswick village school sixty years earlier: Janet and Nigel to the right, Rita to the left. I'd come home. Old skies wrap round me again, the same wild geese are flying.

WILKIE COLLINS

Magdalen at the Window

From *No Name* (1862)

No Name was one of the finest of Wilkie Collins' issue novels. In it he tackled the theme of illegitimacy. Dispossessed after the death of her father, the heroine Magdalen plans revenge on Noel Vanstone, the cousin who has received her inheritance, and pursues him to Aldeburgh. There she succeeds in inveigling him into marrying her. Two days before the wedding, her despair is such that she buys laudanum with the intention of killing herself.

She removed the cork, and lifted the bottle to her mouth.

At the first cold touch of the glass on her lips, her strong young life leaped up in her leaping blood, and fought with the whole frenzy of its loathing against the close terror of Death …

No word passed her lips. Her cheeks flushed deep; her breath came thick and fast. With the poison still in her hand, with the sense that she might faint in another moment, she made for the window, and threw back the curtain that covered it.

The new day had risen. The broad grey dawn flowed in on her, over the quiet eastern sea.

She saw the waters, heaving, large and silent in the misty calm; she felt the fresh breath of the morning flutter cool on her face. Her strength returned; her mind cleared a little…The promise of release which she saw in it from the horror of her own hesitation roused the last energies of her despair. She resolved to end the struggle, by setting her life or death on the hazard of a chance.

On what chance?

The sea showed it to her. Dimly distinguishable through the mist, she saw a little fleet of coasting-vessels slowly drifting towards the house, all following the same direction with the favouring set of the tide. In half an hour—perhaps in less—the fleet would have passed her window. The hands of her watch pointed to four o'clock. She seated herself close at the side of the window, with her back towards the quarter from which the vessels were drifting down on her—with the poison placed on the window-sill, and the watch on her lap. For one half hour to come, she determined to wait there and count the vessels as they went by. If, in that time an even number passed her—the sign given should be a sign to live. If the uneven number prevailed—the end should be Death.

With that final resolution, she rested her head against the window, and waited for the ships to pass.

The first came; high, dark, and near in the mist; gliding silently over the silent sea. An interval—and the second followed, with the third close after it. Another interval, longer and longer drawn out—and nothing passed. She looked at her watch. Twelve minutes, and three ships. Three.

The fourth came, slower than the rest, larger than the rest, farther off in the mist than the rest. The interval followed; a long interval once more. Then the next vessel passed, darkest and nearest of all. Five. The next uneven number—Five.

She looked at her watch again. Nineteen minutes; and five ships. Twenty minutes. Twenty-one, two, three—and no sixth vessel. Twenty-four, and the sixth came by. Twenty-five, twenty-six, twenty-seven, twenty-eight; and the next uneven number—the fatal Seven—glided into view. Two minutes to the end of the half-hour. And seven ships.

Twenty-nine, and nothing followed in the wake of the seventh ship. The minute-hand of the watch moved on half-way to thirty—and still the white heaving sea was a misty blank. Without moving her head from the window, she took the poison in one hand, and raised the watch in the other. As the quick seconds counted each other out, her eyes, as quick as they, looked from the watch to the sea, from the sea to the watch—looked for the last time at the sea—and saw the EIGHTH ship.

She never moved; she never spoke. The death of thought, the death of feeling, seemed to have come to her already. She put back the poison mechanically on the ledge of the window; and watched, as in a dream, the ship gliding smoothly on its silent way—gliding till it melted dimly into shadow—gliding till it was lost in the mist.

The strain on her mind relaxed when the Messenger of Life had passed from her sight.

'Providence?' she whispered faintly to herself. 'Or chance?'

Her eyes closed, and her head fell back. When the sense of life returned to her, the morning sun was warm on her face—the blue heaven looked down on her—and the sea was a sea of gold.

She fell on her knees at the window and burst into tears.

John Everett Millais, *Magdalen at the Window*, 1863.

John Everett Millais was a friend of Wilkie Collins and illustrated the 1863 one-volume edition of No Name. *Here Magdalen is at the window waiting for the ships to pass looking out from the villa North Shingles (probably North House on Wentworth Road).*

LUCY HUGHES-HALLETT

Sciapod (2021)

Lucy Hughes-Hallett is a cultural historian and novelist. Her book on Gabriele d'Annunzio,
The Pike, *won the Samuel Johnson Prize, the Duff Cooper Prize and the Costa Biography of the Year Award.*

He lies on his back, tunic slipping around his hips but round hat still firmly rammed on. One arm lolls negligently, the other is set akimbo as he turns towards the viewer, his face unreadable but his beard that of a man in his prime. Supine, bent knees in air, he is canopied by his prodigious feet, elegantly curved and as long from heel to toe-tip as he is from hat-crown to nearly bare bottom. He is a sciapod, carved into a medieval pew-end in the church of St Mary the Virgin in Dennington, Suffolk.

Sciapods were among the strange creatures described by Ctesias, a Greek of the fifth century BC, who became physician at the court of the Persian King Artaxerxes II. Ctesias wrote a book about India (which he never visited), in which he described headless people with faces on their chests, others with ear-flaps hanging as low as their elbows, hermaphrodites, giants, men with tails, dog-headed people who communicated by barking, one-eyed cyclopses, griffons, unicorns and gold-digging ants.

The sciapods were among the oddest of Ctesias's humanoid beings. They were one-legged but agile, hopping at great speed, and their feet were large enough to act as parasols, shading them from the burning Indian sun. Comical, and oddly endearing (in order to benefit from their built-in sunshades they have to lie in the posture of a baby having its nappy changed) the sciapods lodged themselves firmly in the collective imagination of the West.

When Alexander reached India his men were surprised not to meet them and their polymorphous Ctesian fellows, but subsequent authors dealt with the problem simply by relocating the 'monstrous races': perhaps their home wasn't India after all, but Ethiopia. Pliny the Elder included them in his Natural History, where medieval scholars found them and took them for motifs to decorate their churches, their manuscripts and maps. There are sciapods in the margin of Hereford Cathedral's Mappa Mundi, in the illuminations to a thirteenth-century bestiary, in carvings in medieval churches in Augsburg and Sens, and in the fourteenth-century fictional travelogue of Sir John Mandeville. So persistent was the belief in their existence that Christopher Columbus, arriving two thousand years after Ctesias's lifetime in what he thought was India, was at least half-hoping to lay eyes on the prodigies Ctesias had described.

Sciapod, pew end at Dennington Church.

The Greeks had seen sciapods and the like as inferior aliens. (Those barking dog-people are figments of the same kind of ethnocentric imagination that labelled all foreign-language-speakers 'barbarians'—people whose attempts at communication are just a senseless bar bar bar.)

Christian thinkers, less concerned with physical perfection than their classical predecessors, took a kinder view. St Augustine decided that Ctesias's 'monstrous races of men' (whose existence Augustine didn't doubt) were 'derived from the stock of Adam'. They might be a bit peculiar, but they were human, and had souls. God had made them (or permitted them to evolve) as evidence that deviation from the physical norm was acceptable to him. Whole tribes of people with ears like winnowing fans, or backward-facing feet, could be candidates for admission to heaven, and so could oddly-made individuals. On the tympanum of the twelfth-century abbey at Vezelay the apostles are sent forth by Christ to bring the gospel to foreigners, some of whom have pigs' snouts and others elephants' ears, but all of whom can be saved (albeit violently—it was at Vezelay that St Bernard preached the second crusade). To the medieval mind these marvellous aliens were exotic, not repugnant; instances not of deformity but of difference.

PENELOPE FITZGERALD

Not an Everyday Experience

From *The Bookshop* (1978)

Penelope Fitzgerald's novels are short, spare masterpieces. She won the Booker Prize for her novel Offshore *in 1979, and her last work,* The Blue Flower, *was acclaimed as a work of genius.* The Bookshop, *her second novel, published when she was sixty-one, is based on her experience of running a bookshop in Southwold. Set in 1959 it is the story of Florence Green, a kind-hearted widow with a small inheritance, who risks everything to open a bookshop—the only bookshop—in the seaside town of Hardborough. As Fitzgerald and her heroine were to find, selling books in 1950s rural Suffolk was not easy, particularly if your shop was haunted by a poltergeist, as it was. In this passage in the novel, Florence is returning from her interview with the bank manager.*

Florence Green might be accounted a lonely figure, but this did not make them exceptional in Hardborough, where many were lonely. The local naturalists, the reedcutter, the postman, Mr Raven the marshman, bicycled off one by one, leaning against the wind, the observed of all observers, who could reckon the time by their reappearance over the horizon. Not all of these solitaries even went out. Mr Brundish, a descendant of one of the most ancient Suffolk families, lived as closely in his house as a badger in its sett. If he emerged in summer, wearing tweeds between dark green and grey, he appeared a moving gorse-bush against the gorse, or earth against the silt. In autumn he went to ground. His rudeness was resented only in the same way as the weather, brilliant in the morning clouding over later, however much it had promised.

The town itself was an island between sea and river, muttering and drawing into itself as soon as it felt the cold. Every fifty years or so it had lost, as though careless or indifferent to such things, another means of communication. By 1850 the Laze had ceased to be navigable and the wharfs and ferries rotted away. In 1910 the swing bridge fell in, and since then all traffic had to go ten miles round by Saxford in order to cross the river. In 1920 the old railway was closed. The children of Hardborough, waders and divers all, had most of them never been in a train. They looked at the deserted LNER station with superstitious reverence. Rusty tin strips, advertising Fry's Cocoa and Iron Jelloids, hung there in the wind.

The great floods of 1953 caught the sea wall and caved it in, so that the harbour mouth was dangerous to cross, except at very low tide. A rowing-boat was now the only way to get across the Laze. The ferryman chalked up his times for the day on the door of his shed, but this was on the far shore, so that no one in Hardborough could ever be quite certain when they were.

After her interview with the bank, and resigned to the fact that everyone in the town knew that she had been there, Florence went for a walk. She crossed the wooden planks across the dykes, preceded as she tramped by a rustling and splashing as small creatures, she didn't know of what kind, took to the water. Overhead the gulls and rooks sailed confidently on the tides of the air. The wind had shifted and was blowing inshore.

Above the marshes came the rubbish tip, and then the rough fields began, just good enough for the farmers to fence. She heard her name called, or rather she saw it, since the words were blown away instantly. The marshman was summoning her.

'Good morning, Mr Raven.' That couldn't be heard either.

Raven acted, when no other help was at hand, as a kind of supernumerary vet. He was in the Council field, where the grazing was let out at five shillings a week to whoever would take it, and at the extreme opposite end stood an old chestnut gelding, a Suffolk Punch, its ears turning delicately like pegs on its round poll in the direction of the human beings in its territory. It held its ground suspiciously, with stiffened legs, against the fence.

When she got within five yards of Raven, she understood that he was asking for the loan of her raincoat. His own clothes were rigid, layer upon layer, and not removable on demand.

Raven never asked for anything unless it was absolutely necessary. He accepted that coat with a nod, and while she stood keeping as warm as she could in the lee of the thorn hedge, he walked quietly across the field to the intensely watching old beast. It followed every movement with flaring nostrils, satisfied that Raven was not carrying a halter, and refusing to stretch its comprehension any further. At last it had to decide whether to understand or not, and a deep shiver, accompanied by a sigh, ran through it from nose to tail. Then its head drooped, and Raven put one of the sleeves of the raincoat round its neck. With a last gesture of independence, it turned its head aside and pretended to look for a new grass in the damp patch under the fence. There was none, and it followed the marshman awkwardly down the field, away from the indifferent cattle, towards Florence.

'What's wrong with him, Mr Raven?'

'He eats, but he's not getting any good out of the grass. His teeth are blunted, that's the reason. He tears up the grass but that doesn't get masticated.'

'What can we do, then?' she asked with ready sympathy.

'I can fare to file them,' the marshman replied. He took a halter out of his pocket and handed back the raincoat. She turned into the wind to button herself into her property. Raven led the old horse forward.

'Now, Mrs Green, if you'd catch hold of the tongue. I wouldn't ask everybody, but I know you don't frighten.'

'*How* do you know?' she asked.

'They're saying that you're about to open a bookshop. That shows you're ready to chance some unlikely things.'

He slipped his finger under the loose skin, hideously wrinkled, above the horse's jawbone and the mouth gradually opened in an extravagant yawn. Towering yellow teeth stood exposed. Florence seized with both hands the large slippery dark tongue, smooth above, rough beneath, and, like an old-time whaler, hung gamely on to it to lift it clear of the teeth. The horse now stood sweating quietly, waiting for the end. Only its ears twitched to signal a protest at what life had allowed to happen to it. Raven began to rasp away with a large file at the crowns of the side teeth.

'Hang on, Mrs Green. Don't you relax your efforts. That's slippery as sin I know.'

The tongue writhed like a separate being. The horse stamped with one foot after another, as though doubting whether they all still touched the ground.

'He can't kick forwards, can he, Mr Raven?'

'He can if he likes.' She remembered that a Suffolk Punch can do anything, except gallop.

'Why do you think a bookshop is unlikely?' she shouted into the wind. 'Don't people want to buy books in Hardborough?'

'They've lost their wish for anything of a rarity,' said Raven, rasping away. 'There's many more kippers sold, for example, than bloaters that are half-smoked and have a more delicate flavour. Now you'll tell me, I dare say, that books oughtn't to be a rarity.'

Once released, the horse sighed cavernously and stared at them as though utterly disillusioned. From the depths of its noble belly came a brazen note, more like a trumpet than a horn, dying away to a snicker. Clouds of dust rose from its body, as though from a beaten mat. Then, dismissing the whole matter, it trotted to a safe distance and put down its head to graze. A moment later it caught sight of a patch of bright green angelica and began to eat like a maniac.

Raven declared that the old animal would not know itself, and would feel better. Florence could not honestly say the same of herself, but she had been trusted, and that was not an everyday experience in Hardborough.

ROBIN ROBERTSON

ON TIME

His head's a secret train-set in the attic:
quiet, straightforward, always summer.

The cattle in their fields of baize,
the postman on his bike,

the green sponge trees
by the papier-mâché tunnel, the children

forever waving their stiff handkerchiefs
at the trains that are always on time.

JAMES HAMILTON

Freedom is the Only Manner: Gainsborough's Landscapes

From *Gainsborough: A Portrait* (2017)

Thomas Gainsborough (1727–1788) was one of the most important British artists of the second half of the eighteenth century. Despite being a prolific portrait painter, Gainsborough gained greater satisfaction from his landscapes and is credited as one of the originators of the eighteenth-century British landscape school.

Gainsborough was born in Sudbury, Suffolk, the son of a clothier. He trained in London, and set up in practice in Ipswich about 1752. In 1759 he moved to Bath, and then, in 1773, to London.

Gainsborough's many hundreds of finished landscape drawings, and his liberality in giving so many of them away, testify to the richness of resource that he found in landscape as a subject. They can only have developed with such variety and conviction through long immersion in real landscape. When he made his countless journeys between London and Ipswich, the landscape was always there, changing before him, and challenging him.

Drawing was also a source of freedom, a way for Gainsborough to escape in his head from the distractions of home, the rule of his wife, the challenge of his daughters, the pressure of his portrait-painting business. In Sudbury and Ipswich, landscape painting was part of Gainsborough's stock-in-trade: he took commissions for landscapes and treated them on a par with his portrait commissions. His landscapes had by the early 1760s reached around five feet square and the breadth of the horizontal canvas comes as something of a relief after the strict verticality of the portrait, while to be alone with a landscape painting and not having to share his presence with a sitter must have been a blessing.

Gainsborough constructed his landscapes as tabletop models using broccoli, moss and stones. William Henry Pyne was thirteen or fourteen years old when he first met Gainsborough and watched him at work on his models. This will have been in the 1780s:

> I have more than once sat by him of an evening, and seen him make models, or rather thoughts, for landscape scenery, on a little old-fashioned folding oak table which stood under his kitchen dresser. He would place cork or coal for his foregrounds and make middle grounds of sand and clay, bushes of mosses and lichens, and set up distant woods of broccoli.

Thomas Gainsborough, *Wooded Landscape with a Cottage and a Shepherd*, 1748.

Much of Gainsborough's early work was of the Suffolk landscapes surrounding his home. ''Tis a most delightfull country for a landscape painter. I fancy I see Gainsborough in every hedge and hollow tree,' wrote John Constable half a century later.

There is a further strain in his landscapes which indicates that they represent a kind of relief to him: they are invariably end-of-day, dusk-descending scenes, people or livestock going home, settling in for the evening, a last glimmer before nightfall. In painting landscapes as he did, from models and little studio constructions lit by candles, Gainsborough was settling in for the evening. The end of the day that Gainsborough painted was also the time of day he painted it.

LUCY WALKER

A Safe Retreat: Britten and Pears at The Red House (2021)

Dr Lucy Walker is a freelance writer and researcher. She worked for the Britten Pears Foundation and later Britten Pears Arts for over fifteen years, writing articles and chapters about Britten and Pears as well as editing two books and making numerous films about Britten's music. She has given many public talks on Britten's music and on many other subjects, including opera, film and heritage. She has a PhD in musicology from King's College, London on the operas of Francis Poulenc.

The Red House in Aldeburgh, the final home of composer Benjamin Britten and his partner the singer Peter Pears, is a former farmhouse with multiple nooks and crannies, two staircases, and a rabbit warren of corridors. It has an eclectic jumble of furniture, brightly coloured carpets, vast numbers of books, and an astonishing art collection. It sits within a five-acre plot with an orchard and lawns for tennis and croquet, plus two small bungalows on its outskirts.

For Britten and Pears, who moved there in 1957, the house was a retreat. Their previous Aldeburgh home on Crag Path, where they had lived for ten years, was too visible to passers-by on the seafront and Britten in particular needed more peace, and certainly more privacy. The Red House site as a whole came to include a studio, a library, and offices for staff and was arranged to suit Britten's preferred mode of working, as well as to support his immensely busy schedule of composing, rehearsing, and administering the Aldeburgh Festival. He composed in the studio from mid-1958: it was a converted hay-loft design by H.T. Cadbury-Brown with stunning views of what would have been open countryside at the time. He would rehearse in the library, completed in 1964 and substantial enough to house his Steinway D piano. The Red House became a self-sufficient operation, enabling Britten to remain in Aldeburgh as much as possible. Pears had his own study and rehearsal space in an upstairs room of the house.

While Britten and Pears both travelled a great deal, giving tours across the world, Pears was often away from home by himself. But he was certainly involved in the decoration of the house, choosing carpets in his favourite colours of red and green. Britten was not uninterested in his home's interiors, writing to Pears about Crag Path, 'The walls will be white with an offness of pink' and was known to be keen on architectural innovation. But above all, it seemed he needed to be secure in his domestic setting and accepted by his town—to inhabit a 'warm nest of love' as the poet W. H. Auden sarcastically put it to him once. His life in Aldeburgh with Pears certainly provided that.

It may seem surprising, however, that two men could live together so peacefully in the 1940s onwards given the laws and general public perception of homosexuality at the time. Yet Britten and Pears' life together was hardly a secret. A feature in the 1956 *Woman's Journal* ('Benjamin Britten at home') noted that they shared a house together. Their household accounts reveal that their lives were quite routinely seen as entwined. For example, a receipt in the Britten Pears Archive from O&C Butcher—an outfitters on Aldeburgh High Street, still operating today—had 'shoe repairs (for Mr Pears)' noted at the top of an invoice for Britten's dress shirts.

At the same time, their status as a couple had to remain a secret, and it was never acknowledged throughout their thirty-seven-year relationship. They had become romantically involved in 1939, in the early stages of their three-year stay in the USA. Their early letters to each other are passionate and personal, and at times they refer to each other as if they were any other 'married' couple: 'ever your loving hubbie' Pears signs off on one occasion; while Britten writes, missing Pears in 1943, 'Still, it's not too bad; think of all the other married couples who are separated for everso much longer!!' (Their correspondence also reveals the inevitable rough patches in their relationship: 'God—you blighter!' begins Britten in one letter, furious that Pears missed a telephone call.)

However, homosexuality was illegal in most countries (and remains so in some countries even today), which had long-lasting and sometimes brutal consequences. Britten, not given to much in the way of personal statements—even in his own diaries—made only a few comments in the early 1930s that hint at the struggles he was undergoing. On 5 March 1937 he wrote 'Now is the time for me to decide something about my sexual life. O for a little courage.' And a month earlier, 'Life is a pretty struggle these days—sexually as well.' For Britten, even though he was never explicit about his sexual feelings, the threat of public disapproval and censure for him and for thousands of other men were real and loomed large. And the effects of this on gay men were profound. In 1955 the author Peter Wildeblood, who had been imprisoned for 'gross indecency', wrote a brave account of his life as a homosexual, entitled *Against the Law*, in which he vividly depicts the psychological damage of criminalisation:

> The shadow of fear is a terrible thing: it cripples a man's character and distorts his moral sense. Set us free, and we can at least try to order our lives with decency and dignity; leave us in this shadow, and we shall continue to be bitter, secretive and warped, a persecuted faction incapable of good.

Wildeblood was surprised and touched by the public support he received after publishing *Against the Law*. Indeed, it appeared that the public were often more supportive of changing the laws in the 1950s than were the law-makers. The Home Secretary David Maxwell Fyfe initiated a campaign in 1953 to seek out homosexuals and make an example of them, leading to several high-profile arrests, including John Gielgud, John Cranko and Alan Turing. Turing opted for chemical castration instead of imprisonment. His letters during this experience make for heart-breaking reading and he committed suicide in 1954—a year before the first meeting of the Wolfenden Committee.

This Committee, over a period of two years, investigated the supposed 'crime' of homosexuality (and of prostitution) and published its findings in 1957, concluding with a recommendation that homosexual acts between 'consenting males in private' should not be criminalised under the law. It took another ten years before the law was passed—again, with public opinion clearly in favour of speeding things up.

In February 1966 the Sexual Offences Act passed in the Commons, and eventually received royal assent and became law in July 1967. It permitted homosexual acts to be decriminalised in England and Wales under the conditions recommended by the Wolfenden Report. Yet even then, the law only applied to men who were able to find a private space to conduct their relationships and despite a general public acceptance of the change in law, there remained a great deal of stigma attached to being gay. As Noel Coward wrote in his diary in February 1966: 'The Homosexual Bill has passed through the House of Commons with a majority of fifty-five votes … some of the opposition speeches were so bigoted, ignorant and silly that one can hardly believe that adult minds … should be so basically idiotic. Nothing will convince the bigots, but the blackmailers will be discouraged and fewer haunted, terrified young men will commit suicide.'

There are no remarks on record from either Britten or Pears on the publication of the Wolfenden Report, or on the passing of the Bill. However, and although it may be a coincidence, Britten and Pears did commission a joint portrait from artist Maxwell Armfield shortly after July 1967 which, other than the Kenneth Green double portrait from 1943 (hanging in the National Portrait Gallery), is the only one in existence. Pears suggested to Armfield that he should be depicted with his arm around Britten's shoulder and the original version of the portrait shows just this. Yet although their relationship could now be 'outed', Britten was very reluctant to commit to such a public display of affection. Armfield, mortified at having offended Britten, painted over the arm with reeds. Britten died in 1976, having never publicly commented on his personal relationship with Pears.

After Britten's death Pears became considerably more open, giving a long interview for Tony Palmer's *A Time There Was* (1980) in which he is quite clear that they were together:

> He really was absolutely devoted to me and unbelievably good and kind … It was a quite marvellous relationship and I'm incredibly grateful for it … It was established very early that we were passionately devoted and close and … that was it.

A year earlier he spoke to the American gay magazine *The Advocate*, in which he voiced his hope that one day 'the climate [would] be right for publishing some of

Maxwell Armfield, *Double Concerto at Snape*, 1969.

the most marvellous letters that one can imagine'—those between himself and Britten. The letters were eventually published forty years after Britten died in 2016, under the title *My Beloved Man*.

The strain of lifelong secrecy must have been palpable at times. Pears acknowledged this in a letter to Britten in 1963 where he compares their 'outsider' status to the conventional lives of their heterosexual friends: 'we are after all queer & left & conshies which is enough to put us, or make us put ourselves, outside the pale …'. But in some ways, Britten and Pears were more fortunate than other homosexual men at the time. The 'open secret' of their relationship was delicately balanced, and relied on their discretion, to some degree on their high-profile lives, but also on the 'don't ask, don't tell' attitudes that—paradoxically—allowed discreet relationships to exist under the radar.

A similar example can be found in W. H. Auden's case, after he chose to move to Kirchstetten, a rural village in Austria around the same time Britten and Pears moved to The Red House. He lived there with his partner Chester Kallman, and as Sandra Mayer writes,

> Auden in Austria defied categorisation and took full advantage of the liberating potential of his cultural, social, linguistic, and sexual outsiderdom, which freed him from any pressures to fit in and observe the stifling rules and conventions of village life. Paradoxically, the small scale and the provincial life provided him with a considerable degree of licence that condoned the foibles of the eccentric foreigner and his 'housekeeper'. (From W. H. Auden in Austria, *The Lives of Houses*)

Britten and Pears, with their artistic careers and international reputations, were perhaps seen as sufficiently 'other' to be afforded a certain indulgence that they might not have been permitted otherwise. But whatever the case, for Britten public acceptance was absolutely crucial. On receiving the Freedom of Aldeburgh in 1962 Britten movingly said,

> As I understand it, this honour is not given because of a reputation ... It is—dare I say it?—because you really do know me, and accept me as one of yourselves, as a useful part of the Borough—and this is, I think, the highest possible compliment for an artist.

Aldeburgh gave Britten the domestic security he needed, and at the same time allowed his and Pears's artistic ambitions to flourish. Together, they managed to achieve a remarkable, hard-won, and very touching equilibrium, something that visitors to their former home can detect. The Red House was a comfortable retreat, serving a brilliant artistic mind; an aesthetically pleasing surrounding for a vibrant and sensitive performing artist—and a safe, loving home, against the odds.

KENNETH CLARK

The Other Side of the Alde

From *Tribute to Benjamin Britten on his Fiftieth Birthday* (1963)

Kenneth Clark (1903–1983) was a British art historian, museum director, and broadcaster. He set up the War Artists' Advisory Committee and persuaded the government to employ up to 200 official war artists including Paul and John Nash and John Piper. After running two important art galleries in the 1930s and 1940s, he came to wider public notice on television, presenting a succession of programmes on the arts during the 1950s and 1960s, culminating in the Civilisation *series in 1969.*

I spent the first fifteen years of my life from 1903 to 1918 across the river from Aldeburgh in a house called Sudbourne Hall. It was one of Wyatt's characteristic East Anglia jobs, large and square, red brick outside, pseudo-Adam inside, and has now been pulled down, all but the stables, which were probably the best part.

My parents arrived from Scotland in time for the first of October, when pheasant shooting begins, and left for Monte Carlo on about the 10th of January, when all but the wiliest birds had been polished off. I remained there alone for the greater part of the year.

When my parents departed for Cap Martin and Vichy, I was left to my own devices. I was an only child and should have felt lonely, but in fact I do not remember suffering any inconvenience from solitude. On the contrary, I remember with fear and loathing the rare occasions when some well-wishing grown-up arranged for me to meet companions of my own age. They were always stronger and more resourceful than I was, and were used to a communal life which I did not understand. After an evening of misery, often accompanied by physical pain, I would be delighted to get back to my large empty house, to the library, the billiard table and the pianola. This last was my chief joy. It was of the old-fashioned push-on variety, which was far more controllable than the later built-in models; and I believed that I gave completely personal renderings of the classics. My parents had decided that I should not learn to play the piano, as they thought, quite correctly, that the sound of my practising would annoy them. But by means of buying scores and propping them up on the pianola while I played, I enjoyed the illusion of learning without pain. To this day I might be able to tell a wrong note in most of Chopin's *Preludes*. Chopin was my God, and as I pedalled away at one of his *Ballades* tears would pour down my cheeks.

Only two things marred my happiness: bad food and fear of ghosts. The servants, who naturally despised me and felt in some obscure way that by ill-treating me they were getting their own back on their employers, gave me almost uneatable food, rancid butter and cheese so full of weevils that I remember pieces of it hopping about the table. As for the ghosts, I cannot say I ever saw one in Sudbourne (though I did in another of our houses), but they would swish round corners in the galleried hall, and whimper at my bedroom door. For years my nights were a misery, and I was quite relieved when a homing Zeppelin dropped fourteen bombs in the park, and created a diversion.

My days were all pleasure. Most children suffer from boredom, but I do not remember a dull moment at Sudbourne. I loved the Suffolk country, the heaths and sandpits, the great oaks in Sudbourne wood and the wide river at Iken. To reach these favourite spots I reluctantly mounted a pony. Horses instantly recognize that I am afraid of them, and either bolt or rub up against walls or (most humiliating of all) lie down. However a pony was the only means of getting as far as Butley Priory or the Maltings at Snape, and these were the two romantic boundaries of my world. They were both just off the estate, so, apart from their architectural beauty, they gave me the thrill of a journey abroad.

My greatest treat was a trip to Aldeburgh. For this I was allowed to borrow a governess cart, driven by an elderly groom with Dundreary whiskers and the good Suffolk name of Pryke (I suppose that the housekeeper in *Albert Herring* was really Miss Pryke, but Miss Pike is easier to sing). We would drive to a point opposite Slaughden where a large bell hung from a wooden gibbet. If one rang it long enough a man would row over, grumbling, and take one back. I would then walk to Aldeburgh, have tea at Reading's, and spend the rest of the afternoon on the beach looking for amber, which of course I never found, and collecting pocketfuls of pebbles, which of course lost their lustre by the time I got them home. I usually ended by buying a small piece of amber in Mr Stephenson's shop.

The charm of Aldeburgh is very difficult to define, as I often find when I try to persuade an American or Italian friend to visit the festival. I could not explain to my parents why I liked it so much, and they were slightly annoyed by my frequent request to go there. For some reason I had got it into my head that this was a place where my wits were brighter and my senses more alert than anywhere else.

I have never lost this feeling; and when, almost forty years later, there was a reason for going there again, I felt sure that a piece of myself would be recovered. To my astonishment it had hardly changed, and I found that I, too, had changed much less than I expected: I immediately began to look for amber, although by this time I knew quite well that I should never find it; and I brought back even larger handfuls of fast-fading stones. I found that the delicate music of the Suffolk coast, with its woods straggling into sandy commons, its lonely marshes and estuaries full of small boats, still had more charm for me than the great brass bands of natural scenery, the Alps or the Dolomites. To all this was added the fact that Benjamin Britten had settled there, and made it a centre of inspiration. Others are better qualified than I am to understand the technical mastery of Ben's music; but in so far as it takes some of its colouring from the sea, and the skies and marshes of East Suffolk, I can claim to be an initiate. Grimes and Herring are my compatriots. To sit in Orford church, where I had spent so many hours of my childhood dutifully awaiting some spark of divine fire, and then to receive it at last in the performance of *Noye's Fludde*, was an overwhelming experience. I heard the *Fludde* again at a rehearsal in Orford town hall (where at the age of twelve, I had been sent by my parents to make a patriotic speech); and while the procession of Mice, Crows and Doves was being organized, I reflected on what it would have meant to me if, between the ages of nine and fifteen, such marvellous works of genius had been within reach; and I had been allowed to participate in that more enlightened world which, as I already believed, existed on the other side of the Alde. I do not complain of the rich, sporting, philistine atmosphere in which I was brought up. I can think of many other milieus—clerical, academic or military—in which I should have been far less happy. But from an early age I know that the only society I enjoyed was the society of artists, the society of people whose minds were free, whose senses were alert, and who felt the need to communicate their joy. As people. But to have known them as a child; to have met them simply by crossing the Alde! With what rapture would I have clanged the bell at Slaughden and waited for the reluctant ferryman.

M. R. JAMES

'Oh, Whistle, and I'll Come to You, My Lad'

From *Ghost Stories of an Antiquary* (1904)

M[ontague] R[hodes] James (1862–1936) spent his childhood in Suffolk; his father was the vicar at Great Livermere, north-east of Bury St Edmunds. Brought up in a rectory furnished with images of religious antiquity, many of his most unsettling ghost stories evoke Suffolk landscapes, with their misty light and mysterious marshes. His famous early ghost story 'Oh, Whistle, and I'll Come to You, My Lad' (1904) evokes the Suffolk coast. Burnstow is a thinly-disguised Felixstowe. An Oxbridge professor, Professor Parkins, is staying there on holiday with the intention of improving his golf; but he enters a dream-like world of horror.

He was made welcome at the Globe Inn, was safely installed in the large double-bedded room, and was able before retiring to rest to arrange his materials for work in apple-pie order upon a commodious table which occupied the outer end of the room, and was surrounded on three sides by windows looking out seaward; that is to say, the central window looked straight out to sea, and those on the left and right commanded prospects along the shore to the north and south respectively. On the south you saw the village of Burnstow. On the north no houses were to be seen, but only the beach and the low cliff backing it. Immediately in front was a strip—not considerable—of rough grass, dotted with old anchors, capstans, and so forth; then a broad path; then the beach. Whatever may have been the original distance between the Globe Inn and the sea, not more than sixty yards now separated them.

Professor Parkins, one of whose principal characteristics was pluck, spent the greater part of the day following his arrival at Burnstow in what he had called improving his game, in company with this Colonel Wilson: and during the afternoon—whether the process of improvement were to blame or not, I am not sure—the Colonel's demeanour assumed a colouring so lurid that even Parkins jibbed at the thought of walking home with him from the links. He determined, after a short and furtive look at that bristling moustache and those incarnadined features, that it would be wiser to allow the influences of tea and tobacco to do what they could with the Colonel before the dinner-hour should render a meeting inevitable.

'I might walk home to-night along the beach,' he reflected—'yes, and take a look—there will be light enough for that—at the ruins of which my colleague

Disney was talking. I don't exactly know where they are, by the way; but I expect I can hardly help stumbling on them.'

This he accomplished, I may say, in the most literal sense, for in picking his way from the links to the shingle beach his foot caught, partly in a gorse-root and partly in a biggish stone, and over he went. When he got up and surveyed his surroundings, he found himself in a patch of somewhat broken ground covered with small depressions and mounds. These latter, when he came to examine them, proved to be simply masses of flints embedded in mortar and grown over with turf. He must, he quite rightly concluded, be on the site of the preceptory he had promised to look at. It seemed not unlikely to reward the spade of the explorer; enough of the foundations was probably left at no great depth to throw a good deal of light on the general plan. He remembered vaguely that the Templars, to whom this site had belonged, were in the habit of building round churches, and he thought a particular series of the humps or mounds near him did appear to be arranged in something of a circular form. Then he proceeded to examine an oblong eminence which lay east of the centre of the circle, and seemed to his thinking likely to be the base of a platform or altar. At one end of it, the northern, a patch of the turf was gone. It might, he thought, be as well to probe the soil here for evidences of masonry, and he took out his knife and began scraping away the earth. And now followed another little discovery: a portion of soil fell inward as he scraped, and disclosed a small cavity. He lighted one match after another to help him to see of what nature the hole was, but the wind was too strong for them all. By tapping and scratching the sides with his knife, however, he was able to make out that it must be an artificial hole in masonry. It was rectangular, and the sides, top, and bottom, if not actually plastered, were smooth and regular. Of course it was empty. No! As he withdrew the knife he heard a metallic clink, and when he introduced his hand it met with a cylindrical object lying on the floor of the hole. Naturally enough, he picked it up, and when he brought it into the light, now fast fading, he could see that it, too, was of man's making—a metal tube about four inches long, and evidently of some considerable age.

By the time Parkins had made sure that there was nothing else in this odd receptacle, it was too late and too dark for him to think of undertaking any further search. What he had done had proved so unexpectedly interesting that he determined to sacrifice a little more of the daylight on the morrow to archæology. The object which he now had safe in his pocket was bound to be of some slight value at least, he felt sure.

Bleak and solemn was the view on which he took a last look before starting homeward. A faint yellow light in the west showed the links, on which a few figures moving towards the club-house were still visible, the squat martello tower, the lights of Aldsey village, the pale ribbon of sands intersected at intervals by black wooden groynes, the dim and murmuring sea. The wind was bitter from the north, but was at his back when he set out for the Globe. He quickly rattled and clashed through the shingle and gained the sand, upon which, but for the groynes which had to be got over every few yards, the going was both good and quiet. One last look behind, to measure the distance he had made since leaving the ruined Templars' church, showed him a prospect of company on his walk, in the shape of a rather indistinct personage, who seemed to be making great efforts to catch up with him, but made little, if any, progress. I mean that there was an appearance of running about his movements, but that the distance between him and Parkins did not seem materially to lessen. So, at least, Parkins thought, and decided that he almost certainly did not know him, and that it would be absurd to wait until he came up. For all that, company, he began to think, would really be very welcome on that lonely shore, if only you could choose your companion. In his unenlightened days he had read of meetings in such places which even now would hardly bear thinking of. He went on thinking of them, however, until he reached home, and particularly of one which catches most people's fancy at some time of their childhood. 'Now I saw in my dream that Christian had gone but a very little way when he saw a foul fiend coming over the field to meet him.' 'What should I do now,' he thought, 'if I looked back and caught sight of a black figure sharply defined against the yellow sky, and saw that it had horns and wings? I wonder whether I should stand or run for it …

Luckily, the gentleman behind is not of that kind, and he seems to be about as far off now as when I saw him first. Well, at this rate he won't get his dinner as soon as I shall; and, dear me! it's within a quarter of an hour of the time now. I must run!'

Parkins had, in fact, very little time for dressing. When he met the Colonel at dinner, Peace—or as much of her as that gentleman could manage—reigned once more in the military bosom; nor was she put to flight in the hours of bridge that followed dinner, for Parkins was a more than respectable player. When, therefore, he retired towards twelve o'clock, he felt that he had spent his evening in quite a satisfactory way, and that, even for so long as a fortnight or three weeks, life at the Globe would be supportable under similar conditions—'especially,' thought he, 'if I go on improving my game.'

As he went along the passages he met the boots of the Globe, who stopped and said:

'Beg your pardon, sir, but as I was a-brushing your coat just now there was somethink fell out of the pocket. I put it on your chest of drawers, sir, in your room, sir—a piece of a pipe or somethink of that, sir. Thank you, sir. You'll find it on your chest of drawers, sir—yes, sir. Good night, sir.'

The speech served to remind Parkins of his little discovery of that afternoon. It was with some considerable curiosity that he turned it over by the light of his candles. It was of bronze, he now saw, and was shaped very much after the manner of the modern dog-whistle; in fact it was—yes, certainly it was—actually no more nor less than a whistle. He put it to his lips, but it was quite full of a fine, caked-up sand or earth, which would not yield to knocking, but must be loosened with a knife. Tidy as ever in his habits, Parkins cleared out the earth on to a piece of paper, and took the latter to the window to empty it out. The night was clear and bright, as he saw when he had opened the casement, and he stopped for an instant to look at the sea and note a belated wanderer stationed on the shore in front of the inn. Then he shut the window, a little surprised at the late hours people kept at Burnstow, and took his whistle to the light again. Why, surely there were marks on it, and not merely marks, but letters! A very little rubbing rendered the deeply-cut inscription quite legible, but the Professor had to confess, after some earnest thought, that the meaning of it was as obscure to him as the writing on the wall to Belshazzar. There were legends both on the front and on the back of the whistle. The one read thus:

FLA

FUR   BIS

FLE

The other:

QUIS EST ISTE QUI UENIT

'I ought to be able to make it out,' he thought; 'but I suppose I am a little rusty in my Latin. When I come to think of it, I don't believe I even know the word for a whistle. The long one does seem simple enough. It ought to mean, "Who is this who is coming?" Well, the best way to find out is evidently to whistle for him.'

He blew tentatively and stopped suddenly, startled and yet pleased at the note he had elicited. It had a quality of infinite distance in it, and, soft as it was, he somehow felt it must be audible for miles round. It was a sound, too, that seemed to have the power (which many scents possess) of forming pictures in the brain. He saw quite clearly for a moment a vision of a wide, dark expanse at night, with a fresh wind blowing, and in the midst a lonely figure—how employed, he could not tell. Perhaps he would have seen more had not the picture been broken by the sudden surge of a gust of wind against his casement, so sudden that it made him look up, just in time to see the white glint of a sea-bird's wing somewhere outside the dark panes.

The sound of the whistle had so fascinated him that he could not help trying it once more, this time more boldly. The note was little, if at all, louder than before, and repetition broke the illusion—no picture followed, as he had half hoped it might. 'But what is this? Goodness! what force the wind can get up in a few min-utes! What a tremendous gust! There! I knew that window-fastening was no use! Ah! I thought so—both candles out. It's enough to tear the room to pieces.'

The first thing was to get the window shut. While you might count twenty Parkins was struggling with the small casement, and felt almost as if he were pushing back a sturdy burglar, so strong was the pressure. It slackened all at once, and the window banged to and latched itself. Now to relight the candles and see what damage, if any, had been done. No, nothing seemed amiss; no glass even was broken in the casement. But the noise had evidently roused at least one member of the household: the Colonel was to be heard stumping in his stockinged feet on the floor above, and growling.

Quickly as it had risen, the wind did not fall at once. On it went, moaning and rushing past the house, at times rising to a cry so desolate that, as Parkins disinterestedly said, it might have made fanciful people feel quite uncomfortable; even the unimaginative, he thought after a quarter of an hour, might be happier without it.

Whether it was the wind, or the excitement of golf, or of the researches in the preceptory that kept Parkins awake, he was not sure. Awake he remained, in any case, long enough to fancy (as I am afraid I often do myself under such conditions) that he was the victim of all manner of fatal disorders: he would lie counting the beats of his heart, convinced that it was going to stop work every moment, and would entertain grave suspicions of his lungs, brain, liver, etc.—suspicions which he was sure would be dispelled by the return of daylight, but which until then refused to be put aside. He found a little vicarious comfort in the idea that someone else was in the same boat. A near neighbour (in the darkness it was not easy to tell his direction) was tossing and rustling in his bed, too.

The next stage was that Parkins shut his eyes and determined to give sleep every chance. Here again over-excitement asserted itself in another form—that of making pictures. Experto crede, pictures do come to the closed eyes of one trying to sleep, and are often so little to his taste that he must open his eyes and disperse them.

Parkins's experience on this occasion was a very distressing one. He found that the picture which presented itself to him was continuous. When he opened his eyes, of course, it went; but when he shut them once more it framed itself afresh, and acted itself out again, neither quicker nor slower than before. What he saw was this:

A long stretch of shore—shingle edged by sand, and intersected at short intervals with black groynes running down to the water—a scene, in fact, so like that of his afternoon's walk that, in the absence of any landmark, it could not be distinguished therefrom. The light was obscure, conveying an impression of gathering storm, late winter evening, and slight cold rain. On this bleak stage at first no actor was visible. Then, in the distance, a bobbing black object appeared; a moment more, and it was a man running, jumping, clambering over the groynes, and every few seconds looking eagerly back. The nearer he came the more obvious it was that he was not only anxious, but even terribly frightened, though his face was not to be distinguished. He was, moreover, almost at the end of his strength. On he came; each successive obstacle seemed to cause him more difficulty than the last. 'Will he get over this next one?' thought Parkins; 'it seems a little higher than the others.' Yes; half climbing, half throwing himself, he did get over, and fell all in a heap on the other side (the side nearest to the spectator). There, as if really unable to get up again, he remained crouching under the groyne, looking up in an attitude of painful anxiety.

So far no cause whatever for the fear of the runner had been shown; but now there began to be seen, far up the shore, a little flicker of something light-coloured moving to and fro with great swiftness and irregularity. Rapidly growing larger, it, too, declared itself as a figure in pale, fluttering draperies, ill-defined. There was something about its motion which made Parkins very unwilling to see it at close quarters. It would stop, raise arms, bow itself toward the sand, then run stooping across the beach to the water-edge and back again; and then, rising upright, once more continue its course forward at a speed that was startling and terrifying. The moment came when the pursuer was hovering about from left to right only a few yards beyond the groyne where the runner lay in hiding. After two or three ineffectual castings hither and thither it came to a stop, stood upright, with arms raised high, and then darted straight forward towards the groyne.

It was at this point that Parkins always failed in his resolution to keep his eyes shut. With many misgivings as to incipient failure of eyesight, over-worked brain, excessive smoking, and so on, he finally resigned himself to light his candle, get out a book, and pass the night waking, rather than be tormented by this persistent panorama, which he saw clearly enough could only be a morbid reflection of his walk and his thoughts on that very day.

The scraping of match on box and the glare of light must have startled some creatures of the night—rats or what not—which he heard scurry across the floor from the side of his bed with much rustling. Dear, dear! the match is out! Fool that it is!

BLAKE MORRISON

Covehithe

From *Shingle Street* (2015)

Blake Morrison is a poet and novelist. His memoir When Did You Last See Your Father? *won the J.R. Ackerley Award for Autobiography.*

COVEHITHE

The tides go in and out
but the cliffs are stuck in reverse:
back across the fields they creep,
to the graves of Covehithe church.

From church to beach
was once a hike.
Today it's just a stroll.
Soon it'll be a stone's throw.

And that path we took
along the cliffs has itself been taken,
by winter storms.
The wheat's living on the edge.

What's to be done?
I blame the dead
in their grassy mounds,
the sailors and fishermen

longing to be back at sea
who since they can't get up
and stride down to the beach
entice the sea to come to them.

Bill Jackson, *Covehithe*.

Bill Jackson is a multi-award winning photographer, filmmaker and sound artist.

P.D. JAMES

Superintendent Adam Dalgliesh in Suffolk

From *Unnatural Causes* (1967)

P.D. James (1920–2014) was inspired by her holiday home in Southwold, which became a pivotal setting in the dystopian tale The Children of Men. *Covehithe features in her detective novel* Death in Holy Orders, *and in another of her detective novels,* Unnatural Causes, *her most famous character, detective Adam Dalgliesh, visits his aunt near Dunwich. Dalgliesh is on the verge of a life-changing decision about whether to marry; and it is the landscape of Suffolk which finally makes the decision for him.*

Adam Dalgliesh drove his Cooper Bristol gently on to the grass verge outside Blythburgh church and, a minute later, passed through the north chantry-chapel door into the cold silvery whiteness of one of the loveliest church interiors in Suffolk. He was on his way to Monksmere Head just south of Dunwich to spend a ten-day autumn holiday with a spinster aunt, his only living relative, and this was his last stop on the way.

He had started off from his City flat before London was stirring, and instead of taking the direct route to Monksmere through Ipswich, had struck north at Chelmsford to enter Suffolk at Sudbury. He had breakfasted at Long Melford and had then turned west through Lavenham to drive slowly and at will through the green and gold of this most unspoilt and un-prettified of counties. His mood would have wholly matched the day if it weren't for one persistent nagging worry. He had been deliberately putting off a personal decision until this holiday. Before he went back to London he must finally decide whether to ask Deborah Riscoe to marry him.

Irrationally, the decision would have been easier if he hadn't known so certainly what her answer would be. This threw upon him the whole responsibility for deciding whether to change the present satisfactory status quo for a commitment which both of them, he suspected, would regard as irrevocable whatever the outcome. As he walked to and fro under the marvellous cambered tie-beam roof and smelt the Anglican odour of wax polish, flowers and damp old hymn books, it came to him that he had got what he wanted at almost the precise moment of suspecting that he no longer wanted it.

Half an hour later he closed the church door quietly behind him and set off on the last few miles of the journey to Monksmere. He had written to his aunt to say that he would probably arrive at half-past two and, with luck, he would be

Michael Rimmer, *Blythburgh Angel*, 2015.

Michael Rimmer studied classics at Oxford University before becoming an investment manager and photographer. In 2010 he set out to create the first comprehensive photographic record of every angel roof in East Anglia. He lives in Norfolk and lectures regularly on angel roofs.

there almost precisely on time. If, as was usual, his aunt came out of the cottage at two-thirty she should see the Cooper Bristol just breasting the headland. He thought of her tall, angular, waiting figure with affection. Just over five years ago she had sold her house in Lincolnshire and bought Pentlands, a stone cottage on the edge of Monksmere Head. Here Dalgliesh visited her at least twice a year.

They were no mere duty visits. Already he was looking forward to the satisfaction of seeing her, to the assured pleasures of a holiday at Monksmere. There would be a driftwood fire in the wide hearth scenting the whole cottage, and before it the high-backed armchair once part of his father's study in the vicarage where he was born, the leather smelling of childhood. There would be a sparsely furnished bedroom with a view of sea and sky, a comfortable if narrow bed with sheets smelling faintly of wood-smoke and lavender, plenty of hot water and a bath long enough for a six-foot-two man to stretch himself in comfort. Most immediately, there would be tea before the fire and hot buttered toast with home-made potted meat. Best of all, there would be no corpses and no talk of them. He knew exactly what the holiday offered. They would walk together, often in silence, on the damp strip of firm sand between the sea's foam and the pebbled rises of the beach. He would carry her sketching paraphernalia, she would stride a little ahead, hands dug in her jacket pockets, eyes searching out where wheatears, scarcely distinguishable from pebbles, had lighted on the shingle, or following the flight of tern or plover. It would be peaceful, restful, utterly undemanding; but at the end of ten days he would go back to London with a sense of relief.

He was driving now through Dunwich Forest where the Forestry Commission's plantations of dark firs flanked the road. He fancied that he could smell the sea now, the salt tang borne to him on the wind was sharper than the bitter smell of the trees. His heart lifted. He felt like a child coming home. And now the forest ended, the sombre dark green of the firs ruled off by a wire fence from the water-coloured fields and hedges. And now they too passed and he was driving through the gorse and heather of the heathlands on his way to Dunwich.

The rough track which led across Monksmere Head to Pentlands was usually barred by a heavy farm gate but today this stood open, biting deep into the tall hedge of brambles and elders. The car bumped slowly over the potholes and between the stubble of hay which soon gave way to grass and then to bracken. Now the track wound uphill and suddenly the whole of the headland lay open before him, stretching purple and golden to the cliffs and shining sea. At the crest of the track Dalgliesh stopped the car to watch and to listen. Autumn had never been his favourite season, but in the moment which followed the stopping of the engine he wouldn't have changed this mellow peace for all the keener sensitivities of spring. The heather was beginning to fade now but the second flowering of the gorse was as thick and golden as the first richness of May. Beyond it lay the sea, streaked with purple, azure and brown, and to the south the mist-hung marshes of the bird reserve added their gentler greens and blues. The air smelt of heather and woodsmoke, the inevitable and evocative smells of autumn. It was hard to believe, thought Dalgliesh, that one was looking at a battlefield where for nearly nine centuries the land had waged its losing fight against the sea; hard to realise that under that deceptive calm of veined water lay the nine drowned churches of old Dunwich.

At that moment his aunt appeared at the side of her cottage and gazed up at the headland. Dalgliesh glanced at his wrist. It was thirty-three minutes past two. He let in the clutch and the Cooper Bristol bumped slowly down the track towards her.

It was nearly half-past eight and Dalgliesh and his aunt, their dinner over, sat in companionable silence one each side of the living room fire. The room, which occupied almost the whole of the ground floor of Pentlands, was stone walled with a low roof buttressed by immense oak beams and floor of red quarry tiles. In front of the open fireplace, where a wood fire crackled and spurted, a neat stack of driftwood was drying. The smell of wood smoke drifted through the cottage like incense; and the air vibrated endlessly with the thudding of the sea. Dalgliesh found it hard to keep awake in this rhythmic, somnambulant peace. He had always enjoyed contrast in art or nature and at Pentlands, once night had fallen, the pleasures of contrast were easily self-induced. Inside the cottage there was light and warmth, all the colours and comfort of civilised domesticity; outside under the low clouds there was darkness, solitude, mystery. He pictured the shore, one hundred feet below, where the sea was spreading its fringe of lace over the cold, firm beach; and the Monksmere bird reserve to the south, quiet under the night sky, its reeds hardly stirring in the still water.

Stretching his legs to the fire and wedging his head still more comfortably into the high back of the chair, he looked across at his aunt. She was sitting, as always, bolt upright and yet she looked perfectly comfortable. She was knitting a pair of woollen socks in bright red which Dalgliesh could only hope were not intended for him. He thought it unlikely. She was the most self-sufficient, and least sentimental woman that he knew. Dalgliesh wondered how Deborah would get on with her, what the two women would make of each other. It was difficult to picture Deborah in any setting other than London. He could only see her now against the background of his own City flat, of restaurants, theatre foyers and their favourite pubs. Deborah was not part of his job and as yet she had no place at Pentlands. But if he married her, she would necessarily have some share in both. Somehow, on this brief holiday he knew he had to decide if that was what he really wanted.

Jane Dalgliesh said: 'Would you like some music? I have the new Mahler recording.'

Dalgliesh wasn't musical, but he knew that music meant a great deal to his aunt and listening to her records had become part of a Pentlands holiday. And, in his present mood, he was even ready to try Mahler.

ROGER DEAKIN

Swimming with Otters

From *Waterlog, a Swimmer's Journey through Britain* (1999)

Roger Deakin (1943–2006), film maker, writer and environmentalist, lived at the moated Walnut Tree Cottage, on Mellis Common by the Waveney near Diss. Waterlog, a chronicle of swimming his way round Britain in moats, ponds, rivers and sea, comprises cultural history, autobiography, travel writing and natural history. It has become an influential work, inspiring many to follow in his breaststrokes and take up wild swimming as well as highlighting the importance of connecting with nature.

Next day I met an otter in the Waveney. I swam round a bend in my favourite river in Suffolk and there it was, sunning itself on a floating log near the reed-bed. I would have valued a moment face to face, but it was too quick for that. It slipped into the water on the instant, the big paddle tail following through with such stealth that it left hardly a ripple. But I saw its white bib and the unmistakable bulk of the animal, and I knew I had intruded into its territory; knew also that it was underwater somewhere close, sensing my movements. It hadn't paused to puzzle over my unconventional mode of approach. It just went. It didn't miss a beat. We can scarcely be said to have communed, yet I can replay every frame of the brief encounter in slow motion, right down to the just-vacated wet log rolling back into balance, oscillating slightly, and my own emotions, a mixture of elation at a rare moment's audience with the most reclusive animal on the river (Ted Hughes called it 'a king in hiding') and shame at having interrupted its private reverie.

That otters came within a whisker of extinction in England and Wales during the late fifties and early sixties is well known. It happened suddenly and insidiously. But there are hopeful signs that they are now gradually returning to many of their traditional rivers. It has taken thirty years for the powerful poisons that killed them, organochloride pesticides like aldrin, dieldrin and DDT, to flush out of our rivers, and for people to realise that otters will only thrive in waters that are left wild and untutored, as well as unpolluted, with plenty of wet woodland, untidy wood stacks, nettles, story-book gnarled trees full of hollows, and as few humans as possible.

I was swimming ten miles from the moat, where the Waveney defines the border between Norfolk and Suffolk. It is a secret river, by turns lazy and agile, dashing over shallow beds of golden gravel, then suddenly quiet, dignified and deep. It winds through water meadows, damp woods and marshes in a wide basin that was once tidal from Yarmouth to Diss, close to its source in the great watershed of Redgrave Fen, where its twin, the Little Ouse, also rises and flows off in the opposite direction, into the Fens. With its secret pools and occasional sandy beaches, the Waveney is full of swimming holes, diving stages improvised from wooden pallets, dangling ropes, and upturned canoes pulled up on the bank. Every two or three miles you come to a weir and a whitewashed watermill.

I swam on beyond the otter pool, under some sort of spell. It struck me that the animal's particular magic does not stem so much from its rarity as its invisibility. It is through their puckish, Dionysian habit of veiling themselves from view that otters come to embody the river spirits themselves. Henry Williamson knew this when he wrote his great mythic poem of Tarka the Otter. In the best traditions of spirits, the otter reveals itself through signs. You hunt for their tracks on sandbars, or for their spraint, the aromatic dung they leave behind to mark their territory, like clues in an Easter-egg hunt, under bridges or on the lowest boughs of willow and alder.

That otters were once plentiful in the Waveney was clear enough until recently if you went to the Harleston Magpie, which used to be a principal meeting place for the Eastern Counties Otter Hounds. Before the pub was altered, there were still otter masks and pads on the walls there, and up the road at the De La Pole Arms in Wingfield they have even installed entire animals, mummified in glass cases. One of my Suffolk friends inherited a red and blue tweed hunting coat that would have been worn by a member of the Eastern Counties Otter Hounds. It must have been hot work, hurrying on foot up and down the river bank, and from pub to pub along the valley, in tweed suits. A student of rural customs, he also once saw an otter pad mounted on a wooden shield with the enigmatic inscription: 'Shanghai Otter Hounds, Wortwell Mill, 1912'. Quite serendipitously, he stumbled on the explanation in a bookshop the following year, looking through the memoirs of an officer of the Shanghai Police, Maurice Springfield, who, it seemed, had been the Master of the Shanghai Otter Hounds, and bought some of the dogs in Suffolk around 1912 to take back with him to China. He must have been allowed to hunt them with the East Anglian contingent, perhaps by way of a road test, running down the unfortunate otter at Wortwell Mill.

In the autumn of the year before, I had crossed Suffolk to Westleton Village Hall one Saturday morning to attend a training session in animal tracking organised by the Suffolk Wildlife Trust so that we could take part in a survey of the Suffolk rivers for otters, mink and water voles. About forty of us sat in the hall studying slides of their footprints, and learning more about their ways. Small plastic tubs containing otter and mink shit were solemnly passed round. It was a bit like a wine tasting. You waved the poos under your nose, sniffed, then passed on the sample to your neighbour. Our tutor described otter spraint as 'fragrant', with something of the quality of jasmine tea, but perhaps an added nuance of fish oil and new-mown hay. A sample of jasmine tea was also circulated. You need a good nose to be a successful otter detective. We took it on trust from our tutor that otter spraint is also 'tarry and tacky'. Mink, on the other hand, have, or do, 'scats'.

Scats look quite like spraint, but smell like burnt rubber or rotten fish. I felt the aesthetics of the matter posed some threat to our scientific objectivity.

That afternoon, we had all gone down to the Eel's Foot at Eastbridge, within sight of the Sizewell B nuclear power station, and walked along the bank of the Minsmere river in a crocodile looking for real live otter spraint. The Minsmere otters, no doubt observing all this from the safety of some hollow tree, would have witnessed the unusual spectacle of forty humans queuing to lie full-length on the bank and sniff small dollops of poo, making appreciative sounds. Someone spotted a bubble and all forty of us froze, bright-eyed and bushy-tailed, but it was just a bubble. I find I have since rather gone off jasmine tea.

I had met my Waveney otter downstream of Mendham Mill, near where I began my swim, diving in from a lush meadow where giant puffballs grow in late summer, once in such profusion that I mistook them at first sight for a flock of sheep, or the naked bottoms of swimmers. The breaststroke had again served me well by being so silent. I swam on downstream, over festive streamers of waving ribbon weed, brushed by the floppy leaves of yellow waterlilies, through endless meandering bends, past swans that hissed, but swam away, and turned off into the still, secret world of one of the drainage channels that run in straight lines across the flood meadows. It was five feet wide, full of moorhens and humming with insect life. Damselflies of all hues and patterns courted each other madly right in front of my nose, quite unconcerned. They even flew about in flagrante, performing the extraordinary feat of flying and copulating at the same time; a kind of insect Mile High Club. Huge dragonflies, some blue, some brown, hawked up and down the water right over me, or perched undisturbed on lilies. As I pushed through between the reeds, rows of bubbles rose ahead of me as eels sank deeper into the mud, or where a moorhen had dived and was swimming off underwater. Eels are the favourite food of otters, and the most nutritious of all fresh-water fish.

Helen Napper, *Waxing Moon*, 2020.

Helen Napper is known for her paintings of intense and intimate still lifes and of swimmers, the sea, the marshes and the creatures that wander through them. The scenes she depicts are as often imbued with saturated colour as they are immersed in muted grey tones that capture the coastal hues she sees from her home in Aldeburgh where she has lived, painted and swum every day since The Great Storm of 1987.

OLIVIA LAING

A Late Frost *(2021)*

Olivia Laing is a British writer, novelist and cultural critic. She is the author of five works of non-fiction, To the River, The Trip to Echo Spring, The Lonely City, Funny Weather *and* Everybody, *as well as a novel,* Crudo. *In 2018, she was awarded the Windham-Campbell Literature Prize for non-fiction and in 2019, the 100th James Tait Black Memorial Prize for* Crudo. *In 2019 she became an elected Fellow of the Royal Society of Literature. She moved to Suffolk in 2020.*

A late frost, gone by nine. The wood pigeons are making nests and the white ribes glows against the yew. When we first saw the garden it was January, a dank day, rain in the air. Ivy had grown up above the walls in dense ramparts, blotting out the light. I walked ahead, scouting for treasures. A skeletal tree peony, festooned with shining black seeds. Leucojums, which resemble snowdrops from a giant's garden.

The bones, as designers like to say, were very good. The garden was entirely surrounded by walls and occupied about a third of an acre, nearly encircling the house. It felt much larger because it had been divided into a series of compartments by cunning hedges of beech and hornbeam and yew. One of these enclosed spaces had a Mediterranean feel, with a quatrefoil pond, two cypresses and a run of hibiscus trees. There were vast unpruned figs against a curving eighteenth-century wall of soft pink Suffolk brick. In another space, tucked between the house and pub, there were fruit trees and a decrepit greenhouse, and at the end there was a wild enclosure full of rotting cherries and a medlar tree, its centre covered with a circular black tarpaulin that marked the site of a wedding marquee.

All my life, I'd been looking for this garden. It was as if it had materialised directly from a children's book: the coughing pheasant, the heavy air drenched with the scent of a daphne. It was impossible to look at the tangles of a banksia rose without remembering Mary from *The Secret Garden* scraping at brown twigs and crying out, *it's wick, it's wick.* It was a garden to vanish into, the sense of benign neglect adding to its Green Knowe charm. You could lose yourself inside it, an ocean away from the world.

Lockdown intervened, and we didn't see the garden again until the late summer. What had looked in winter like promise had curdled into a bad spell. The old walls had vanished beneath a luxuriant curtain of bindweed. Bamboo had ramped out of control. The garden had been laid out in the 1960s by its long-term inhabitant Mark Rumary, once the head designer at Notcutt's, the venerable Suffolk nursery. I'd seen photographs from its immaculate heyday in back issues of *Country Life* and *The English Garden*. The beds were orderly back then, the planting intricate and unusual. Ever since we'd first seen it, I'd been researching what Rumary had grown, making hopeful lists of Carpentaria, pineapple broom, even an acuba from Chopin's grave. But I hadn't bargained for what a decade of neglect could do. The beds were full of couch grass. The soil was rock hard and the consistency of Muscovado sugar.

I'd been told to do nothing in the first year, and especially not to remove any plant I didn't recognise. Instead, I edited. For month after month, we turfed out rubbish, stripping first the bindweed then the ivy, rediscovering bed edges, rooting out nettles and grass. Every week we drove to the dump with rubble sacks stuffed full of corpses of shrubs that had died and been left to rot where they stood. The beds were choked with self-seeded comfrey and alkanet. There were red and white striped dahlias crammed into every available space, a misguided attempt at jollification that only contributed to the chaos. Skeletal roses attested to the impoverished soil. There were autumn weeks of scraping off moss and replacing it with a duvet of manure, trying to improve conditions. Lots of the trees looked half-dead, and in October I understood why when clumps of golden mushrooms appeared, the fruiting bodies of the dreaded honey fungus, which feeds off roots, and was killing a beautiful cockspur thorn and threatening the magnolia. So that was why the ribes died the day we arrived, keeling over, unable to cope in the drought.

Every winter, in every garden I have had, I've thought that nothing will come back. I drew plans for new borders, planted fritillary and species tulips in the little orchard, hired a tree surgeon to bring out the dead, sat on my hands and waited. The hellebores arrived first, ghostly and glowing, in greens, creams, mauves, even striped like a blackcurrant ripple. There were hardly any crocuses, but thousands of snowdrops. The great torch of the daphne was lit, and its fragrance filled the garden until the magnolia took over. Crown imperials emerged, and the remnants of what must once have been an entire blue carpet of scilla. Primroses, bluebells, star of Bethlehem. I pruned and pruned, cutting into old wood, rewarded a few weeks later with a clean flush of green. The soil was, as Mark Rumary had promised, as fine as sugar, the worst possible soil to garden in, 'easy on the back and heavy on the heart'. I didn't mind. The greenhouse was rebuilt and filled with pelargoniums and sweet pea seedlings. I fed the box and planted roses: Rosa mundi, the lovely striped apothecary's rose that Derek Jarman grew at Prospect Cottage; Shropshire Lass, good for a north wall; and Mermaid, a favourite of Vita Sackville West, to keep company with the fig that had come from a cutting from Sissinghurst.

And now it's now, which is to say April, with its miscellany of weather. Pink fists of peonies, the lavish, going-nowhere leaves of autumn crocuses, which won't deliver their abundant promise 'til next September. The magnolia is browned by the hail but remains triumphant, a big ship in sail. The daffodils are over, the tulips yet to start. Yesterday as I drank my coffee by the pond I saw something on the path, a greenish oblong object I couldn't place. It was a bird's nest, tumbled from a branch. The outer layer was lichen. Beneath it was a cushion of moss packed with silky feathers. Someone's carefully maintained home, intricate and lively. I tucked it into the fig.

Ffiona Lewis, *Maidens on Marigold*, 2020.

Ffiona Lewis qualified as an architect in 1990 before turning to painting. Her pictures tread a fine balance between figuration and abstraction, with scenes that are stripped of people but nonetheless allude to a human presence. Her paintings are typical for their bold, dynamic strokes, with Lewis using a palette knife to both add and remove layers of paint.

MELISSA HARRISON

Winter in Suffolk

From *The Stubborn Light of Things* (2020)

A Londoner for over twenty years, moving from flat to tube to air-conditioned office, Melissa Harrison knew what it was to be insulated from the seasons. Adopting a dog and going on daily walks helped reconnect her with the cycle of the year and the quiet richness of nature all around her. She records the world around her in her nature diaries.

16 November 2019

I have come to a place of extraordinary silence. Having lived in rural Suffolk for the last two years I thought I knew quiet, but now I've bought my first house, a cottage four miles north in a village significantly further from any main roads—and the difference is astonishing. Now, if I wake at night, the silence feels as though it's actively pressing on my ears. Lying in pitch-blackness (we have no street lights), utterly deprived of sensory input, is strangely disquieting. Yet the constant hum of background noise is a very recent development. For most of our history, total silence—and total darkness—would have been nothing unusual at all.

This new quietness has made me more aware of sound, from the mysterious creature that processes across my roof each night to the rain gurgling relentlessly in the gutters and the noise the wind makes as it rushes through the last of the ash leaves, tattered and yellowing.

Sound is such a vital part of our relationship with nature, and yet—apart from birdsong—it's so easily overlooked. You can look away from something you're not interested in, but you can't 'listen away'—noises are taken in and processed regardless. We have an auditory relationship with the natural world that persists despite our modern lack of attention to it. Tuning in to sound is a deeply atavistic pleasure.

Dusk is my favourite time to go out walking. As the light fades, the night shift clocks on: rabbits come out to feed, owls call from the copses and spinneys, and foxes, deer, hedgehogs and badgers can sometimes be seen. In summer bats begin hunting as darkness falls, and in spring there is the evening chorus to serenade you, almost as joyful and riotous as at dawn. As the human world quietens down, it can feel as though the natural world wakes up.

But there's another reason I love to be out of doors at day's end. Here in Suffolk traces of the past are everywhere, from horse ponds glinting like mercury among the stubble fields to labourers' cottages like mine with woodsmoke curling from brick chimneys hundreds of years old. In the half-light of dusk, the old lanes empty of traffic, it's possible to leave behind the present day with its frightening uncertainties and enter a world in which heavy horses worked the land, the seasons turned with comforting regularity and climate change was unheard of. Political and social nostalgia may be dangerous, but ecologically it's unavoidable. At dusk—if only briefly—one can imagine that the world is still unharmed.

25 January 2020

Winter sun slants low over Suffolk's stubble fields, cold but golden, and casting long shadows. It gilds the brown back of the kestrel as she hovers over a hedgerow, looking for the ultraviolet trails left by the urine of voles passing along their habitual runs. It backlights the tall ears of a hare racing for the wood margin, making them glow pink, and gleams in dustily at the end window of the old barn where, on a beam beside its numbered box, the white owl roosts.

Cold, though. The light may be gold, but Suffolk's rich brown ploughland is silvered with a hard frost.

At night the wood pigeons leave the fields and roost in the village's conifers and other evergreens. Returning from the pub with my torch, I startled several, sending them exploding out of the foliage with much clapping of wings and the characteristic whistling noise their feathers make in flight. They're perfectly capable of dropping silently out of a tree on the far side of an approaching human; this loud take-off is a non-vocal avian alarm call, designed to communicate danger to others. We now know that a specially modified outer wing feather creates the piping sound.

9 May 2020

Twice in recent days I've got up before sunrise and headed out to hear the dawn chorus, taking a field recorder so I can capture it for the podcast I'm making to keep people in lockdown in touch with the natural world. In towns and cities robins are often the first to give voice, often while the sky is still black; here in Suffolk it's been the job of the skylarks, hanging over the dim fields.

I was cheered to hear the notes of yellowhammers from the hedges. One of the few birds to sing right through to late summer, they soundtrack August strolls along hot country lanes and walks on sun-baked, gorse-clad uplands. Once they were known as scribble larks or writing larks for the intricate patterns on their eggs.

These grain-eating birds have been in steep decline across western Europe since 1980, and the issue seems to be one of winter survival. Once, they could feed on grain spilled on stubble fields in colder weather, as well as weed seeds from 'unimproved' hay meadows, but agricultural intensification has vastly reduced both stubble and weeds. Properly planned, consistent agri-environment schemes are vital if we are not to lose farmland birds like yellowhammers from our countryside, and with them part of our shared cultural heritage: that age-old, deeply evocative song.

When your life's work is trying to connect people to nature, seeing so many tuning in to birdsong, revelling in rain showers and hungry for the rites of spring is deeply satisfying. Suddenly, it seems, there's space for the small, seasonal pleasures that sustain some of us, but which have gone unnoticed by many, stuck on the exhausting treadmill of travel and shopping and work: the first swift, the heady scent of lilac, a blackbird's evening song.

If we could take one thing from this nightmarish period and carry it into whatever world is to come, I'd choose this fragile new awareness, this new need for nature, this sudden new love.

NORMAN SCARFE

Islands

From *Suffolk in the Middle Ages* (1986)

Norman Scarfe (1923–2014) was an eminent historian who devoted much of his life and talent to Suffolk history. He was instrumental in the founding of the Suffolk Record Society, editing the journal of the Records Society. He worked with the Suffolk Preservation Society and Suffolk Historic Churches Trust and helped establish the Museum of East Anglian Life at Stowmarket. He became chairman of the Centre of East Anglian Studies at the University of East Anglia.

The earliest verbal records of Suffolk are its place-names. They face us on sign-boards every two or three miles; more frequently in Suffolk than elsewhere. We are apt to look rather blankly at them, for we need a dictionary—E. Ekwall's *Concise Oxford Dictionary of English Place-Names*—to get the hang of most of them. In Suffolk, most of them go back at least to Domesday Book, so one depends on his expertise in Old English, Old Scandinavian, etc. The surprising thing, though, is how little they have changed over all the centuries. Despite amusing variations in the spellings of the same name by the Domesday scribes, the place-names we use today are easily identifiable in the great record of 1086. These names provide valuable clues for our detection of the past.

Eyes

Do you think of islands when you think of Suffolk? I, for one, did not. Yet eight fairly well-known Suffolk place names embody the Old English word for an island (*eg*, which has become *-ey*, and Eye itself). Centuries of draining marshes and improving water-courses have lowered the river-levels and removed or reduced the original watery surroundings that distinguished these places. But once you are alerted, you will have no difficulty in seeing that the market-town of Eye, in the middle of Suffolk, is built on a small island, surrounded by low-lying, willow-growing, sedgy land. (Much of it is the 'Town Moor', which in Suffolk means Town Fen, or Marsh: A. H. Smith shows how in the eastern fens 'moor' came to mean 'marsh'.) In the years 1066–1071, when the Conqueror's magnate, William Malet, built his castle here and laid out the market-place, he chose the place for its defensible 'island' qualities—those of a moat.

Kersey is no longer easy to think of as a 'cress-island', though visitors always remember the water-splash a little higher up-stream, where it crosses the village street below that steep church-path. The cress-island was eclipsed during the Middle Ages by the fulling-mill beside that stream, so that 'kerseys', popular textiles, entered early into the imagination of Shakespeare: 'Russet yeas and honest kersey noes' (*Love's Labour's Lost*). So did next-door Lindsey, in the same way as 'linsie wolsy' in *All's Well*; for at least one of Lindsey's three running brooks must have turned a fulling-mill: in the twelfth century one of them was used to fill the moat of Adam of Cockfield's 'adulterine' castle—which was built, perhaps, on the original 'island'.

The most startling of Suffolk's -*eys* is Bawdsey, at the northern lip of the Deben estuary. As you descend and rise from Stangrove Hall and the Alderton 'mainland', on the one road leading into Bawdsey, you easily perceive how it stood islanded by the river and the sea. But a most tantalising enigma lies hidden in the first part of the name, which Ekwall reveals as 'Baldhere's island'. Whoever this particular Baldhere may have been, we can hardly ignore his namesake Balder, Odin's son, in Scandinavian mythology, slain by the inevitable mistletoe spear and sent blazing out to sea on his funeral ship as in Matthew Arnold's 'Balder Dead'—not an inspired poem, but an endlessly evocative title. Bawdsey's name by itself might have prepared us, years earlier, for the uncovering of the great burial-ship seven miles up river at Sutton Hoo. (*Hoo* is a hill-spur, and Sutton, south-*tun*, southern estate.) Perhaps this explains why it has proved so hard to find a body in the ship-burial at Sutton Hoo.

SUSAN OWENS

On Constable

From *Spirit of Place: Artists, Writers and the British Landscape* (2020)

Susan Owens is a writer and art curator. Her most recent books are The Ghost: A Cultural History *and* Spirit of Place.

The unemphatic farmland of Suffolk and Essex where Constable grew up, the cornfields, river, windmills, watermills, towpaths, millponds and locks, inspired him more than the most dramatic scenery. He went on a sketching tour to the Lake District in 1806—a rare excursion for him into conventional 'picturesque' territory—but the watercolours he brought back in his portfolio were oddly unfocused, as though (try as he might) he was not quite able to get to grips with the Lake District. Whether or not 'the solitude of mountains oppressed his spirits', as his first biographer claimed, remains a moot point. But it is obvious that his heart was not really in it. Where his art came fully alive was in familiar farmland—industrial landscapes, even—and his imagination was caught by the sorts of details that would have horrified his contemporaries brought up on the dictum that it was best to generalize, to adopt the classical 'grand manner' and shun mundane, unelevated subjects. Writing to a friend in 1821, he listed his favourite bits of the country—several of the very features that, fifty years earlier, had so appalled William Gilpin: 'the sound of water escaping from Mill-dams [...] Willows, Old rotten Banks, slimy posts, & brickwork. I love such things'. Constable's sketchbooks are full of these seemingly insignificant details, to be salted away in his studio, sometimes emerging many years later when he wanted to add a broken-down bit of fencing to a towpath scene, or a stumpy pollarded willow. After he married and his visits to East Anglia became less frequent, these records became all the more precious, the pungent lifeblood of his art bottled up and stored in his Charlotte Street studio.

Sketchbooks were essential during the long summers Constable used to spend with his family at East Bergholt, before his marriage in 1816—they fitted neatly in his coat pocket as he walked the fields for hours at a time, stopping to sketch not only landscape details and vistas, but also the labourers and livestock that caught his eye. But no matter how skilfully he could record the turn of a cow's head or the angle of a scythe slung over a work-weary shoulder with his pencil, graphite could not capture nature on the move: foliage blown about on a breezy day, a drifting cloud, a patchwork of light and shadow changing the colour of a lane. So, although it was less convenient, he decided to take his oil paints outdoors. He worked as neatly as he could, resting his paint box on

John Constable, *Boat-Building near Flatford*, 1815.

his knee and pinning his sheets of paper to the inside of the lid (you can still see the pinholes in the corners). And he sat down to sketch, choosing to paint the sandy corner of a Suffolk lane on a windy day, his flicking brushstrokes deftly describing birds in flight. He studied dock leaves and undergrowth and a section of mossy tree-trunk bathed in pale sunlight; his art, he once wryly observed, 'is to be found under every hedge and in every lane, and therefore nobody thinks it worth picking up'. One stormy evening he painted barges on the Stour at Flatford Lock, the sky almost as dark as the water. In years to come he would take his paint box on to the uplands of Hampstead Heath, where with quick strokes of a thick brush he could record cloud formations before they drifted away or changed shape, and study how they related to the tossing foliage beneath.

At least once Constable attempted to complete an entire composition out of doors, setting up his easel in front of his father's dry-dock at Flatford Mill on the navigable river Stour in the early autumn of 1814 and sitting down on a bank to paint as, below him, a barge was constructed. He knew when it was time to return home at the end of the day when, from his vantage point, he saw smoke rising from the kitchen fire. It was not the first time industry had dominated a landscape, but this picture was so full of information that it verged on the didactic—he shows a man planing a shaped timber, and a cauldron in which pitch is being heated, prior to caulking the hulk. One almost expects every piece of equipment and activity to be labelled with a letter that corresponds to a printed key. Although the ghost of Claude seems to be hovering about the surrounding trees and distant hills, *Boat-building near Flatford Mill* was an outspoken statement about what land-scape looked and felt like to those who lived and worked in the country, and about what landscape art could be if only artists and the picture-buying public would stop being so obsessed with a few areas deemed to be picturesque. Constable was the son of a wealthy miller brought up working in a business it was understood that he would one day take over—it was only when his younger brother Abram stepped in that he was freed to go to London to study at the Royal Academy Schools. So he knew how windmills worked, was so interested in ploughs that he painstakingly drew regional variations in his sketchbooks, and could tell you the week of the year by the colour of ripening corn in a picture. As he grumbled to a friend in 1821, 'The Londoners with all their ingenuity as artists know nothing of the feeling of a country life (the essence of Landscape)—any more than a hackney coach horse knows of pasture'. His entire career can be seen as a struggle to rede-fine landscape—to rethink it as something that embraced the local, the everyday, the industrial, the inhabited.

RICHARD MABEY

The Suffolk Nightingale

From *The Barley Bird* (2010)

The Barley Bird is based on Richard Mabey's 1993 book Whistling in the Dark. *Mabey realised that his memorable experiences of nightingales were in Suffolk. For five decades Richard Mabey has been a pioneering voice in modern nature writing, from the rediscovery of foraging that led to* Food for Free *to the encyclopaedic* Flora Britannica.

This is where the great coloratura recitals happened, the birds singing deep into parched heathland nights, or breaking the silence of icy May dusks. This is no geographical accident. Suffolk is probably, after Kent, the best English county for the bird, which relishes its ancient coppice woods and bushy coastal heaths.

It's early May, a nightingale moon. I'm perched in a narrow lane above the Stour valley in Suffolk, listening to the birds. The landscape is already drained of colour, caught in that moment between light and dark when distances and outlines blur. I try to focus on the tumulus of scrub in front of me, but it seems to be dancing with phosphorescence. I know this is just my eyes playing tricks, but it gives the undergrowth an oddly insubstantial feel, quite out of keeping with the brilliant clarity of the song that is pouring from it.

It's my first nightingale of the year, and a coloratura bird into the bargain. It has a clipped, Latin style, full of deft phrases which are turned this way and that and drawn out into short, fading tremolos. As the moon rises, changing from hazy orange to platinum white, the singing becomes more assured. The sound is astonishingly pure and penetrating, broken with teasing, theatrical seasons. I realise I am rooted to the spot, standing in the middle of the lane and barely noticing the cars edging past.

No other bird song can match these outpourings under the May full moon. Even by nightingale standards they seem more eloquent and passionate than at any other time of the spring. Perhaps this is just a flight of fancy on my part, a touch of moonshine. But it's a critical moment in the bird's year. Ever since early April nightingales have been migrating back to Europe from their wintering quarters in tropical Africa, running the gauntlet of bird catchers and Mediterranean storms. The advance guard are almost all male birds, and since their arrival they will have been scouting out nesting territories in heaths and woodland thickets and river valleys.

The females follow a week or so later, choosing warm, clear nights for migration if possible. These nights in early May mark the crescendo of the nightingale's courtship. Territories are settled, female birds are on the move and choosing mates, and the last waves of new arrivals are winging in. No wonder the males' songs seem so intense: they are serenades to tempt the females down from the sky.

I heard my first Suffolk nightingale some twenty years before that enchanted evening. I'd bought a cottage in the Blyth Valley—my very first house—and had moved in on another hot May evening. I'd driven up from the south, and all through the tracts of heathland between Aldeburgh and Blythburgh nightingale phrases flew, disembodied, into the car. That night I lay in bed with the windows open and was transfixed to find that my own house had nightingales on tap. One was singing in the little patch of heather and gorse that began fifty yards from the garden, the other up the lane, in the churchyard of Wenhaston St Peter, with its exuberant sixteenth-century wall-painting of the Last Judgement.

I wish I could say that I was reminded of another phrase from Keats' Ode— 'The voice I heard this passing night was heard/ In ancient days …'—but I wasn't too familiar with nightingale poetry then. Nor can I recall being stirred to passion or melancholy or any of the emotions supposedly aroused by, or contained in, the bird's song. What I felt was more earthily romantic. I had fetched up on this per- fect spring evening in a landscape suffused by rhapsodic sounds that I knew were as special to this eastern heathland—the English *maquis*—as the lilt of the curlews on the coastal saltmarshes. They felt like a benediction—or a password.

I knew too that East Anglia was the only part of England that had a vernacu- lar name for the nightingale. It was called the Barley-bird, because its arrival coin- cided with the sprouting of the barley. Suffolk even seemed to be contradicting the sad decline in nightingale numbers which had begun at the start of the twentieth century. In a national census in 1980, 367 singing males were located in Suffolk. When the survey was repeated in 1991, the total had risen to 881, which may have represented a sixth of the entire English population. East Suffolk, especially, felt like the *axis mundi* of the nightingale world.

MICHAEL HAMBURGER

In Suffolk

From *Collected Poems* (1998)

Michael Hamburger (1924–2007) was a noted German-British poet, critic, memoirist and academic. He was known in particular for his translations of Friedrich Hölderlin, Paul Celan and W.G. Sebald from German, and his work in literary criticism. Hamburger settled in East Anglia with his wife, the poet Anne Beresford. They lived in an ancient house in Middleton surrounded by fruit trees, especially apple trees, cultivating what Hamburger himself termed 'obsolete and obsolescent' varieties of apple, such as Royal Russett and Orleans Reinette. These he propagated not from the normal method of grafting, but from pips, one from a core harvested in Ted Hughes's garden. W.G. Sebald made a memorable visit to his friend Michael's house which is described in The Rings of Saturn. *This is the first in a sequence of ten sections.*

IN SUFFOLK

So many moods of light, sky,
Such a flux of cloud shapes,
Cloud colours blending, blurring,
And the winds, to be learnt by heart:
So much movement to make a staying.

So much labour, with no time for looking,
Before trees wrenched free of ivy
Behind lowered eyelids began
To be ash or alder or willow.

So much delving down
With fork, spade, bare hands
To endangered roots before,
Weighed, breathed in, this earth
Made known its manyness
Of sand, humus, loam,
Of saturation, and so
Began to permit a tenure.

Landscape? Not yet. Even now,
Though more than a year of weathers
Has rushed, crept through the trees,

Annabel Gault, *Winter Garden*, 2006.

Annabel Gault has lived and worked in East Suffolk for over thirty-five years. Her garden near Leiston is a constant source of inspiration and ideas.

Leaved, stripped, torn off
Old boughs, snapped
Trunks of the newly planted.
In its burgeoning froze
This young medlar? Bending it,
Ripped the fine roots?
Other weathers will tell;

Let a dark glow red perhaps
Come again from the copper beech
Through translucent foliage, in May;
Deepen again the blackness
Of conifer woods, and pierce it.

Later perhaps, out of changing shapes,
A landscape will seem to grow,
Seem to cohere: a system
Of marsh and heath, of meadow
And forest, all veined
With waterways, roads. Not yet.

Winter. A night long
Gales tried the house. Rain
Found a way in. A gutter's
Jagged end hangs loose.
Iron sheets from a roof
Jam the holly hedge.
A telephone pole
Bars the lane to the village.

But bright the eastern sky
Breaks. Blue rivulets
Streak the grey north.
Mild or harsh, the day
Will only be itself.

Snow brings in snipe
To the sodden lawn
Pocked with molehills. Their bills
Jerk, prodding by inches
Down to the mud between clumps.
Now a tomcat prowls
The verge. They cower,
Motionlesss, merge in the cleared ruts.

Fieldfare alights, to fight
With blackbird, song thrush
Till a gull swoops down,
Then a jackdaw, to rob them and fight.
Only lapwing keeps aloof,
Stalks at the far end.

Sunshine, a quick thaw.
And all are gone. A gust,
And even the sparrows, robins
Are not to be seen or heard;
But in the distance, wind-blurred,
Lapwing's, gull's cry.

HELEN MACDONALD

Sun Birds and Cashmere Spheres: the Lost Orioles of Lakenheath, Suffolk

From *Vesper Flights* (2020)

Helen Macdonald is a writer, naturalist and maker of TV documentaries. Her book H is for Hawk *won both the Samuel Johnson and the Costa Award.*

I only saw them once. I didn't know I'd never see them again. I assumed they'd be eternal, like Pan Am, and the Soviet Union, and so many other things in the world that existed before I was born. I went out early that morning, sun glowing faintly through stratus, and drove northwest until shapes rose syrup-slow on the far horizon. They looked like buildings, like aircraft hangars or warehouses, but they were stands of poplars planted in the peaty loam of low-lying Suffolk in the 1950s by Bryant & May, the safety match manufacturers. Disposable plastic lighters and cheaper wood imports had turned these trees into economic relics. But the plantations were beloved of birders, because they were the only place in the country you could see breeding golden orioles. They were legendary birds. I'd read about them for years. They're dazzlingly pretty—the males buttercup yellow with shiny black wings and a strawberry-red beak, the females soft olive green—but much of their glamour came from their rarity. If you live somewhere other than Britain, you might see orioles all the time. There are many in the Americas, and golden orioles are common garden birds in countries across the Palearctic. But in Britain we only had this one tiny outpost: a handful of breeding birds in stands of trees by a railway line a few miles from an American airbase where nightingales singing in scrubby roadside copses vie with the roaring of F-15 fighter jets on training circuits. Before I knew better, I had imagined inland Suffolk to be a bucolic, soft landscape, all woodsmoke and Constable and cattle grazing under the ghosts of vanished elms. But when I moved to East Anglia I was delighted to discover how wrong I'd been. Because this part of Suffolk is different. It is particoloured and peculiar, vaguely uncertain of itself, a perpetual work in progress. Forestry blocks, flooded fields, drainage ditches and twisted pines, poplars, reeds, American flags, biker cafés, rabbit-cropped turf and flint-faced cottages. It's one of my favourite places on Earth.

I'd arranged to meet my guide by the entry gate to RSPB Lakenheath. I'd never met him before, but there wasn't much doubt that he was the man in a woollen hat waving at me with a pair of binoculars. Peter was a friend of a friend, an expert on these orioles and he had, it turned out, been sleeping in his car all night on site waiting for daylight. He told me I'd missed the bitterns booming in the reedbeds at dawn, that it was the strangest of sounds, like someone blowing across the top of a deep and wide-necked bottle. But, he continued, the orioles were still singing. And as we walked down the dew-soaked track towards the wood, I heard them, fluting, rich, melodic phrases that cut across distance and the rattle of leaves and the loud chatter of singing reed warblers as if they were drifting in from an impossibly remote place. That place of distance felt like the past, the birds speaking softly of history. Chaucer wrote of a bird called Wodewale, which has been variously identified by experts as a woodpecker, a woodlark, or an oriole. I'm sure it's the latter, for the word itself is a beautiful phonetic approximation of an oriole's song: Wo-de-wal-e, wod-de-wal-e, a phrase like the curl of the cut ends of a gilded banner furling over the page of an illuminated manuscript.

It was easy to hear orioles. Seeing them was a different matter. The Suffolk poplar plantation resembled, somehow, a scaled-up table-top cardboard theatre set, and peering into it pulled me into all manner of perspectival tricks and traps. Rows of equally-sized grey, columnar trunks marched back to vanishing points in the dim distance, and because poplar branches begin high up, the arches where the leaves met between the rows of trees seemed part proscenium, part cathedral buttress. It was noisy, too, with a near-continuous rattle and clatter. Poplar's heart-shaped leaves are arranged in little fists of long, flexible petioles that make them twist and flap, flag-like, in the least breath of wind. The whole forest looked as if were made of torn paper, and somewhere in its leaves were orioles. They called, moved. Sang, then called again, moved unseen to a distant tree, called again, made a different call, a sharp cat-call hzzzt! moved, called, sang, and then moved once more. They stuck to the very tops of the tree canopy, and after a while I began to wonder if they could throw their voices. We stood there for a very long while, binoculars raised, necks getting cricked, and we saw no orioles at all. Driving home, I held the memory of their song with me like a hot pebble in the palm of one hand. I hadn't been disappointed by my morning in the poplars. Even so, I knew I needed to come back and try again.

This was fifteen years ago, in 2006, and our little East Anglian population was about to blink into nonexistence. At this point the outpost was only about forty years old: its first colonisers had came here from Holland in the 1960s, where they nested in trees in the Polders just like these. They must have crossed the North Sea and found themselves somewhere that felt like home. They quietly thrived. By the 1980s there were about thirty pairs, but there was already concern about their future, for many of the most expansive poplar stands in the area were scheduled to be felled. People clubbed together to form a group to study, survey, and help protect them, and some new poplar belts were planted in hope of future colonisation. But the largest block of trees was hewn down all the same, and their numbers plummeted. This coincided with the beginning of a wider decline in oriole populations across their northern range in Holland, Denmark, Finland. It might have been the effect of environmental changes in the Congo, where orioles spend their winters, or perhaps because increasingly early springs in Europe have led to a mismatch in timing between the emergence of the insects that orioles feed upon, and when they are most needed to feed their young. In Britain the end came fast. Three years after my visit, only one nest remained, after which there were no more British-bred orioles. They had been a visitation, living in a little snippet of economic history, settling gold on the papery branches, making the fens obliquely glorious with their song. We never thought of these birds as immigrants; this was no Lost Colony. We thought of them as lost natives, and cherished their foothold in our time.

I returned to Lakenheath a week later in hot, thundery darkness just before sunrise. The site had been turned into a bird reserve a few years earlier, and the carrot fields around the poplar plantations had been flooded and planted with phragmites reeds. My walk to meet Peter ran through these reeds, passing patches of unreflective water, flat pools with surfaces matte with milky pollen-dust, tiny froglets scrambling away from my feet, the grass running with scores of minia-ture, urgent amphibians. Though beautiful, reedbeds are unsettling places. Unlike deserts and open water, they're not inimical to supporting human life except in a very literal sense. You can walk across deserts, foot by foot. You can't walk on water at all. With reedbeds, who knows? Their stalks are spiky and soft at once, and reedbeds do, in some places, become islands, as in the Danube delta, and sail off in matted arks of rot and life. They're delicate, different and faintly dangerous places. Let no one underestimate the strange effect on human psychology of not knowing whether the ground underfoot is ground at all. Unless you have special, local knowledges, reedbeds can be as forbidding and as lethal as mountains.

As I looked over the reeds I heard a pinging sound, then four or five small, long-tailed birds flew in little musical slurs across the water and landed to catch like little spherical burrs in the reeds right in front of me. They were bearded reedlings, birds utterly reliant on stands of phragmites like these. The adults raise a couple of families a year, and this was a brood of adolescents let loose upon the reeds. Adult male bearded reedlings are legendarily glamorous, possessing grey cowls and long black moustaches. But these youngsters weren't in grown-up dress; they were sleek and fawn-coloured as if they made of very expensive cashmere, and some-how wearing long, black velvet evening gloves. Their tiny waxen beaks resembled the heads of all-weather matches, and set in a thumb-smear of sooty kohl were strange, pale eyes that caught the light oddly as they clambered among the reeds. Their movements were bewitching. They're birds built for a world of verticals. Their legs are long, black and glint like obsidian, and they have huge, cartoon bird feet. Orioles forgotten, I stood and watched the little cashmere balls bouncing up and down in the reeds, and was delighted to see that quite often a bird hopped from one reed stem onto two, grabbing one stalk in each foot before sitting there happily doing the splits to pick reed seeds from the nearest overhanging frond.

This time Peter had brought the technology, had set up a telescope on the bank and already trained it on the nest. The nest adhered to the tree the way that papery burnet moth cocoons adhere to stems of grass. It was shaped something like a half coconut woven carefully from a hammock of thin grass and slung between two whippy branches sixty feet high in the air, and it was like no nest I'd seen before, although for a long while I couldn't see it at all. Through the telescope there was barely enough ambient light for depth and modelling to appear, but as the sun rose higher, what I saw became something like looking into a Magic Eye picture. Here was a circle, and in it a thousand angles of stalk and leaf and scraps of shade at various distances, and every straight stalk or branch was alternately obscured and revealed as the wind blew. I began to feel a little seasick watching this chaos, but then, as magically as a Magic Eye stereogram suddenly reveals a not-very-accurate 3D dinosaur, the muddy patch just off centre resolved itself into the nest.

As soon as it happened I tensed with the effort of not losing it again. The telescope's focus was slightly out for my short-sighted eyes, so it required physical effort to keep what I saw from derealising back into nonsense. I wanted so much to see an adult oriole leaping onto the nest to make it real, the gaping mouths of begging chicks emerging from inside it, the flapping of newly-grown feathers. But nothing happened.

If there were birds inside that nest, at this time of year they'd be close to fledging and leaving it, I thought, so why couldn't I see anything in it move? They'd be restless, surely, at this hour? I surrendered the telescope to Peter along with my misgivings, spread my coat on the grass and sat down. Our mood grew sombre as we came to suspect, then believe, then finally know that there was nothing in this nest at all. It had been exceptionally windy the previous day, so we wondered if the young had fallen from the nest. After thinking this, there was no question but that we needed to go into the wood and look for the chicks that might be underneath the tree.

I shrugged my coat back on. The wood was at least five feet deep in stinging nettles. I'd done a lot of birding, and walking, and hawking, in nettles, and knew that the correct way to treat banks of big nettles is to wear reasonably thick clothes and not give a cuss for them. Wade through and be damned. It's like the Red Sea miracle— with faith, they'll part harmlessly in front of you. But what I wasn't used to dealing with was nettles emerging from a swamp. We stepped through rushes growing etiolated through wet black mud, and across places where the ground was so wet there was no vegetation at all, was something akin to quickpeat. But mostly we walked in nettles, their stems so densely packed that neither of us had much idea of what was beneath them as we struggled through. The poplar branches here were low, permitting us only a tiny tunnel of clearance between the top of the stinging nettles and the thatch of twigs and leaves. It felt like river caving, tilting our chins upward to the foot and a half of air between water and rock. It was claustrophobic, intense, the greens rich and dark, and it felt very far away from England. Like Louisiana, perhaps. Mosquitoes descended on us, swarms of big Anopheles whose delicate stripes and long noses drifted purposively towards our faces. We halted at the nest tree, kicked carefully about. There was nothing beneath it but nettles. I slapped away one mosquito after another, noticed there was blood all over my hands.

Then we heard an oriole. It wasn't the oriole's otherworldly song, but a series of short, rasping calls. Then, very softly from the foggy, papery green, a soft hoot hoot hoot was sent back to it—the contact call of a chick. Then came the glorious sweeping flute of one of the parents as he swept in from nowhere to feed. And that's when I saw him. Finally, I saw my oriole. A bright, golden male. It was a complex joy, because I saw him only in stamped-out sections, small jigsaw pieces of a bird, but moving ones, animated mutoscope views. A flick of wings, a scrap of tail, then another glimpse—this time, just his head alone— through a screen of leaves. I was transfixed. I had not expected the joyous, extravagant way this oriole leapt into the air between feeds, the enormously decisive movements, always, and the little dots like stars that flared along the edge of his spread-wide tail. It's hard to comprehend that in all these views through my binoculars, he was never more than the size of a fingernail at arms length. But then a fingernail at arms length is, I guess, exactly the size of the visible sun.

GEORGE EWART EVANS

The Wisdom of the Bees

From *The Pattern under the Plough* (1966)

George Ewart Evans (1909–1988) was a Welsh-born schoolteacher and writer who became a dedicated collector of folklore and oral tradition in the East Anglian countryside from the 1940s to 1970s, and produced eleven books of collections of these materials, including Ask the Fellows who Cut the Hay. *He is widely regarded as the 'grandfather' of British oral history, although he always said that the term 'oral history' reminded him of 'the filing cabinet of a well-equipped dentist'.*

The close link of the bees with the household or family of their owner is a feature of northern mythology; and the custom of 'telling the bees' was practised in many north European countries until recent years. It was a common practice among the old rural community in East Anglia, and here is a typical account of it taken from a man who was born at Stonham Aspal, Suffolk: 'If there was a death in the family our custom was to take a bit of crêpe out to the bee skeps after sunset and pin it on them. Then you gently tapped the skeps and told the bees who it was who had died. If you didn't do this, they reckoned the bees wouldn't stay, they'd leave the hives—or else they'd pine away and die.'

It is clear from other sources that up to sixty or seventy years ago in East Anglia the beekeepers regarded the bees as highly intelligent beings and treated them as such: 'the wisdom of the bees' and 'the secret knowledge of the bees' were more than just poetic phrases to them; they believed they were true to the letter. In the Suffolk village of Debenham there was an old beekeeper who regularly talked to his bees and claimed to be able to interpret their response by the pitch of their buzzing. It is certain that bees are very responsive to different tones of the human voice, and this is probably the reason for the country belief that bees are peace-loving beings and will not stay with a quarrelsome family. Similarly it is likely that it is the basis of the injunction that 'you must never swear in front of your bees'. A Suffolk man said: 'My grandfather was a bit of a rough diamond, and he wasn't above letting a few words fly in front of us children when he felt like it. But he would never use bad language when he was near his bees. He'd always be on his best behaviour then!'

But to return to the old beekeeper: 'James Collins treated the bees as members of the family. He as a retired thatcher and he used to come and work the bees, as he said, at the saddler's where I was apprentice. This was well before the First World War. I used to carry the box up for him when he was going to smoke the bees out, and I was able to observe him pretty closely. If there was a tempest

David Gentleman, *Mr Thompson's Bees*, 2013. Ink drawing from *The Pattern under the Plough*.

about—if the air felt thundery in any way—he wouldn't go near the bees. And at any time before approaching the hives he'd stand back and listen, to find out how they were getting on. Then he'd look to see which way they were travelling, so that he wouldn't get in their line of flight. He'd watch them quietly; and he often told me how he had a good idea where they'd been taking their honey: if they came to their hives low, they'd most likely have come off a field of clover. If they had been working on fruit trees they'd come in much higher. It wouldn't do to get in their line of flight: you'd be sure to get stung. The old man told me in this connection: 'If the bees come near you don't start beating the air: leave 'em. Don't fight the bees; the bees will allus win.'

'It's true. The bees will stop a horse. And I thought of what Jim Collins said when I heard what happened over at Stonham. Just by the Maltings there was a man cutting clover with a cutter and two horses. Everything was going on well till the machine broke down. The worst part about it was that it stopped right in the line of flight of some bees who were working the field of clover. They attacked the driver and he straightaway made a bolt for it, leaving the horses standing there. Both horses were stung unmercifully. One of them died soon afterwards; and the other one—I saw it myself—was so bad and its head so swollen up with the stings that it had to be supported in its stable by a kind of sling fixed to the roof.

'But Jim Collins was the cleverest man I knew at bees. He used to talk to them quietly when he was at the hives; and he reckoned he could tell when they were about to swarm by the different sound of their buzzing: how they answered his talk. As I say, he treated the bees as members of the family as though they were friends; and I never knew him to be stung. Although the bees and the hives really belonged to Mr Rumsey, my master, Jim reckoned that he was their owner: the bees, he said, belonged to him. He could manage them; and he used to say that if he went away and left his hat hanging on one of the trees in the garden, the bees would never leave. If they swarmed they wouldn't go farther than the garden. He wore a hat with a veil when he was working his bees but often as not the veil used to be drawn back on his hat and nowhere near his face and his neck. There is a story that another Debenham beekeeper once took a swarm of bees in his hat; and then put the hat on and walked home. And after knowing Jim Collins I can well believe the story's a true one.'

But the bees not only knew the voice of their owner but also his particular smell: one beekeeper told the writer: 'Whenever I go to the barber's I've always to tell him: "Nothing on, thank you." If he were to put lotion on my hair, however nice it smelled, the bees wouldn't think much of it at all. I know from experience that if I approached their hives with scented lotion on my hair it would make them angry.' The bees in fact should be treated at all times, so is the belief, as if they were people; and people who were very ready to take offence if not treated properly. They must not be bought or sold or even taken or given as a present. A beekeeper may give away a hive, and later the recipient will find a way of unobtrusively repaying the kindness either with an appropriate gift or with some worthwhile service.

The Legend of the Black Dog of Bungay (1577)

There are frequent reports of sightings of this terrible ghostly dog of East Anglia. The name Shuck derives from the Old English word *scucca*, which means devil or fiend, from the root *skuh-* terrify.

On 4th August 1577 at Blythburgh, Black Shuck is said to have burst in through the doors of Holy Trinity Church to the sound of a clap of thunder. He ran up the nave, past a large congregation, killing a man and a boy and causing the church steeple to collapse through the roof. As the dog left, he made scorch marks on the north door which can be seen at the church to this day.

The Reverend Abraham Fleming's famous account continues the story on the same day.

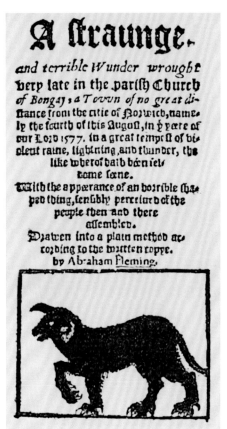

THEA SMILEY

The Wolf Pits

Adapted from *The Last Woodwose* (2019)

Thea Smiley is a Suffolk writer. Born in Ipswich and married at the end of Southwold Pier, she has lived near the village of Bramfield for most of her life. Her poetry has been shortlisted for the Bridport Prize, her short stories published in anthologies, and her plays include The Return of the Wildman *and* The Last Woodwose, *produced by Wonderful Beast theatre company.*

In the twelfth century, the inhabitants of Woolpit, a village not far from Bury St Edmunds, found two children near the wolf pits, after which the place was named. The children wore strange clothes, spoke an unknown language, and their skin was green. The first chroniclers, William of Newburgh and Ralph of Coggeshall, described it as 'a wonder'. This is a new retelling of that wonderful tale.

The deep pits were covered with a layer of leafy branches and lined with planks so no wolf could dig its way out. My parents told me not to go near them but, one morning, I heard howling and was drawn to the edge. Down on the dark earth, surrounded by broken sticks, a wolf prowled back and forth. I crouched beside the pit to watch as it ripped the flesh from an old sheep carcass, ate, and licked its paws.

I returned often to see the wolves. Asleep, they appeared harmless. But I liked to hear their rumbling growls, and let them jump and snap at my dangling feet. When the carcass writhed with maggots, I fed them crusts of bread and slivers of meat until my parents found out.

'Serve you right if the wolves eat you,' they said.

Once, I tried to help a wolf escape by coaxing it up a branch. I was caught by the old woman who lived nearby. She told my father and his face strained with rage.

'Why would you want to release a killer in the village?' he said.

He beat me and I was forbidden to visit the wolf pits again.

The sun was fierce one afternoon as I carried his lunch to the fields. As soon as I was out of my mother's sight, I took a swig of cider. It was cool and tasted of sharp, green apples. My father would be thirsty after a morning's scything. If he noticed some missing, I'd tell him I had stumbled and spilt it. I scuffed my bare feet along the dusty path and, when I stopped to take another swig, I heard whining coming from the wolf pits. I crept across the dry grass and peered in.

Two, small green faces stared back. They looked like children, siblings, a little younger than me. They wore patterned clothes which made my own brown tunic seem rough and muddy, and their skin was the pale green of sage leaves. I wondered if they'd tunnelled up from an underground world or fallen from the sky.

'Come away from the wolf pits, Maud!' shouted my father from the field. I ran along the path and told him what I'd seen. His scowl deepened.

'Don't lie.'

'It's true,' I said, 'There are two green children in a pit.' Overhearing this, the harvesters put down their scythes and followed me.

As we gathered above them, the children cowered in the darkest corner.

'I can just make them out,' said an old man, shading his eyes.

'Where?' said the others, jostling to see.

My father picked up a stick and tried to poke the children. They moved into the sunlight and everyone gasped.

'So green.'

'Where have they come from?' one man asked.

'Perhaps they're little folk,' said another.

'They'll bring bad luck,' said my father.

After a moment, the taller child spoke, her voice soft and clacking like leafy saplings. No one could understand her. The smaller child pointed to his mouth and whined.

'Maybe they're hungry,' someone said.

I dropped the cloth bundle into the pit.

'That's my food, Maud!' shouted my father.

'Let them have it,' said the others. 'They look half-starved.'

Cautiously, the children opened the cloth and took out the bread and cheese. They sniffed it but didn't eat.

'How about an apple?' said a man, tossing one at their feet. They picked it up, looked at it, then put it down.

'Let's take them to Sir Richard,' said the old man, 'See what he makes of them.'

The others agreed, so we set off for the manor house.

On the way, we passed a field of broad beans. I picked a few stalks and ate the beans as I walked along. When we reached the grand house, Sir Richard de Calne strode out to see us off. He was about to speak when he saw the green children, and fear flickered across his face.

'What in God's name are they?' he asked, staring at their skin. The harvesters told him how they'd found the children, and explained that they were harmless and hungry. Sir Richard sent for food, and it was soon brought before them. But, although they seemed hungrier than ever, the children still wouldn't eat.

Then, the girl caught sight of my bean plants and held out her hands. I gave them to her, and she and her brother split the stalks open. Finding them empty, they moaned. So, I showed them how to open the pods and, when they saw the fat beans, they crammed them into their mouths as though they hadn't eaten for weeks. We fetched more, and the children ate until they were so full they fell asleep. I didn't want to leave them, but my father insisted. We thanked Sir Richard and returned to our village.

The next day, when I was sent to milk the goats, I ran to the manor house to see if the children were still there. I searched everywhere and found them locked in a stable. I slid back the bolt and let them out. Having slept well on the hay, they had more energy. They smiled at me, and we chased each other around the garden until the servants told me to go home.

The following day, when I was sent to dig up potatoes, I went to see the children again. We played hide and seek all morning. Later, my mother asked where I'd been and why I'd returned empty-handed.

'Don't be naughty, Maud,' she said, 'or you'll get a beating.' But it didn't stop me. Whenever I could, I stole away to see my new friends.

After a few weeks, my parents decided I was old enough to go into service and make money for the family. So, I started work for Sir Richard and, between tasks, I taught the green children rude words and tricks. We put live mice in the cook's pots until she complained, and Sir Richard said:

'If you want to stay, you need to behave.' Then, he sent for a priest to teach the children right from wrong and, to save them from sin, he asked the priest to baptise them.

The day of their baptism was cold and windy. The children were dressed in their best clothes and taken to the village church. As I watched them walk down the drive, I could hear the boy coughing. He seemed small and thin as he pulled his coat around him. That night, the poor boy coughed himself to death.

I found his sister curled in a corner. I held her hand and told her stories about my life and the wolves, how they'd howled for the wild. Sitting side by side, she began to confide in me. She said she and her brother had come from a land where everything was green and dimly-lit. They'd been tending their cattle when they came across a cavern. Inside, they heard bells and followed the sound until they emerged into sunlight. Overwhelmed by the brightness and warmth, they lay down to rest. When they awoke, they were trapped in the pit.

'It was strange,' she said, 'I can't explain it.'

After her brother's death, Sir Richard told the girl she had to earn her keep. He said she would work as a servant and he called her Agnes, so he could summon her. He kept us busy from dawn until dusk. But, at dusk, she and I would sit in the orchard and talk, or paddle in the stream, and on cold nights we'd huddle by the kitchen fire and eat. Over the years, she ate all sorts of food and her skin grew less green.

One hot summer, I asked Agnes to keep watch for me while I rolled in the hay with the stable boys. I never got caught, but she did, and she got a reputation for being wanton. So, Sir Richard decided to marry her off to a gentleman from Kings Lynn. Before we knew what was happening, she was leaving.

The last time I saw Agnes, she was dressed in white, her cheeks flushed and pretty. We held each other and said farewell, and she wished me all the best for the birth of my first baby. I heard she settled in to her new life, and only two of her children had a green tinge to their skin.

As for me, I married Ralph, a stable boy, and had many children. Sometimes, I take them to the wolf pits, and explain that those pits gave the village its name, though there are fewer wolves now than there used to be. I tell them the story of the green children of Woolpit. Then we howl to scare the villagers and run away.

PAUL HEINEY

A Political Crisis for
the Suffolk Punch (1990)

In the early 1990s, Paul Heiney decided to become a farmer. He had fallen in love with the Suffolk Punch, the great carthorse of East Anglia, and wanted to experience life alongside them, and better understand the culture of the working horse and the men who worked them. He set out to create a small Suffolk farm of the kind recognisable any time up to middle of the twentieth century, before 'modernisation' eclipsed them. Having found a farm, untouched since those times and still complete with a traditional stable, Heiney set off on the exhausting business of learning to plough, sow, reap and mow with his three Suffolk horses. He never thought it would be easy, nor did he ever expect that politics would play such an important a part in stable life. His diary, published in The Times *during Mrs Thatcher's resignation crisis, records:*

The only item in our old stable that relates in any way to the latter half of the twentieth century is a transistor radio. I switch it on for the early morning news and more often than not it stays switched on. However, I have decided that I must be more careful about leaving it blaring. The political upheavals of the last weeks have proved infectious, and the farm is now in the midst of its own leadership battle. To predict the outcome, you need to know the contenders for the crown and the deviousness of the electoral system.

When we had only two Suffolk Punches life was simple. Punch was premier. Punch is a good-looking horse, intelligent but self-willed. For a decade he has been paired with Star as his deputy: as good a workhorse as you could wish for. Star has never been known to be bad-tempered, or ever refused to pull with all his might. I heard that a previous owner had accidentally driven Star into a ditch so deep that it needed the fire brigade to drag him out. When the rescue team arrived they found a peaceful old Star, up to his knees in mud, eyes half closed, blissfully enjoying the fresh grass growing up the sides of the deep drain and blaming nobody. It took a crane to lift him out, after which the old statesman was put back between the shafts and off he ambled as if nothing had happened. It was his finest hour. When he dies we may have to have him sculpted in bronze.

But as in politics, so in the farmyard: it is not always the best man that wins. For most of his working life the downtrodden Star has been governed by his chippy companion, Punch. Punch can be bad-tempered. When it is time for work, he will fling his head to the rafters thus making it almost impossible for me to get his collar over his head. When ploughing, he will irritatingly stop halfway along the furrow if he thinks it is time he had a rest. You may curse, even scream, at him

Installation view, Sarah Lucas, *Perceval*, Aldeburgh Festival, Suffolk, 2011.

Sarah Lucas is a contemporary British artist known for her kinesthetic photographs, performances, and sculpture. She is part of the generation of Young British Artists who emerged during the 1990s. She lives 'tucked away down a long country lane, behind a Baptist church in Suffolk'.

but he shows his mastery of you by insolently moving off as slowly as he knows how, but only when he is good and ready. Damned old hoss! Back at the stable he ruthlessly reaffirms his status by pawing the concrete floor with his front feet if he is not fed before the others. He knows that, to a farmer who has to pay ever-increasing blacksmith's bills, nothing grates like the sound of needless scraping of a £10 iron horseshoe.

The old ruler reigned unchallenged till the spring when our new young horse arrived: Blue. The political ground beneath Punch's broad hooves was shifting, and he wasn't happy. Equine teeth were bared and those who feel wounded by current political back-biting can think themselves lucky they didn't have a jealous Punch coming at their spines, mouth wide open.

Punch, at fifteen, is looking older now. It is rare for him to go ploughing. Sensing that Punch may be losing his grip, Blue seized his opportunity and the farmyard suddenly found itself in the grip of a leadership crisis.

As with most animals, it usually kicked off at feeding time. We have a hayrack at which Punch and Star used to feed together, with Blue only approaching when they had finished. But I noticed he was now beginning to stand his ground and if he gets there first he will not budge. It means more aggravation from a disgruntled Punch who deals with it by strolling over to his rival's hay and piddling on it. His political technique would be the envy of even one of Thatcher's ruthless Chief Whips.

It is still uncertain which of them will emerge from this contest as leader. When I open the stable door in the morning, I closely observe the order in which they all file through. Blue, I'm sorry to say is still last. Surprisingly, Star is often first. Perhaps that dark horse will make it after all.

Harry Becker, *The Muck Cart*, c. 1913.

Harry Becker, the son of a German immigrant, was born in Colchester in 1865. His artistic talents were noticeable from a young age, and at fourteen he was sent to the Royal Academy of Antwerp for formal training. He finished his education in Paris where he was greatly influenced by the Impressionists, in particular Edgar Degas whose use of mixed media and emphasis on light on stained canvases interested Becker.

From 1886–1894 Becker lived in the Minories in Colchester where he painted watercolour portraits as well as landscapes in both watercolour and oils. In 1894 he moved to London to open his studio where he became well known for his lithographs and dramatic graphic work. In 1902 he married Georgina Waddington, a fellow artist, who gave birth a year later to their daughter, Janet. In 1913 they settled in Suffolk where he would remain until his death in 1928, shunning the commercial art world in favour of painting the rural landscapes and people he so loved. During his lifetime Becker received a number of high-profile commissions most notably one in 1908 for a large mural in the central hall for a new department store owned by Gordon Selfridge. However, the commission was later cancelled due to disagreements between Becker and Selfridge due largely to Becker's contempt of commercialism.

Becker spent much of his later years living in near poverty, a poverty that is reflected in his use of materials: reusing old canvas and scraps of paper. Despite this he spent much of his time trying to buy back paintings he had sold earlier in his career.

ROBERT BLOOMFIELD

Ploughing in Spring

Extract from *The Farmer's Boy* (1800)

Robert Bloomfield (1766–1823) was known as 'the first of the Rural Bards'. Born in Honington in Suffolk, the son of a tailor, he worked as a labourer on a nearby farm before moving to London to become a shoemaker. One of his first duties as a boy was running errands and reading aloud from the newspapers to the men as they worked in their garret in Bell Lane, educating himself and becoming a voracious reader. Much of this poem, The Farmer's Boy, *his masterpiece, was composed while he worked at his cobbler's bench, keeping long sections in his head before they were written down. Suffolk squire and radical editor Capel Lofft championed it and prepared it for publication in 1800 with woodcuts by Thomas Bewick, without Bloomfield's knowledge. It describes rural life with all its hardships, but much of its contemporary success may be ascribed to its innocently cheerful account of farm labour as it follows the boy, Giles, in his seasonal work. The poem contains Bloomfield's notorious condemnation of Suffolk cheese: 'Too big to swallow, and too hard to bite.'*

The poem was an instant bestseller. John Constable admired it, using couplets from it as titles for several paintings. John Clare was influenced by it. It brought Bloomfield the scorn of Lord Byron, who referred to him and his brother as the 'cobbler-laureats'. And it brought him noble patronage: the Duke of Grafton supported him with a pension of one shilling a day when his next ventures—selling books and making Aeolian harps—failed.

'Twas thus with GILES: meek, fatherless, and poor:
Labour his portion, but he felt no more;
No stripes, no tyranny his steps pursu'd;
His life was constant, cheerful, servitude:
Strange to the world, he wore a bashful look,
The fields his study, Nature was his book;
And, as revolving SEASONS chang'd the scene
From heat to cold, tempestuous to serene,
Though every change still varied his employ,
Yet each new duty brought its share of joy.

Where noble GRAFTON spreads his rich domains,
Round Euston's water'd vale, and sloping plains,
Where woods and groves in solemn grandeur rise,
Where the kite brooding unmolested flies;

The woodcock and the painted pheasant race,
And sculking foxes, destin'd for the chace;
There Giles, untaught and unrepining, stray'd
Thro' every copse, and grove, and winding glade;
There his first thoughts to Nature's charms inclin'd,
That stamps devotion on th' inquiring mind.
A little farm his generous Master till'd,
Who with peculiar grace his station fill'd;
By deeds of hospitality endear'd,
Serv'd from affection, for his worth rever'd;
A happy offspring blest his plenteous board,
His fields were fruitful, and his harm well stor'd,
And fourscore ewes he fed, a sturdy team,
And lowing kine that grazed beside the stream:
Unceasing industry he kept in view;
And never lack'd a job for Giles to do.

FLED now the sullen murmurs of the North,
The splendid raiment of the SPRING peeps forth;
Her universal green, and the clear sky,
Delight still more and more the gazing eye.
Wide o'er the fields, in rising moisture strong,
Shoots up the simple flower, or creeps along
The mellow'd soil; imbibing fairer hues
Or sweets from frequent showers and evening dews;
That summon from its shed the slumb'ring ploughs,
While health impregnates every breeze that blows.
No wheels support the diving pointed share;
No groaning ox is doom'd to labour there;
No helpmates teach the docile steed his road;
(Alike unknown the plow-boy and the goad;)
But, unassisted through each toilsome day,
With smiling brow the plowman cleaves his way,
Draws his fresh parallels, and wid'ning still,
Treads slow the heavy dale, or climbs the hill:
Strong on the wing his busy followers play,
Where writhing earth-worms meet th' unwelcome day;
Till all is chang'd, and hill and level down
Assume a livery of sober brown:
Again disturb'd, when Giles with wearying strides
From ridge to ridge the ponderous harrow guides;
His heels deep sinking every step he goes,

Thomas Bewick, *The Farmer's Boy*, 1800.

Till dirt usurp the empire of his shoes.
Welcome green headland! firm beneath his feet;
Welcome the friendly bank's refreshing seat;
There, warm with toil, his panting horses browse
Their shelt'ring canopy of pendent boughs;
Till rest, delicious, chase each transient pain,
And new-born vigour swell in every vein.
Hour after hour, and day to day succeeds;
Till every clod and deep-drawn furrow spreads
To crumbling mould; a level surface clear,
And strew'd with corn to crown the rising year;
And o'er the whole Giles once transverse again,
In earth's moist bosom buries up the grain.
The work is done; no more to man is given;
The grateful farmer trusts the rest to Heaven.
Yet oft with anxious heart he looks around,
And marks the first green blade that breaks the ground.

ADRIAN BELL

The Christmas Market in Bury St Edmunds

From *Corduroy* (1930)

Adrian Bell (1901–1980) was an English journalist and farmer, and the first compiler of the Times *crossword. In 1920, the young Bell was sent by his father to live with a farming family in a Suffolk village near Bury St Edmunds. He was twenty, his health was not good, and he was under pressure from his father, the news editor of the* Observer, *to get a 'proper job'. In* Corduroy, *he records the daily life of the farmers around him, and his own growing realisation that farming was to be his own future.*

The next Wednesday was Christmas sale day at Stambury [Bury St Edmunds] and Mr Colville took me with him to see it. The town was full of cars and farmers. Inn yards were crowded with gigs. The market-place was at one end of the town, a vast space divided up into pens and selling-rings under cover.

Dealers hailed Mr Colville near the entrance with, 'I've got a pretty bunch of heifers this morning that would just suit you, sir,' and 'Do you want to see some real fine beasts, now?'

There was a great bustle of unloading, penning, and marking the creatures. Whichever way I turned I seemed to find a herd of bullocks charging down upon me.

The pens near the rings contained the fat beasts, and were garnished with holly and laurel. A piece of mistletoe (somebody's joke) dangled over the auctioneer's head. The bidders, simulating unconcern, nodding imperceptibly, shot occasional flashing glances to spot their rivals. It was a battle royal of butchers for the prestige of having a carcase with a red rosette hanging in their shops, a carcase split, showing inner qualities of meat and fat corresponding to those outward proportions for which he had been famous. Butchers who cater for farmers have a clientele of connoisseurs, and at Christmas-time something extra special is expected.

'Turkeys be damned,' said Mr Colville before this brave show of creatures, 'give me beef and plum pudding.'

What, indeed, was turkey to him, who had pheasants or partridges for the pointing of his gun? Not cooked in camera in an oven, either, but turning upon a spit close above brilliant wood embers on the old hearth in the scullery, well basted, hissing and browning, their flavours sealed within them. His wife kept turkeys for the Christmas trade; all day their melancholy calling filled the air.

'Their row gets on my nerves,' said Mr Colville more than once. 'Thank God when they're sold and gone. I don't want to see one again for a long while, least of all on Christmas Day.'

The first prize steer made £85, the second £80. Mr Colville pointed out to me the points of good bullocks—'Tails well set up, and good wide backsides on 'em, Now, these are a nice lot, a choice little bunch, all roan. They'll sell; roan is always a favourite colour.'

I was all eyes and ears, and tried hard to differentiate in this matter of backsides and tails, but for lack of practice could not. Whenever I expressed an opinion I found I had been led away by some irrelevance of smooth or rough coat.

We inspected the Christmas show of pigs. As I cast my eye across the market, congested with fat beasts, it seemed almost incredible that in a few days' time the human mouth would have devoured the lot, and all these prize bullocks, pigs, turkeys, become assimilated into humanity.

It was half past one, and smells of cooking wafted across the market-place.

'I don't know how you are, but I begin to feel a bit peckish,' Mr Colville remarked.

I agreed that lunch would be welcome; I began to feel chilly with long loitering and looking. We passed down a street where I saw lofts full of trussed hay, where granary doors stood open, revealing sacks and hanging chains. We entered a dim hall of beer-barrels, and so came by a back way, familiar to farmers, to the Three Tuns Inn, and mounted wooden steps from the courtyard to a lofty chamber where the Market Ordinary Luncheon was to be had.

The floor was of scrubbed boards, the walls whitewashed. A long table went down the centre of the room, and at one end was a serving-table on which stood various joints, with spirit-flames beneath them keeping them hot. Behind this the landlord and his wife were stationed, wielding carving-knives worn thin as rapiers, while aproned wenches went to and fro with plates and dishes.

We had roast beef and brown beer. It was a variegated throng; corn merchants in smart suits, with button-holes, sitting next to tradesmen snatching half an hour in the market-day rush. The merchants were leisurely, oracular; the tradesmen swift of speech; the farmers wryly humorous, but interested mostly in their luncheon. I saw Sam Sneep, a bearded farmer, eating of his own bullock.

After the beef we had bread and cheese and celery. The farmer never eats biscuits with cheese. The actual menu of the market luncheon was soup, joint, sweet and cheese, two and threepence. The price was based, I think, on the fact that the farmer does not take a sweet. I noticed small bowls of stewed apples and custard, but they were untouched. They seemed to be included merely to swell the menu, for every farmer shook his head and reached for the cheese at the servant's mentioning the effeminate word 'sweet'.

Mr Colville's father came in towards the end of our meal, a bit short of breath and glad to sit down. He said, 'I've been coming to Stambury market for fifty years, and I've only missed twice in all that time.'

Jason Gathorne-Hardy, *Taking Bids I: Poultry and Game Auction*, 2004.

Jason Gathorne-Hardy is a Suffolk based artist living and working at White House Farm in Great Glemham, Suffolk. His work includes drawings of livestock and wildlife alongside landscape painting using natural pigments and more recently, narrative drawings.

Another, even older, told me he had been an attendant there for fifty-five years, and in his early days they used to take their places at the table according to the number of bottles of port they drank at a sitting—the three-bottle men at the top, the one-bottle men at the foot. 'In those days we used to do all our business in the morning, and sat a-drinking and card-playing the rest of the time, till very near the next morning.'

After lunch we went to the Corn Exchange. Within was a vast chamber, the roof chiefly of glass. A deep hum of many persons talking filled the air. Row upon row of desks stood each a few yards from another, with a merchant's name and trade inscribed on the front. Behind stood the merchant himself.

Mr Colville had a sample of barley with him, which he offered to a merchant. The man opened the bag, and, having gazed upon the barley, plunged his nose into it, to which, when he lifted his face, several grains adhered. He poured it in and out of his hand, cracked some grains with his teeth, then asked the price.

'Seventy shillings,' said Mr Colville, in an uncompromising tone.

'Heavens, man, what are you thinking of—not this sample?' returned the merchant. He held up the bag. 'I'll bid you once, and more than it's worth—sixty shillings.'

Mr Colville shook his head, and taking the sample, walked away. He showed it to another merchant, who offered him fifty-seven shillings, and a third, who offered him fifty-five. Thereupon Mr Colville returned to the first merchant, remarking on the way, 'I don't reckon he'll stand word.' He didn't. His bid was now a shilling less per coomb, but agreement was at length reached by the mutual concession of sixpence.

Mr Colville now said, consulting his watch, 'I have a business appointment in five minutes. Perhaps you would like to look round the town. I'll meet you in the Old Butter Market at four o'clock.'

Stambury was a fine and ancient town, containing squares of Georgian houses, and churches in the noble Suffolk style. It had its polite street, where on days other than market-days the country gentry shopped, and large cars rested, and carriages, too, of unusual shapes with technical names, while grooms stood at the heads of horses. Although the motor-car was universal, there was a certain pride, among those that had the money and ability, in driving a prancing grey in a yellow gig through the streets, with floating whiplash and all.

To be a master of the horse, round Stambury, was like being a master of life. The children of the great drove in their own miniature tub-carts with shaggy ponies, and the grocer came out of his three-gabled shop in Churchgate Street and waited on them when they stopped outside.

There was also an agricultural tailor in this vicinity who cut breeches just suitable for a farmer's better occasions—not exaggeratedly Newmarket, nor yet unassumingly narrow, but with a hint of style about them. The chief shopping-place of the day was the Old Butter Market. Here beef and pork and poultry were turned by the alchemy of the coin to feminine adornments, tobacco, silks and scents. Here wives and daughters strolled.

Where this joined the agricultural neighbourhood stood a shop devoted to clothing of a rural kind. A line of dickeys hung down the window. Some were blue, with a pattern; some striped. There were both soft and stiff ones, the former with a system of tags at the corners for fixing. The most interesting kind were those which were compounded with a collar. This was in two halves. You put it round your neck; the two parts of the dickey met upon your chest; you buttoned them together, and in a trice were both collared and shirted. Then, putting on your better coat to hide the make-believe, you were ready for market. On your

return, you had merely to unbutton and whip it from your neck, and you were in working trim to milk the waiting cows. They were only a shilling each.

There were corduroy coats with black velvet collars, stiff blue trousers, scarves and ties for 'courting' in, of sugary hues. There were underclothes, also, but of a grim hairiness.

What a packing up was going on before starting home—a fitting of one another in, wife and daughter, and the neighbour who was being given a lift. Fringes of rugs were tucked in, doors slammed. The sun was setting; it seemed to have dissolved and dyed the air. The sky had a bronze glow, purple-hazed where a plume of smoke expanded. The air was nipping.

Jason Gathorne-Hardy,
Watching the Bidding, 2004

I went home for Christmas, of course. I returned to London, to a world of narrow sky and no darkness, to find the old life half strange already. My brown Sunday boots seemed uncouth there, and I was asked to change them, as they would ruin the carpets.

I noticed most keenly the brilliance of electric light after oil lamps, and the absence of anything worn, or uneven, or overgrown. Interiors had the illusory quality of flashed scenes of a midnight storm. In fact, the whole Christmas sojourn had a flashed effect, flat and unrooted, with people gesturing and smiling as in a charade.

WILLIAM KENDALL

Lady Eve Balfour (2021)

Lady Eve Balfour was a trailblazing agriculturalist of the twentieth century whose ideas on soil and the vital role it plays in human health were ahead of their time. As a consequence of prevailing beliefs about food production, only a handful of people in the world were aware of the importance of her work during her lifetime and even fewer knew about it in Suffolk, the county she called home for the last seventy years of her long life.

William Kendall grew up in an East Anglian farming family and farms organically in the same village where Lady Eve lived the last decades of her life. He never met her but has been inspired by her determination and vision. He is an entrepreneur and campaigner for better food and nature. He was a recent High Sheriff of the county and is a Deputy Lieutenant.

The public sometimes finds fault with estate agents, but we can thank the one who, in 1919, sent particulars of a farm for sale in Haughley, Suffolk when their client, Eve Balfour, had requested details of farms to let in Sussex. Eve had been running a small farm unit as part of the war effort in Monmouthshire. This, and the fact that she had earned one of the first ever diplomas in agriculture from Reading University to be awarded to a woman, provided her with the certainty that she wanted to devote her life to farming. Even though Eve remarked that nothing would induce her to move to Suffolk, she also conceded that she had never been there, and the county's flatness at least meant that 'ploughing would be a Mug's game'. With only days left before the sale of 157-acre New Bells, Haughley, Eve set off on the 200 miles in a pony and dog-cart with Mary, her elder sister cum business partner. As was so often the case in her long life, her determination and ever-expanding network of friends and supporters ensured that she did reach Suffolk in time and could find the £25 an acre asking price. The farmhouse was semi-derelict: a forgotten, timbered building with no services and water drawn from its stagnant moat. On entering the damp interior for the first time, Eve, ever positive, thought it 'wonderfully large and airy'. She was twenty-one and had just taken possession of the place which would soon host the world's first scientific experiment in organic farming and first centre of the Soil Association.

Eve had enjoyed a privileged upbringing on the Balfour family estate in East Lothian. Her much-loved, childless uncle Arthur had been Prime Minister and her father Gerald, also a statesman, would eventually inherit his brother's earldom, meaning that Eve became Lady Eve. The family was famous for its forthright approach in an age when the ruling classes were forthright by definition. Lesser mortals would have wilted in Balfour company. Aged eight she objected to the cruelty of a pheasant shoot and was advised by her father that she should become a vegetarian. After establishing what vegetarianism was, she decided to do just that and mostly followed the principles for the rest of her life. Her interest in the countryside and farming was evident from an early age and by the time she was twelve her parents had accepted that this would be her vocation. Fortunately, at that stage, they had not realised the amount of patient, financial support her pioneering work would demand over the years.

Eve set about trying to turn the new farm to profit. The slump in the interwar years made this almost impossible. Her family, who were not rich and even less so after the Wall Street Crash, were annually persuaded by her optimism to bail her out. As this source of funds began to run dry, she discovered, for someone who could barely spell, an improbable talent as a writer of detective stories. She and a friend kept things afloat for a few more years by writing several successful novels. Her harshest literary critics were her family finding new opportunities for withering one-liners. A titled aunt told Eve's mother that it would be 'better for her to occupy her days selling good milk than in defiling the "Springs of English"'. Eve did in fact sell good milk via a milk round in Ipswich but prices were too low to avoid the need for other income.

Looking back over her life Eve was always someone in pursuit of a cause. In 1929, the now forgotten Tithe War broke out with struggling farmers refusing to pay their absurdly historic dues to wealthy institutions. Farms were forcibly entered by county constables stiffened by burly bailiffs who seized assets which could be sold to settle the unpaid tithes. Lady Eve became a powerful advocate for the underdogs at the local disturbances which sometimes developed. Her aristocratic status was assisted by her physical stature. She was a tall, strong woman with a stentorian tone. With her Eton crop and farmer's clothes she was often mistaken for a man. Once, after being fined thirty shillings by the Stowmarket magistrates for letting her dog bite a postman, she asked for his ripped trousers to repair and then wear for herself.

In 1943 she published *The Living Soil.* At the same time, she transferred the Haughley farm into a trust to run ground-breaking scientific research into chemical-free farming practices. The central thesis was to examine the soil's ability to deliver the fertility necessary to grow good food with natural processes and without artificial inputs. The book, although often revised, has rarely been out of print since and became the bible of the organic movement. The Haughley experiment showed that for twenty years the land became progressively more fertile even though nutrients were lost every time a crop was taken off. In the end the project ran out of funds and the research ended. The newer members of Lady Eve's Soil Association were at odds with the need for scientific evidence and relied more on ideology to promote their goals. Her firm belief that a truly healthy soil would lead to a healthy population when fed off its produce was, at that time, lost on the majority. Most people were convinced by the promises which promoted the so-called Green Revolution and by the wonders of processed food. Lady Eve

Eve Balfour on her Ferguson tractor, about 1925.

remained unperturbed. She toured the world meeting her growing band of disciples who knew she was right and were often proving it on their own land. She had by then bought a cottage in Theberton on the Suffolk coast where she spent the last thirty years of her life. She continued to travel extensively until she was ninety. She was awarded an OBE days before she died in January 1990. Lady Eve's last home can be found at the end of a leafy lane in Theberton. Outside is a piece of tree trunk with 'Eve's Cottage' in simple painted letters.

W.G. SEBALD

The Sailors' Reading Room, Southwold

From *The Rings of Saturn* (1995)

W.G. Sebald (1944–2001) was a German writer and academic. In 1970 he became a lecturer at the University of East Anglia and lived near Norwich ever after.

Now, with an advancing chill in the air, I sought the familiarity of the streets and soon found myself outside the Sailors' Reading Room, a charitable establishment housed in a small building above the promenade, which nowadays, sailors being a dying breed, serves principally as a kind of maritime museum, where all manner of things connected with the sea and seafaring life are kept and collected. On the walls hang barometers and navigational instruments, figureheads, and models of ships in glass cases and in bottles. On the table are harbourmasters' registers, log books, treatises on sailing, various nautical periodicals, and several volumes with colour plates which show legendary clippers and ocean-going steamers such as the *Conte di Savoia* or the *Mauretania*, giants of iron and steel, more than three hundred yards long, into which the Washington Capitol might have fitted, their funnels so tall they vanished into the low-hanging clouds. The Reading Room at Southwold is opened every morning at seven (save only Christmas Day) and remains open

A Game of Cards in the Sailors' Reading Room.

until almost midnight. At best, it attracts a handful of visitors during the holidays, and the few who do cross the threshold leave again after they have taken a brief look around in the uncomprehending way characteristic of such holidaymakers. The Reading Room is thus almost always deserted but for one or two of the surviving fishermen and seafarers sitting in silence in the armchairs, whiling the hours away. Sometimes, in the evenings, they play a game of pool in the back room. Apart from the muffled sound of the sea and the clicking of the balls there is nothing to be heard then, except perhaps, from time to time, the slight scratching noise made by a player priming his cue and the short puff when he blows off the chalk.

Whenever I am in Southwold, the Sailors' Reading Room is by far my favourite haunt. It is better than anywhere else for reading, writing letters, following one's thoughts, or in the long winter months simply looking out at the stormy sea as it crashes on the promenade. So on this occasion too I entered the Reading Room to see whether anything had changed and to make notes on things that had occurred to me during the day. At first, as on some of the earlier visits, I leafed through the log of the *Southwold*, a patrol ship that was anchored off the pier from autumn of 1914. On the large landscape-format pages, a fresh one for each new date, there are occasional entries surrounded by a good deal of empty space, reading, for instance, Maurice Farman Bi-plane N'ward Inland or White Steam-yacht Flying White Ensign Cruising on Horizon to S. Every time I decipher one of these entries I am astounded that a trail that has long since vanished from the air or the water remains visible here on the paper.

CRAIG BROWN

Thorpeness Scrapbook (2021)

Craig Brown is a writer, critic and satirist, famous for his parodies. His book on The Beatles,
One, Two, Three, Four *won the Baillie Gifford Prize in 2020. He lives in Aldeburgh.*

Thorpeness reminds me of a stage-set. For most of the year, the stage remains unpopulated and then, all of a sudden, roughly halfway through July, it becomes home to a noisy summer variety show, full of youngsters having fun and their anxious parents doing their level best to stop their youngsters from having too much fun.

It is a war the parents can never hope to win. Thorpeness is a village designed with children in mind. They are the masters of this little universe. Not long ago, out on the Meare, I remember seeing a little boy of about ten in a boat with a dog, rowing briskly away from the Pirate's Castle, leaving his frantic parents stranded behind. 'Oh come on, Orlando—joke over!', his father kept yelling, as the boy disappeared into the distance.

There is a distinctly English middle-class, Joan Hunter-Dunn, air to the summer season in Aldeburgh. The air is riven by the sound of people shouting to each other in loud, posh voices: shouting for help with the unpacking, or requests for more Extra Virgin Olive Oil, or for directions towards a lost tennis-ball. Friends of ours call it 'Braywatch'.

Thorpeness may have recently celebrated its centenary, but there is a timeless quality to it. Children turn into parents and parents turn into grandparents, and they keep coming back, generation after generation. I have noticed that when people talk about it, they grow a little misty-eyed, and the word 'First' often crops up: it was where they first played tennis, or where they first played Bingo, or where they had their first snog. This last category seems unusually large, suggesting that Thorpeness has, over the years, become something of a Finishing School, or, perhaps, more accurately, a Starting School, for lusty adolescents.

Orlando's parents aside, it is, in my experience, almost impossible to feel unhappy in Thorpeness, particularly on the Meare. It is a fairytale place, somehow always that little bit larger than you remember it, a watery haven for the vanishing art of time-wasting. Whenever I take a boat out on it, this ditty pops into my mind, unbidden:

'Row, row, row the boat, gently down the stream,
Merrily, merrily, merrily, merrily, life is but a dream'.

Life often spills into dream in this very unusual village, benevolently loomed over by The House in the Clouds, which must surely be one of the most outlandish structures in the world. I have heard tell that it was actually built as a bungalow for hoarders, who needed a six-storey basement for all their odds and ends. We rented it ourselves once, and a very enjoyable week we had there, but I remember being surprised by quite how many huffy complaints there were in the visitors' book about the number of stairs. What on earth did they expect?

When you step into Thorpeness, you take a step away from everyday life. It has a Peter Pan quality about it. It is somehow unsurprising to discover that J.M. Barrie had a hand in the design of the Meare. It also has the air of a private kingdom. Even the ducks and the swans of Thorpeness give the impression of being in on some sort of shared joke, though the joke may well be on you if you lay out your picnic too close to a swan's nest.

Thorpeness was specifically built as a holiday village, which makes it quite a rarity and gives it its other-worldly feel. Keith Waterhouse once said that Brighton looks as though it's a town helping the police with their inquiries. In the same way, Thorpeness looks as though it's a village waiting for a pantomime to begin. One half-expects Mother Goose to appear on the balcony of the Country Club, or Rapunzel to put her head through an upper window in The House in the Clouds, ready to let down her hair.

And odd things do happen at Thorpeness. In 1996, the village hit the headlines after the local police had been chasing a car that was being driven erratically. It turned out that the driver was a ninety-year-old retired farmer called Leslie Evans. PC Derek Baldry was later to tell a packed courtroom exactly what happened.

'He pulled into the golf club car park and PC Scanlan stood in front of his car with his hand up and said "Stop" three times. Evans just waved at us, revved up and headed for the golf course, sending players on the course diving for cover.' PCs Evans and Scanlan were obliged to commandeer a golf buggy in order to give chase, but Mr Evans gave them the slip by the side entrance at the 6th hole. He was arrested the next day at his home in Saxmundham.

'Mr Evans was a member here until two years ago', commented the Golf Club president, 'and is known for being a little eccentric.'

This strikes me as the perfect Thorpeness story. Where else in the world would the police commandeer a golf buggy to chase a ninety-year-old tearaway? Everyone becomes young again in Thorpeness. For the past hundred years, Thorpeness has had a touch of Toytown about it, and with any luck it will continue to do so for the next hundred years.

ELIZA ACTON

Eliza Acton (1799–1859) was born in Sussex but spent most of her youth in Suffolk. She was brought up in Ipswich, where her father worked at St Peter's Brewery in Dock Street. While still a teenager herself, she opened a boarding school for young ladies in Claydon (later moved to Great Bealings and then Woodbridge). She is credited with writing the first cookbook aimed at the domestic market, Modern Cookery for Private Families *(1845). In it she introduced such innovations as lists of ingredients and cooking times, concepts which we now take for granted. Eliza Acton's hot punch sauce is introduced here by one of Britain's favourite cooks.*

DELIA SMITH

Eliza Acton is my most favourite cookery writer because you know by reading the book that she has actually cooked all the recipes herself and I've always felt disappointed that Mrs Beeton's book sort of eclipsed hers. It is a truly wonderful book and has been used by me for over fifty years.

Serves 6

1 large orange
1 lemon
110g caster sugar
25g plain flour
50g unsalted butter, softened
2 tablespoons rum
2 tablespoons brandy
175ml medium sherry

First prepare the orange and lemon zests, and to do this it's best to use a potato peeler and pare off the outer zest, leaving the white pith behind. What you need is 4 strips of each zest measuring approximately 5 × 2.5 cm. Then, using a sharp knife, cut the strips into very thin, needle-like shreds. Now pop these into a medium-sized saucepan, along with the sugar and 275ml water, bring everything up to a slow simmer and let it simmer as gently as possible for 15 minutes.

While that is happening, squeeze the juice from the orange and lemon, and in a separate bowl, mix the flour and butter together to form a paste. When the 15 minutes is up, add the orange and lemon juice, along with the rum, brandy and sherry, and bring it all back up to a gentle heat. Now add the paste to the liquid in small, peanut-sized pieces, whisking as you add them, until they have dissolved and the sauce has thickened. Serve the sauce hot in a warmed serving jug, and if you make it in advance, re-heat it gently without letting it come to the boil.

Friday 18th September

I often wonder about poor old Snooks. He sits by the boat pond and the bin, thinking, thinking. Does he remember why he is there? Does he remember the doctor and Dora? Is he thinking about them all the time? It's a nice place to be on a Summer's day, but how does it feel in Winter, all alone? and at his back the cold, cold sea.

Emma Chichester Clark, *Snooks and Plum*, 2017. Pen and watercolour drawing from *Another Year of Plumdog*.

Emma Chichester Clark is a children's book illustrator and author, who has published over sixty books. Her blog recorded the daily life of Plum, her dog, in Plum's own words and Emma's illustrations. Emma and Plum now live in Aldeburgh, where the bronze statue of Snooks by Gwynneth Holt stands beside the model boating pond. Snooks, who got his name from the tinned fish imported from Africa in the Second World War, was a dog owned by local doctors Robin and Nora Acheson. He used to accompany the doctors on their rounds in Aldeburgh where they practised from 1931. Dr Robin died in 1959. Dr Nora continued to practise medicine, including teaching first aid to the lifeboat crew, until her death in 1981.

RALPH OF COGGESHALL

The Wild Man of Orford

From *Chronicon Anglicanum* (c. 1187–1224)

Orford with its twelfth-century castle can claim one of the Suffolk coast's most curious pieces of history—the story of a wild man captured in the nets of local fishermen. Ralph of Coggeshall, writing in the Chronicon Anglicanum *in 1200 describes briefly, but very vividly, the events:*

James Dodds, *The Wild Man of Orford*, 1995.

It happened that some fishermen who were fishing in the sea caught a wild man in their nets. The wild man was completely naked and all his limbs were formed like those of a man. He was hairy and his beard was long and pointed. Around the chest he was very rough and shaggy. The castellan placed him under guard, day and night, and would not allow him to return to the sea. He eagerly ate anything that was brought to him. He devoured fish raw rather than cooked, squeezing the raw fishes in his hands until all of the moisture was removed and then eating them. He did not wish to talk, or rather did not have the power to talk, even when suspended by his feet and tortured. On being led into the church, he showed no sign of belief or of reverence and he did not genuflect or bow his head when he saw anything holy. He always sought out his bed at sunset and always lay there until sunrise.

He was allowed to go into the sea, strongly guarded with three lines of nets, but he dived under the nets and came up again and again. Eventually he came back of his own free will. But later on he was never seen again.

Ralph noted that people didn't know if the wild man was a 'mortal man, or some fish pretending human shape, or was an evil spirit hiding in the body of a drowned man'.

He continues: 'So many wonderful things of this kind are told by many to whom they happened.'

JULIA BLACKBURN

Searching for Doggerland

From *Time Song* (2019)

Julia Blackburn has always collected things that hold stories about the past, especially the very distant past: mammoth bones, little shells that happen to be two million years old, a flint shaped as a weapon long ago. Time Song *brings many such stories together as it tells of the creation, the existence and the loss of a country now called Doggerland, a huge and fertile area that once connected the entire east coast of England with mainland Europe, until it was finally submerged by rising sea levels around 5000 BC.*

1

I am looking out across the North Sea on a calm day. The surface of the sea is like a covering of grey skin, breathing softly in and out.

As I stand here, the water that separates me from the mainland on the other side begins to retreat, as if a plug has been pulled. A vast country emerges: low hills and wide valleys, the twist and turn of rivers, the scoop of lakes.

At first the country appears limp and without colour, but then a shiver of life moves through it. The birds flying overhead spiral down to settle and pause on their journey. Seeds take root. Reed beds and salt marshes spread out like shadows across the young mud. Tiny trees appear on higher ground. The rivers are again flowing and fish are racing down them towards a more distant ocean. The old lakes are filling up and animals are moving in, exploring the territory; humans, too, since this is a human time.

I fail to catch the moment of the change taking place, but now the sea is rising. Peninsulas become islands, islands disappear without trace, rivers break through the banks that defined them. The lower lands are flooded and even before they fall, the trees on higher ground are killed by the salt water in which they stand. The animals and the humans must escape if they are to survive. For a while the marshes and reed beds remain, but then they go under.

I am on a beach close to the shoreline and looking out across the breathing surface of the North Sea. Slabs of thick, peaty soil containing the roots and broken stalks of those reeds from long ago lie scattered on the sand. I pick up a piece of mammoth bone, brown and heavy and still showing the honeycomb that once carried blood and lymph through the living body. I pick up a shell that has been turned into a stone. I look for flints worked into the shape of a weapon or a tool.

It's getting late. I go home.

— 153 —

2

I live close to the sea and the sea I live close to covers a country we now call Doggerland. This country has been through many incarnations: hot and dry, wet and marshy, cold and ice-bound, but for most of its long time it has in one way or another connected England with mainland Europe.

Much of the fragmented evidence of what this country once was is hidden under the sea, but there is also a lot to be found scattered in the sands and clays and gravels of the land. Deep time lies beneath my feet and if I were to dig into the earth I would witness the past unfolding in layers.

The coastline here is delicate and unprotected; a storm can easily break off great chunks of the soft cliff to reveal lines of brightly coloured sands, a string of dancing shells followed by a band of gravel and then of clay. Bones as well. Just a few weeks ago I found a fossilised piece from the jigsaw of an ancient sea creature, lying below a field where carrots were being harvested, and once I found a human skull, packed tight with soil in which the roots of little plants were growing.

I have been gathering these broken treasures for many years and as I look at them, or rearrange them in different configurations, they seem to become part of my own thought process, part of who I am.

Yesterday, I went, as I often do, to the nearby village of Covehithe. It has an eighteenth-century church standing within the ruins of a much older church. A narrow road passes the church and heads straight for the sea, but it has no final destination because it has snapped off like a piece of biscuit right at the cliff edge: a layer of tarmac and concrete sticking out over the drop beneath, changing shape after each new succession of high tides.

I followed the path from the village to the coast. Gulls were dipping and holding themselves steady in the air as if they had little hooks in their backs attached to elasticated strings. A kestrel: a glint of tawny feathers. The last of the sand martins.

I slept for one night on the sand of this beach with my first husband beside me and our second child stirring in my belly. We lay on a duvet and under a duvet and I remember the slowness of the sunset and geese creaking and crying in long skeins above our heads. The noise of them stepped over into my dreams.

It must have been around the same time I saw two friends entering the shallow sea hand in hand and laughing and it had never occurred to me before that they were also young in their way, even though they were already as old as I am now. She had recently been treated for a cancer which almost killed her and in order to pull herself through the process of recovery she started to build a flint wall in her garden and every day she went to the beach and chose a big flint and carried it to the car and brought it back and cemented it in place and slowly her strength returned to her as the wall grew.

Once I noticed a tiny black thing as hard and shiny as polished jet, tightly embedded in the sand of the cliff. I pulled it out like a thorn and it appeared to

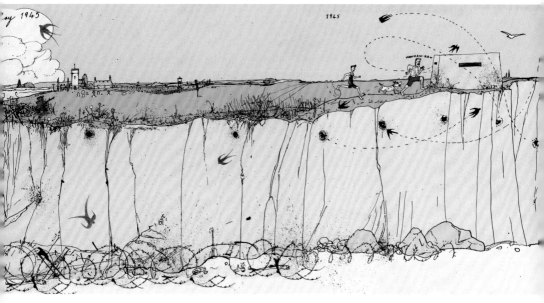

David Hughes, *The Pillbox*, 2015.

David Hughes' graphic novel is part ghost story and part murder mystery set on the coast near Covehithe and Southwold. On holiday in Suffolk, a boy and his dog discover a World War II pillbox half buried on a deserted beach. When he returns the next day with his parents, the pillbox has disappeared.

be a fossilised chrysalis. I could see the tightly folded wings and little circles under which lay the still-closed eyes of a creature that never got round to splitting out of its prison and emerging as a moth or a butterfly.

I found my first piece of mammoth here: an almost complete section of vertebra. I keep it on a window ledge, next to a beautiful stone axe from this same beach and another one which my son, who was stirring in my womb while I listened to the geese, picked up a little while ago in the mud of the Thames, close to Tate Modern. There have been so many Thames Picks, as they are called, found along that stretch of the river that people think they were not lost accidentally, but were offerings to whatever gods were interested in such gifts.

Yesterday the coast looked very battered. Big pieces of land had tumbled down, some of them tufty-topped with fresh grass or with the Chinese lantern shapes of a recent sugar beet crop. Within the side of the wounded cliff I could see the arterial systems of drainage pipes and rolls of barbed wire from the defences of the last war or the war before that one. Things here often appear magically out of nowhere and then vanish with an equal magic. Recently a concrete pillbox settled its awkward weight on the sand like a prehistoric creature, and it reminded me of the last scene in *Planet of the Apes* when Charlton Heston thinks he is back in the dawn of time but then he sees the arm of the Statue of Liberty sticking up out of the sand, along with the spiked crown and the 1920s haircut, and he realises he has arrived in the future and the sand is covering the city of New York.

A friend told me of the nuclear command bunker which lies under the lawn of a garden in the village. Everything is hearsay but it seems it was built during the Cold War and is connected to its twin on the Dutch coast. It is three storeys deep, with enough room to hold thirty important people and enough dry and tinned food to feed them for thirty years. He took a series of photographs inside the bunker with an infrared camera. One of them shows a dour 1960s domestic interior in which a bulbous television set stands close to two stiff armchairs upholstered in that plastic material called leatherette. The other is of a printed notice on a wall with practical information about what you must and must not do, next to a very amateur oil painting of the church and a pinkly flowering cherry tree, all of it set against the bright blue of a summer sky, so the underground people need never forget the look of the world they had lost. I keep thinking of the bunker and how every year it is being brought closer and closer to the cliff edge, until the day comes when it will begin to topple down on to the beach and maybe strangers with no idea of what it once was will stare at the debris and take away anything they consider worth saving.

ROBERT MACFARLANE

Orfordness

From *The Wild Places* (2007)

Robert Macfarlane's journey to find the last wild places left in Britain has become a classic. Here, he sets off with his friend Roger Deakin, author of Waterlog, *to explore the unique and shifting spit of Orfordness.*

Roger and I drove on together to Orford Ness.

In the eleventh and twelfth century, Orford was a thriving port, protected from the North Sea by the comforting arm of the Ness. Then that arm turned murderous. Over the course of several centuries—accurate time-telling is difficult with regard to these shingle formations—it extended down the coast, and strangled the port. Without the flushing action of regular tides, which were deflected by the Ness, the harbour silted up, making it impossible for deep-bellied ships to reach the quays. Orford was turned into a small-boat harbour only, dead to trade.

The weather had been deteriorating since we left Walnut Tree Farm; the yellow dawn of Blakeney curdling into a sour grey day. To reach the Ness you must be ferried across the River Ore. As we stepped from the ferry on the pontoon on

David Gentleman, *Pagodas*, Orford Ness, 2007.

the Ness's shore, it was clear that the Ness was in a wild state. The tide was incoming, and brown currents swirled beneath the pontoon, making it squeak and shift. The easterly wind had strengthened. Looking across the Ness from the pontoon, it was impossible to tell where brown desert gave way to brown sea. The horizon was lost, dissolved into a single rolling beige of shingle, sea and sky. Two Harriers blasted overhead, moving due south, leave a sandpapery roar in the air. We set off to walk the spit.

For eighty years the Ness was owned by the Ministry of Defence, which prized its natural security cordon as well as its uniformity and expanse. So it was that like many other larger deserts—the Great Victoria in Australia, the Kizil Kum in Kazakhstan, the Mojave Desert in America—the Ness became a site for ordnance testing. Bomb ballistics and weaponry experiments were conducted on the Ness during the First and Second World Wars, and in the 1960s, nuclear detonation devices were trialled in specially built concrete structures now known as the Pagodas. In big concrete halls, the Ness military scientists would stand British fighter planes, and then fire enemy bullets at them from fixed cannon, attempting to locate weak points, and to see how the planes could be better armoured.

All across the Ness, enigmatic military structures still protrude from the shingle —pre-fabricated barracks, listening stations, beacons, watch-towers, bunkers, explosion-chambers. Unexploded ordnance still lies around. It is forbidden to step off certain cleared pathways through the shingle, which have been made safe, and marked out with a rust-red dye and blood red arrows. By the sides of the pathways we were following lay military debris: twisted sprays of tank tracking, a shattered concrete block, and an exploded boiler, whose inch-thick iron casing had flared into bright rusted thick petals: warnings not to stray.

It is hard to be on the Ness, and not feel its militarising influence upon one's vision. That day, everything I saw seemed bellicose, mechanised. A hare exploded from a shingle divot. Bramble coiled and looped like barbed wire and orange lichen camouflaged the concrete of pillboxes.

Roger and I walked out to the mid-north of the Ness, halfway between its inner and outer coasts, and there we climbed up on to the roof of the Bomb Ballistic Building, a black chunky structure which had been used for observing the fall of ordnance from planes. From the summit of the building, we gained a harrier's-eye view of the Ness—or a Harrier's-eye view. To our west, cupped on its landward coast, were salt-meres: Lantern Marshes, Kings Marshes. To the north was the gleaming puffball of Sizewell B, oddly bright on this overcast day. Disappearing into the southern haze was the Ness's distal point, probing ever further down the coast—a thin finger indicating the way to Dungeness. And to the east was the outermost edge of the Ness, where its grey-brown stone shaded into the grey-brown water.

Laid out below and around us, much as it would have appeared to the First World War bomb-watchers, was the main expanse of Ness. Seen from this height, the landscape's own logic became more apparent. There were the longitudinal shingle ridges, running and curving its full length—the Ness's storm-born growth rings. Cutting across these were other less regular ridges made by the vehicles of the bomb-disposal teams. These were the marks of the clean-up operation; of the desert's decontamination. The man-made lines and the storm lines swooped and arced and intersected with one another, to create a single vast fingerprint of shingle, stretching as far as I could see.

GRIFF RHYS JONES

Windsong

From *Semi-Detached* (2006)

Griff Rhys Jones is a comedian, actor, writer and television presenter. He was born in Wales, and now lives in Suffolk. He continues to sail whenever he can. 'Every single ruddy holiday' was spent sailing with the family in a succession of boats. Here he remembers his father's last boat.

Windsong was almost entirely flat-bottomed; though thirty feet long she drew no more than two and a half feet. One evening, we crept up the Butley River. It was a creek around behind an island at the mouth of the Ore, and no more than twenty feet across for most of its surprising length. It could be described as little more than a drain, in a wide expanse of utterly flat marsh—not a reedy exotic marsh, but a sharp grassed, unforgiving matted expanse of half-land, crazed with runnels like a large version of a baked mud puddle. We could not see this. The boat sat low between the banks. We motored slowly forward for two, perhaps three miles, twisting onwards. There wasn't room to pass another boat, but we wouldn't meet another boat. No boats came up there any more, though half-way up we passed a red-brick quay where, until the Second World War, Thames barges, mammoth sixty-foot wherries with tan sails, would have tied up to take hay to London. Here the land began. The tidal river unexpectedly widened. The bank built up on the northern side into a twenty-foot-high cliff which met a sea wall snaking in from somewhere towards Orford. We anchored, probably in the middle of an oyster bed.

In the last of the light I rowed away from the boat. When water is completely calm the oars break mirrors. The rowlocks squeak and rattle as if being recorded in a studio. The dinghy and the rower seem to be overpowered, scooting into glassy motion at the slightest tug. I pulled up on the shore and climbed up the sandy cliff and sat under some crouched trees, which seemed to mark the beginnings of liveable land. Away on the other side of the sea wall was a low cottage with a single light in the window. Ahead to the south and west, the Suffolk fields rolled up and out towards Butley woods where I knew there was a priory, originally served by the river. I couldn't see it. It was dusk. What I could see was miles of fading, almost medieval landscape. I waited there as it got dark under the blackening trees, an oil lamp on the boat reflecting on the water like a connecting thread. I can hardly think of any other moment in my life which has encompassed such perfection: the solitude, the beauty, the sense of the journey made and the simplicity of the place. I got back in the dinghy, pulled the thread in and rowed back to the intimacy of the little cabin. It was what my father wanted from it all. He gave that to me.

Thirty-five years on, I went to take a look at *Windsong* while they were laying her up at the end of the 2004 season. It was a difficult yard to get to, upriver of the tide mill in Woodbridge, crossed by a railway line, and dirt tracks, where the Suffolk Heritage Coast dumped its chair manufacturers, plant storage and sausage makers. The place for a beating-up in a low-budget cop show. The winter facilities were little more than a couple of sheds and a crane, in a field full of boats on sticks.

I sat on the blue-covered bench seats, my father's upholstery wearing dramatically well, and as I looked around and praised aloud the cosy ergonomics of the neatly arranged shallow interior, I was thinking that I had libelled my own father in the cause of filial mockery. He hadn't loaded the boat with woodwork until it sank beneath his carpentry. His additions, like the little bookcase, and the 'tidy', were positioned with a good eye and discreetly made in dark mahogany. They looked good. It was good that the boat that he lavished such attention on was going to continue. It was good that what seemed to matter most to him, his claustrophobic, neat cabin, where he liked to 'get a fug up' and hide from the world, retained his stamp. Out on deck again under scudding clouds I paused for a second. I could see down to the bend in the river, where, fifteen years ago we had gone out in a boat and scattered his ashes.

Kate Giles, *Burrow Hill, Towards Gedgrave Marshes*, 2008.

Kate Giles is a contemporary artist whose work for many years has focused on the landscape of her native East Anglia.

BOBBY GROVES

Butley Creek

From *Oyster Isles* (2019)

Bobby Groves is the Head of Oysters at the London restaurant Chiltern Firehouse. His book—part travel writing, part social history—takes us on a tour of the British and Irish oyster.

Ipswich has long been a prosperous town within touching distance of healthy oyster beds. Before the Normans arrived, Lenten food restrictions dominated the springtime for medieval Christians and the church also enforced fish days (usually on a Friday but sometimes Wednesday or Saturday). It cannot be a coincidence that a correlation existed between the natural distribution of oyster beds and the recorded wealth of Anglo-Saxon England in Ipswich.

The Butley Creek river remains unspoilt. The surrounding marshland is home to a thriving biodiversity of British birds and mammals, with seals often seen gliding through the water and oystercatchers flying overhead. It is a calm and quiet backwater that time has forgotten and the tranquillity makes it a perfect environment for oyster growing.

The Pinneys farm the area throughout the year in harmony with the changing seasons. In summer, the oysters grow and the fishing boat will catch lobster, crab and sole, while in winter the oysters concentrate on survival and the day boat will bring in cod and skate. The Pinneys have farmed oysters here since the late 1950s, when Richard Pinney left London to look for a quieter life in the Suffolk countryside. Once settled, he decided to restore the old oyster beds in the creek next to his cottage. He imported oysters from Portugal to see if they would grow as a potential business and they loved their new home. Today, Bill and his family run the operation along with Irene, all working in different parts of the business—a world-class smokehouse, a shop, a busy wholesale set-up, day-boat fishing, oyster farming and a top-quality restaurant.

The rock oysters are grown initially in small blue mushroom boxes suspended from homemade rafts (five mushroom boxes stacked one on top of the other under a floating wooden board) anchored to the bed of the river. The home-made set-up is ingenious, one that Bill Pinney has made almost entirely from recycled materials. Once the oysters grow big enough, they are transferred to standard mesh bags and submerged again to feed on the nutrients suspended in the water. Once they reach a certain size, the oysters are then scattered on to the bottom of the river where the shell grows stronger and the oyster sits filtering happily until it is fished and rowed to shore.

Laurence Edwards, *The Creek Men*, 2008.

For nearly two decades Suffolk-born sculptor and caster Laurence Edwards's studio was at the head of the creek at Butley Mills. This is where he made this giant trio of Creek Men in 2008 using mud from the river to model these eight-foot high figures, which he then cast into bronze using the lost wax method. Once completed they were then towed on a symbolic voyage up the River Alde to Snape Maltings for the Aldeburgh Festival. They stayed moored in the marshes raising and lowering with the tide for the next year. His latest sculpture, the twenty-six foot high Colossus, Yox-Man, now stands beside the A12 at Yoxford.

Bill's approach, which embraces sustainable, low—or no—impact animal husbandry, is a shining example of how oyster farming serves as a great model for good food acquisition. Mankind over the past twenty years or so has become increasingly more careless when it comes to the environment, and Bill has many stories—and warnings—about the negative effects of man's impact on biodiversity around the south-eastern coastline, which becomes a persistent theme for all sustainable farmers for whom the purity and cleanliness of the natural world is paramount. Bill had been aware of the potential problem with plastics for thirty years or so, but 'it always fell on deaf ears', he told me, until it was picked up by Sir David Attenborough, beamed into people's living rooms on a Sunday night, and instantly became a top priority for government and local authorities.

Bill is a man who knows and understands the waters around his region, and is in tune with the effects of tiny changes in the ecosystem around him. These tiny changes are warning signs of bigger, more critical impacts, and we need to listen to Bill and others like him to ensure we are doing all we can to protect the treasures that the natural world has given us.

Livelihoods depend on it—as well as the health and wellbeing of humankind who operate at the top of the food chain. Destroy one part of that chain, and the whole network will fall apart.

There are on-site purification facilities that take a minimum of forty-two hours to complete before the oysters are washed, hand graded and lovingly packed for market. From tide to table, the entire production process takes about two to three years and causes virtually no negative impact on the environment.

The essence of the creek and this location is embodied in the taste of this oyster. The flavour has a hint of sweetness in the meat that varies throughout the seasons, tasting best in the autumn and spring. The Butley Creek environment gives the flesh and liquor a vegetable, grassy note with a slight cucumber finish that reflects its East Anglian environment. There is no overbearing salty flavour, as the oyster is from a river where it takes on the constant flow of nutrients coming downstream from the river's source in the Rendlesham Forest, through Bill Pinney's patch and on to the North Sea.

The beauty of the smoking at Butley Creek is the simplicity of the process. It is an art form that I truly believe the giants of the fish-smoking industry would never be able to rival. One key factor (and it is no secret) is that, after being salted, the smoking of the fish is done right through the meat. Although this sounds ridiculously simple, you would be surprised how many people these days are just imbuing the product with a hint of smoke for flavour, and not taking the trouble to reduce the water content. Of course, they do this to keep the weight up and so make more money. At Pinney's of Orford, it is the simple and honest process that is the foundation for their success as smokers.

KARIN ALTENBERG

Navigating Home (2021)

Karin Altenberg is originally from Sweden and first moved to the UK in 1996. She is a writer of fiction and non-fiction and an occasional translator. She has a PhD in archaeology and her background as a landscape archaeologist has influenced her writing.

On an afternoon in early March, I was standing amongst daffodils and crocked gravestones, looking up at the round tower of St Mary the Virgin in Wortham. A Saxon tower, friends told me, part of the defences against raiding Vikings. It was the first warm day of the year, that pale ochre sunshine that makes the landscape seem soft at the edges, as if it's disappearing or turning magically into another place or time. An illusion, of course, as the English flint of the tower walls soon confirmed, but that sense of the land—that place—revealing itself would stay with me.

I had only been to Suffolk a couple of times before, but this visit was significant. We had, in ways that still seem unfathomable to me, become the custodians of a seventeenth-century cottage on Wortham Ling, an expanse of ancient common grazing, complete with heather, gorse and boxing hares. The previous inhabitant, a friend, had described the view from the cottage as 'staring every evening into the Neolithic Period'. I hadn't yet found my bearings in this landscape but the tale about the round tower and the Vikings grounded me—it was the kind of story that would make my mind draw maps.

Hidden behind a copse of silver birches was the River Waveney, which rises at Redgrave Fen and flows eastward towards Great Yarmouth. The modern course of the river passes only eight hundred metres away from the tower: a mere stream, but in the tenth and eleventh centuries it would have been easily navigable by low-hulled Viking ships. The Norse may well have come here, sailing the very border between the South folk and the North folk on their way to Thetford or Ringmere Heath (the *Hringmaraheiðr* of the Skaldic Verse). Today, the tower sits on slightly raised ground, like a skerry in a sea of arable land—a perfect place for a beacon or a watchtower from which to spot the advancing heathens for miles.

I grew up in a landscape where the wealth generated from those Viking raids still manifests itself in the early churches, place-names and rune-stones commemorating thanes, journeys and battles. The ground around my hometown of Lund in southern Sweden is laden with some of the largest hoards of Æthelred 'crux coins' in Scandinavia. This is where part of the *Danegeld* ended up. Lund was founded by the Danish king Sven Tveskägg (Forkbeard) around 990. Forkbeard was the son of Harald Blåtand—the Bluetooth who had united Denmark some thirty years previously and converted to Christianity, recognising a swift way to strengthen his rule and advance trade. (More recently, Bluetooth gave his name to the wireless technology developed at Lund University in 1994.) Forkbeard, as shrewd a politician as his father, built the first church in Lund, establishing a bishopric, where the English priest Gotebalt strived to make the locals abandon their pagan ways. This was a clever move, providing Forkbeard with a new pow-er-base associated with the Danelaw in England and marking his independence from German leaders. I was about six years old when I first peered down into the pit as this church was excavated, fascinated by the grinning skulls and bits of skeleton emerging from the ground.

Forkbeard was a nation-builder with imperial ambitions extending across the northern sea-worlds and riverways. By the year 1000, he had ousted (and probably murdered) his father, conquered southern Norway in one of the largest sea battles in Viking history and founded the bishopric in Lund. Now his 'mod-ern' realm enclosed the North Sea from the east, south and north. From here he could only go west—to East Anglia. *The Anglo-Saxon Chronicle* records the arrival of 93 ships in 991 and the subsequent Battle of Maldon where a local army was destroyed. Æthelred the Unready was forced to pay £10,000 to make the Norse invaders depart. This was an ill-advised move; Æthelred ended up paying almost £137,000 in *Danegeld* over the next fourteen years. The poem *The Battle of Maldon* describes how a Norse herald, with 'threat in his throat', offers a fair warning:

> The swift-striking seafarers send me to thee,
> bid me say that thou send for thy safety
> rings, bracelets. Better for you
> that you stay straightaway our onslaught with tribute
> than that we should share bitter strife.
> We need not meet if you can meet our needs:
> for a gold tribute a truce is struck.

The extortion money increased Forkbeard's power around Lund as his allies grew richer. In 1013, after the St Brice's Day massacre (another one of Æthelred's rash initiatives), Forkbeard launched a full-scale invasion of England and, after Lon-don capitulated—commemorated, possibly, in the nursery rhyme '*London Bridge is Falling Down*'—he was crowned the first Scandinavian King of England on Christ-mas Day. As it happened, he died four weeks later of natural causes (they say), and was succeeded by his son, Canute the Great. Forkbeard's remains were eventually brought back across the North Sea—his *Mare Nostrum*—and buried in his church in Lund.

Almost 1000 years later, as I watched the shadows of this church emerge out of the ground, I was becoming aware that I shared this place, my hometown, not just with the people I saw in the streets every day, but with all those who had lived there through the course of time. When I was a little older, my father and I would

Tessa Newcomb, *Sweffling Church*, 2009.

Born in Suffolk in 1955, Tessa is the daughter of artist, Mary Newcomb. She attended the Norwich School of Art from 1972 and the Bath Academy of Art in 1976. The Suffolk countryside and country events feature predominantly in Newcomb's paintings; she lives in Suffolk.

cycle around the landscape in search of rune-stones. Dad, a linguist, would read me the runes. The sound of the Old Norse was thrilling. Many of these stones were raised to commemorate men loyal to Forkbeard. This is where he recruited warriors for the attacks on East Anglia, and this is the land where the English silver was invested and buried by those who made it back. The stones told tales of death, valour and loyalty, infused with the magic power of those runes. They never failed to fuel my imagination. Conjuring up images of all the layers of past human life was greatly comforting to me, a kind of *eiderdowniness* of shared humanity. It was no coincidence that I became an archaeologist.

Jacquetta Hawkes, the more-celebrated archaeologist, understood the cultural landscape in the way that I did as a child—its layers and depth—and perceived time as cultural distance. 'It is only the pathetic shortness of human life that gives each individual a sense of the permanence of his background,' she wrote in 1951. No one can claim direct kinship with the people of the distant past, but we are all united in this cultural distance of time. To me the exploration of the past is an exercise in empathy, a way of becoming conscious of what it is to be human in another time and place.

Let's return to the Saxon tower at Wortham. *Historic England*'s listing describes it as possibly eleventh-century: '[a] 3-stage west tower with a diameter of 29 feet and 62 feet high is said to be the largest Norman round tower in England, originally possibly a watchtower for St. Edmund's Bury.' So not a Saxon tower built in defence against Forkbeard and his Vikings. I had imagined too far; I had been seduced by this flinty *madeleine* and forgotten the facts. And yet, I can sense it, the connection between my childhood landscape and this place that is still so new to me—there is a kind of affinity or recognition, not just through the shared course of the past but in the heathland, the rolling fields and the huge sky that reminds me of the cultural landscape around Lund. So, the tower may be Norman—but its fabric contains everything that happened here over time: 'the past should be altered by the present as much as the present is directed by the past,' Eliot wrote in his essay, *Tradition and the Individual Talent*, from 1919.

Archaeology is about exploring absence, looking for the imprint of human life, that which was left behind, the shadows of existence; it's about sifting through obscure sediment until meaning, or some kind of truth, emerges into the light. Putting my hand to the round tower in Wortham that March afternoon, I hoped perhaps to transform the materiality of the cold flint into a more intimate distance, which is as close to experience as we can get. I was searching for that *consciousness*, which would transform me from a foreigner into someone who could find a home here. The people who lived on the Ling throughout the course of time were different from those of us who live here or visit today, with different ideas, values, beliefs, joys and sorrows—in this respect they are foreign, just like me—but we share this thickly layered place, this common home.

As we walked back across Wortham Ling, I found the rusted old shoe of a donkey or was it just the heel plate of an old boot?—it hangs now above our door, for luck, and auld lang syne.

DIARMAID MACCULLOCH

A Government Inspector in Henry VIII's Suffolk

Adapted from *Thomas Cromwell* (2018)

Professor Diarmaid MacCulloch is an English historian, specializing in ecclesiastical history and the history of Christianity. He moved to Suffolk as a boy when his father was appointed rector of Wetherden. He is the first patron of the Suffolk Archives Foundation. Since 1997, he has been Professor of the History of the Church at the University of Oxford.

Writing my recent biography of Thomas Cromwell brought me many pleasures, not least renewing my acquaintance with a panoply of early Tudor folk, some Great and Good, others neither. One of the most entertaining in the latter category brought me back to Suffolk: a young priest emphatically gone to the bad. His comeuppance at the hands of Henry VIII's chief minister came in spring 1535, and exposed an extraordinary eight months of scandalous impersonation in the provinces, worthy of Nikolai Gogol's outrageous creation the failed civil servant and would-be playboy Ivan Alexandrovich Khlestakov. This Tudor Government Inspector *avant la lettre* was named James Billingford. He was from a respectable Norfolk gentry family with links to Thomas Duke of Norfolk, but also bizarrely an Edmund Billingford, probably his elder brother, became one of Cromwell's extended gentry entourage—whether before this episode or after is not certain.

In the 1520s James Billingford had become Rector of South Elmham St George in Suffolk, presented to the living by Thomas Bateman, a local gentleman who is likely to have been his brother-in-law. Bateman enjoyed a lease of this benefice from the Bishop of Norwich, the redoubtable but by then elderly Richard Nix. Billingford was a graduate of either Oxford or Cambridge (most likely Cambridge), for when an ecclesiastical court sat for Elmham deanery in the 1520s, he was described as 'Magister', implying a university degree. Many have been content that their lot has fallen in that fair ground of little Suffolk parishes known as 'the Saints', all Elmhams or Ilketshalls, but not Master Billingford. One can imagine the deep boredom of a high-spirited young graduate in his Waveney valley rectory, under the beady eye of his relations, and with a couple of curates to do any real work that proved necessary.

South Elmham was a principal lordship of Bishop Nix, and one of the Bishop's main manor-houses was actually in Billingford's parish. Maybe it was after witnessing the collapse of the aged bishop's resistance to Archbishop Thomas Cranmer's metropolitical visitation in September 1534 that the Rector of St

George had the idea of embarking on a wild adventure of deception and extortion from the monasteries of England. If his brother was already by then linked to Cromwell, by now the King's chief minister and increasingly involved in the affairs of the Church, family talk could also have provided inspiration for James's enterprising parody of visitation.

James Billingford was evidently adept at namedropping and acting like a gentleman. Banking on the state of nerves about possible monastic dissolutions which was already apparent in monasteries up and down the country, he went on tour claiming to be the official representative or relative of various prominent people—usually Cromwell, but the names of Queen Anne Boleyn or the Duke of Norfolk were also dropped on occasion. He kept himself and his Osip-like attendant in high style on their Tudor road-trip; there were some riotous evenings dicing and carding in assorted hostelries, amid the serious business of intimidating abbots. From early in Billingford's campaign that September in his native East Anglia, two letters crudely forged in Cromwell's name survive in the minister's papers. They demanded money with menaces from a couple of Norfolk monasteries (Horsham St Faith and Coxford), since 'the King of his regal power' was undertaking selective dissolutions, and reform of clergy abuses. The letters have deceived some modern historians into thinking they represent Cromwell's authentic methods of procedure; whether their amateurish production equally duped the monastic heads of house is not clear.

Despite some near-misses from increasingly annoyed authority that winter, it was May Day 1535 before Billingford's extended spree of deception in the Midlands fatally collided in Oxfordshire with cold scepticism from one of Cromwell's friends, a local JP called Anthony Cope. Billingford, cornered in Banbury gaol, at first tried to present it as all a big joke to that gentleman (who happened to be a classical historian of some distinction, used to dissecting tall tales), before resorting to dark talk of all the monastic conspiracies he could reveal to Master Secretary Cromwell. Cope reported it all to Cromwell in a spirit of grim humour, and recommended a merciful discharge for the 'poor lad' his servant—but not Billingford.

James's own fate is alas unknown, though when the commissioners for the Valor Ecclesiasticus did their work that same spring, listing all the church property of the realm, one of his former curates was now listed as Rector of South Elmham St George in his place. Billingford was no longer in Elmham, at least. Where was he: at the end of a rope, or in some dank prison cell, or possibly just on a tavern floor, cards and tankard in hand? So far, we do not know. It must be said that Thomas Cromwell had a distinctly soft spot for wild young men whom the rest of the world deplored—maybe he remembered his own adventurous early days as far away as Italy, and hazarded that some of them combined wildness with talent.

Cromwell certainly recognised that Billingford's remarkably long-lasting scam needed remedying by something more official and systematic—not least to quell widespread confusion and demoralisation which the trickster's pseudo-visitatorial adventures caused among regular clergy. The royal progress of Henry VIII and Anne Boleyn in summer 1535 provided the perfect launchpad for Cromwell in his capacity as Vice-Gerent in Spirituals (effectively the King's deputy in the new Church of England) to undertake an unprecedented investigation into the religious corporations of the realm. The visitation was far more comprehensive than has been understood until the recent research of Dr Anthony Shaw: over seven months, the visitation commissioners visited over 85 per cent of the kingdom's religious houses and secular cathedrals, hospitals and major chantry colleges, including colleges in Oxford and Cambridge Universities.

The self-crafted Government Inspection by the Reverend James Billingford, sometime of South Elmham St George, was part of the prehistory of this major enterprise of Henry VIII's Reformation. When Cromwell's commissioners turned up at successive monastic gateways, armed with the Vice-Gerent's detailed instructions, I wonder how many Abbots cast their minds back ruefully a few months to the supposed Government Inspector with his fine words and his urgent need of horses and cash?

DAVID GENTLEMAN

The Yellow Digger

From *In The Country* (2014)

David Gentleman has spent over thirty-five years inhabiting a sixteenth-century end-of-terrace house on the edge of a small rural village in mid-Suffolk. It has provided a place where he could paint, surrounded by fields and woodland, next to a small stream.

If you look for them, Suffolk abounds in fascinating things—left-over relics, often alluring like the primitive-looking oddities of traction engines and the beautiful and subtle curves of old wooden carts, now preserved and cherished for the craftsmanship and ingenuity amounting to artistry that went into them. There are many examples of these—barns, carts, a maltings pay-shed, along with good historic photos of the people who used them—in the Museum of East Anglian Life at Stowmarket. Other less hallowed remains have survived simply because they are durable or indestructible. There is a wartime Nissen-hut on the edge of our village which has become increasingly skeletal as its corrugated iron cladding rusts away to nothing, each year leaving more open spaces for the dense plants to push up through. It is now impenetrable.

David Gentleman, *The Yellow Digger.*

Bits of heavy farm machinery often remain for years tucked away and over-grown in out-of-the-way corners of fields, probably because they might still come in handy or have been forgotten or are too much trouble to move away, until one day you notice that they have suddenly and inexplicably vanished. Their derelic-tion is part of their charm.

In the seemingly disused, weedy and undesirable corner patch of a field beyond the church, this tall Wellingtonia, the church tower, the digger and the slowly disintegrating plastic silo all make good silhouettes against the sky. Nearby are fragments of old breeze block walls sheltering rotting bales of straw. Such left-over corners make good places for our children to play in and hide. In summer they are full of baby rabbits—I once saw a buzzard flapping heavily away from here with one in its beak. Here I could draw undisturbed, enjoy the changing light and the wild plants flourishing. Now it's gone I even miss the yellow digger.

ROSE TREMAIN

Lady Muck of the Vegetable World

From *The Road Home* (2007)

Several of Rose Tremain's novels are set in Suffolk. This story concerns Lev, a middle-aged immigrant who was recently widowed. He leaves his home, Auror, a village in an unspecified eastern European country, after the sawmill he works at closes down. Soon after, he travels to England to find work so he can make money to send to his mother and his five-year-old daughter, Maya. In this passage he gets a job on a Suffolk farm. Advice on the 'proper picking of asparagus' came from Jack Rosenthal, who farms near Middleton.

'Midge' Midgham brought the old Land Rover round to the three caravans at seven thirty in the morning. He picked up his foreign workers and drove them out to his thirty-acre asparagus spread, where the tractor and rig waited.

The tractor had to haul the rig in a straight line down the furrows. No use letting it buck or slide out of alignment. And it had to go nice and slow, letting the asparagus cutters—the human hardware—keep pace. Housed in the wide steel arms of the rig were plastic crates: five, six in a line, depending on how many cutters were following. The system was simple but effective. The cutters bent down and cut with a knife, making sure there was no wastage, that they sliced each stem just under the earth—not a prodigal inch above it—massed a bunch of stems in their left hands, as if they were gathering flowers, then laid the bunch carefully in the crates, spears all facing the same way. In the old days, hundreds of man-hours had been wasted decanting the full trugs carried by the pickers into boxes at the field's edge. With the rig, the asparagus was cut and crated in one smooth operation. Twice a day, the crates were loaded into the Land Rover and driven down to the chiller in Midge's barn.

The owner of the spread had to be vigilant, that was all. Midge drove the tractor with his big belly squashed up against the wheel and his neck half bent round most of the time, keeping watch on how the cutters were working. If he saw anybody throwing the spears into the crates, he'd yell at them.

'Now, yew listen up,' he'd told them on their first day. 'Asparagus en't sugar beet! It en't blusted Brussels sprouts. It's got a good pedigree. It's Lady Muck of the vegetable world: grows overnight, needs harvesting fast, or it go to seed. And it damage easily. So yew treat it with respect. Yew tug your forelocks to it, or you'll be off this blusted farm.'

Midge told his farmer friends at the Longmire Arms: 'These bors from Eastern Europe, they're used to field work. At home, as kids, I reckon they'd be up at dawn to feed the family chickens, same thing after school, milk the cows, water the cabbages, all that carry on … So they're decent pickers, see, because they understand the land.'

Of the two young Chinese men, Sonny and Jimmy Ming, Midge said: 'Denno 'bout them. Can't seem to get their tongues around the language. And Sonny Ming, he cuts too high up the stem because he's dreaming half the blusted time. But they're good natured. I give 'em that. Laugh a lot, they do. Den't know what at, but who cares? And they never seem to mind the rain.'

But this year Midge had only seven cutters when he could have done with nine or ten, because the asparagus was showing up nice, after a spring that had been just wet enough and after his seaweed mulch, spread on in late autumn, had been broken down by hard winter frosts. The crop had just the right amount of body to it—stems not too fat nor too spindly—and this April was warm; you could practically see the stuff growing. So when Vitas came to him and asked him to take on his friend, Lev, a man in his forties, he'd said, 'Awright by me, Vitas, if he don't mind sharing a van with the Mings. And if he'll put his back into it.'

Lev didn't mind sharing the leaky old caravan. There were no curtains at the windows, so most mornings Lev woke at six, when it got light. He made tea on the two-ring burner and usually took the mug outside, to escape the fug of the caravan, to watch the sun come up behind a stand of poplars and feel the fresh air on his face.

It rained often. The field where the vans stood was always muddy, from the trudging back and forth of the gang of workers. This half-acre of mud reached to where a washing line sagged between two posts, usually draped with towels, cheap bed linen, frayed T-shirts, grey underwear, took in a rubbish heap of pallets, boxes, timber offcuts, lengths of grey piping, steel brackets and plastic shelving, and a Portaloo, narrow as a phone box, jacked up on some concrete blocks. Once a week, the toilet was emptied and refilled with olive-green detergent, sharp in your nose as a dry martini.

Drinking tea and smoking, Lev walked out to where the grass shone with dew, towards hawthorn hedges and a field of raspberry canes, still almost bare of leaf. Beyond the canes, a lush meadow on rising ground, where Midge's geese sometimes wandered, bickered and lay down, like snow-white meringues. Beyond this, the poplars and the big sky. Standing in this place, Longmire Farm, in the quiet of morning, Lev now and again felt something of what Vitas had described to him—that it was alright, better than a thousand other places, despite the mud, like a corner of England from long ago.

But his back ached. Not just from bending all day in the asparagus fields but from the bed he'd been allocated. Everything in his caravan was old, worn, used, stained. Lev slept on a block of petrified foam-rubber, which, in the daytime, was kicked upwards into a rigid fold, to form bulky bench seating for a pull-down Formica table. The foam was upholstered in a prickly brown weave. Lev's thin nylon undersheet slithered around on this weave. All night, his body itched and rolled about.

One morning, after a night of almost no sleep, Lev attempted to ask Midge Midgham for something—a soft blanket or quilt—to put between the sheet and the foam, but he knew that Midge was selectively deaf, so he wasn't surprised when the man simply turned away from him and strode towards the waiting tractor.

And so the morning would roll on, Lev's world shrinking to the grey-brown furrows, the green stems, snapping cleanly under the knife, wild weeds in the ditches, sun or rain on his back, diesel fumes from the tractor sullying the freshness of the air.

There was a kind of camaraderie in the line. Lev liked to hear his own language pass from voice to voice. It reminded him of beating the woods behind Auror for rabbits and pigeons when he was a boy. Sometimes, breathing in the diesel smoke, he caught a memory-whiff of the Baryn mill, half expected to look up and see his old friends standing at the edge of the wood: ghostly faces under hard hats.

The afternoons felt long. On fine days they worked nine, ten hours. Worked till the light began to go, till the rooks began to shuffle in the high trees, till the Lady Muck became almost invisible in her green sheath. Then they fell into the Land Rover, mute, aching, hungry, and were driven back to the caravan. Took turns at the hot shower, a big empty walk-in space, fixed up by Midge next to the chiller. Heated up the cheapest tinned stuff they could buy—ravioli, baked beans, mulligatawny soup—and spooned it in like starving children, bulked out with thick-cut bread. Slaked their sugar-thirst with canned peaches, mandarin oranges, Mars bars. Wandered outside to smoke, if the night was fine, and stared at the stars, clear and bright, over the quiet land.

The wind kept blowing over Suffolk.

PAUL BINSKI

The Thornham Parva Retable

From *A Guide to the Retable* (2003)

Dr Paul Binski is a British art historian and Emeritus Professor of the History of Medieval Art at the University of Cambridge.

The famous fourteenth-century gilded and painted Retable that graces the altar of St Mary's church is one of the most miraculous survivals of the art of the English Middle Ages. This is the second oldest altarpiece to survive from medieval England, and one of only a handful now existing from the entire Middle Ages in this country (others are to be found at Westminster Abbey and Norwich Cathedral).

Made of painted oak, the Thornham Parva Retable is the sort of object that was to be found in English churches of all ranks in the Middle Ages—and exactly the sort of thing that was to be destroyed during the English Reformation of the sixteenth and seventeenth centuries. Yet this extraordinarily beautiful painting survived the religious turmoil of these centuries largely unscathed.

The Retable is now in a secure glazed wooden case over the high altar in the chancel. It was originally intended to be seen at this sort of height, and in this sort of position over an altar. However, this particular retable was not in fact made for the church at Thornham Parva. Lord Henniker's staff had found the Retable in 1927 in a stable loft at Thornham Hall, not far away. Like many medieval works of art, by the nineteenth century its importance and beauty were long forgotten, its value as a stout piece of oak timber being much greater. A beautiful medieval altarpiece had become no more than a bit of Suffolk farmyard junk. Its resurrection in the 1920s and location in the church here in effect saved it for posterity.

What we see is a low wide rectangle consisting of painted and gilded timber, which consists of a row of carved canopies, an arcade of pointed Gothic arches supported on round columns. Over the row of arches is stylized carved and gilded foliage. Within the arcade stand the figures of saints, long and slim in form with small heads and graceful swaying postures. No two figures are quite alike, for it was important to identify and differentiate the saints by the attributes they hold. In medieval fashion, the saints are anachronistically imagined in then-contemporary costume as if present before the eyes of the beholder in the here and now. The overall impression is of rich dark gold for the frame and grounds, and of deep reds, browns and greens with a few dark blues—the harmonious colours of autumn.

The central compartment of the arcade depicts the Crucifixion of Christ; to either side is, literally, the company of heaven, the 'cloud of witnesses', in the form

The Thornham Parva Retable (detail).

of the saints, ten in all if we count Mary and John by the Cross. Each saint stands under one of the arches of the arcade, and the figures are elegantly and politely arranged in pairs, turning to one another as if in a heavenly conversation.

Here we take just two of the saints: in the right-hand half comes the regal image of St Edmund (d. 869), the martyred Anglo-Saxon king whose relics lay at Bury. Edmund was the most important local Anglo-Saxon saint aside from St Etheldreda at Ely. Next to Edmund is St Margaret of Antioch, a formidable crowned early martyr whose elegant figure tramples on the dragon which swallowed her up; she completes the job by skewering it with her preaching staff. We might never have guessed from this that Margaret was the patron saint of childbirth because she escaped from the stomach of the dragon.

It is clear that the panel was originally made for the church of the Dominican Priory, and probably for its high altar. All the evidence—dendrochronology and style—points to an origin in East Anglia at some time around 1330.

The style in which the figures are painted looks very much like works of art made in or for East Anglia at around this time—a period of great prosperity in this region when East Anglia was producing some of the most interesting art in northern Europe. The chequerboard pattern on the grounds of some of the saints here alternate with grounds entirely gilded over. The taste for chequers can be found elsewhere in East Anglia at just this time, as in the flint flushwork and heraldic patterns on the gatehouse at Butley Priory in Suffolk. The fourteenth-century eye loved alternating patterns like these, and the Retable is found to be full of them, if looked at patiently.

MATT GAW

Nightscape

From *Under the Stars* (2020)

Matt Gaw is a poet, writer, journalist and naturalist who lives in Bury St Edmunds. He works with the Suffolk Wildlife Trust. Under the Stars *is a celebration of darkness, and a protest against the growing pollution of artificial light.*

For more than an hour now I have tramped through the forest that grows a few miles from my home, its familiar ruler-straight rides sparkling with fresh spring snow that still falls in fat, bumblebee flakes. The trees drooping, smoored and smothered.

Now the world is about to transform again. Night is coming. Darkness will soon cover the forest as surely as any snow.

I can't remember the last time I was out at night. Not just out, camping, running or toddling home from pubs, but really out; walking and watching as the light fades, experiencing darkness creeping up with each passing minute, from mountain to meadow.

It was my ten-year-old son who had inspired this impromptu outing. The other day, as he argued for a later bedtime, he told me solemnly that the average human will spend twenty-six years of life asleep. Although he was still ushered complaining to his room, his words wormed their way into my brain. They made me realise that my experience of night was one of eyes moving sightlessly against lowered lids rather than a view of the changing shades of the nocturnal hours. Although he might not have meant it as such, it was also a rebuke; a reminder that for all my life's apparent fullness, it was in fact being only half lived. And so, here I am. Venturing into the darkness.

I've never really considered exploring the nightscape before. To me night has always been a dark and gloomy place. A solid, black bookend to day that inspires fear and anxiety. But here among the trees, cloud and snowglow, I can already see that night is not just one long stretch of unforgiving darkness, any more than daytime is constant bright blue sky. Night is full of its own subtle shades of light, capable of illuminating the landscape and inspiring in us a sense of connection and wonder. I feel a tingle of delight at the realisation that almost by accident I've ghosted into a different world.

Certainly, the way the night was lit up has stayed with me. I wonder how it would have appeared without the clouds; how the soft slide from day to night would have been different; how starlight, glinting hard off snow, would have expanded the night beyond a tree-lined horizon. But the clouds were also part of

Frances Crickmore, *Town Fox at his Favourite Puddle*, Lowestoft, 2021.

Wildlife photographer Frances Crickmore has always been an avid wildlife enthusiast. She lives in the Waveney Valley where she photographs the wildlife around her dairy farm at Bungay and has been doing so for the last ten years, posting them for her many followers on Instagram.

the magic, obstructing the glow from towns: the streetlights of Bury St Edmunds to the south and of Thetford to the north.

On our relatively small but densely populated island, there are up to nine million streetlamps (one for every eight people). Their glare, when combined with that of twenty-seven million homes, offices, warehouses and factories, is scattered by atmospheric particles to create a sickly orange skyglow capable of blotting out the nocturnal interplay of natural light—the ever-present glare of electricity chases away darkness and snuffs out the stars.

I've walked around my hometown of Bury at night many times since that first snowy walk in the woods. Apart from when the pubs, restaurants and clubs kick out, it's rare to see another human on foot round here after dark. The town at night empties. A complex social structure disappears with the sun, to leave a network of roads and paths, littered with fag ends, reflective crisp packets and the droopy skins of used condoms. It is a place patrolled by cats, some of which follow me for miles at a time, meowing forlornly as if all have forgotten them.

These areas belong to the local wildlife at night. But while the streets might be devoid of people, they're still full of their artificial lights.

The same is true across the country. Dark nights are on the wane. Just 21.7 per cent of England has pristine skies according to a survey by the Campaign to Protect Rural England. The highest levels of light come from towns and cities, major roads and airports, but light pollution spreads into the countryside too. It is there in everyday, run-of-the-mill places like Bury St Edmunds.

I stand at the top of a new business estate that has been built on higher ground to the far east of the town, a place of grass bunds bristling with plastic-wrapped saplings and warehouses, which although empty are busy with light. I've seen wildlife up here earlier in the year, while the last building was being finished off. Skylarks sang over the snark of angle grinders biting into metal and hares raced over the rough grass between warehouse and road.

Tonight there is little obvious movement. I clamber up onto a bank and look west, back the way I've come. The divide between old and new lighting is clear to see. Around half the town, the Victorian suburbs, the older estates, twinkles sodium orange, while the other half, wrapped in a shell spiral of brightly lit road, is white with LEDs. The clouded sky above the town buzzes with light.

The more we look, the more damage light pollution seems to do, its impact far-ranging, running up and down the food chain, changing the time flowers bloom, how beetles navigate and hunt. While the bright lights of humans create biological chaos for us, the same is true of wildlife. Light and the retreat of night doesn't just impact on single species in isolation, but on whole ecosystems.

ALBERT GRANT

An Adventure (2021)

Albert Grant was born in Barbados in 1934, and came to Ipswich in 1955. He became Ipswich's first Black councillor and mayor. Albert also founded the Ipswich Caribbean Association. He was made an OBE for his services to ethnic minorities in 2000.

The British government came to the Caribbean islands looking for labour to service its railways and hospitals, and a lot of us took the chance and came to England. For us, brought up in the colony of Barbados, it was the mother country so we just got on the boat and went. I was a young man and it was an adventure.

I was encouraged to come to Ipswich because I knew a man who left Barbados and got work here. I got in touch and lodged with him in Ipswich until I started work. I got a job as a forklift driver and then moved to Cranes where I became a boiler fitter. Finding work was easy but it was difficult finding somewhere to live. There were only three or four big houses in Ipswich prepared to take West Indians. I shared a room with two other chaps, so there were twelve people living in each house. We were a curiosity to people here.

I liked Suffolk straight away because it was very much like Barbados, apart from the weather, of course. You have to understand that I was brought up like an English boy in Barbados, the only difference was the colour of my skin. Our education was English, in fact, I knew more about England than the English people I met when I did National Service. It dawned on me then that the standard of education in Barbados was higher than that received by many people here. However, I could talk to people because we had read the same books and in Barbados we were encouraged to speak 'proper English' to get on at school. I felt at home at once.

There were a lot of American military servicemen here when I arrived in Suffolk, and there was tension between the white and the black soldiers. This resulted in fights within the pubs in Ipswich and because of that some pubs refused to serve black people. However, it was better here than in the big cities like Birmingham where black people faced hostility and racism from gangs of teddy boys.

I met my wife Ena in Ipswich whilst in a cinema queue. She's also from Barbados. At the time Ena was working in a steam laundry and we've been married for sixty-two years now. We are blessed with six children, ten grandchildren and five great grandchildren. My children and grandchildren have done fantastically well—amongst the talents, I've got a lawyer, a nurse, a midwife, a musician and psychologist. All but one of my children have stayed in Suffolk and we're a close family with gatherings every bank holiday and for birthday celebrations.

I was a founder member of the Ipswich Caribbean Association which started after Enoch Powell's 'Rivers of Blood' speech. We could see how prejudice and racism were getting worse and wanted to support each other and challenge racism. My father had been involved in politics in Barbados and so I wanted to get into politics here. With widespread racism and being one of the few black men interested, I had problems joining the Labour Party at first but eventually they let me in. I got involved in everything I could and gained a lot of experience over the years I served as Councillor. It was a fantastic experience becoming Mayor of Ipswich. I could knock on every door in this town and get a hearing. I've spent my whole adult life here in Ipswich and although I've travelled all over the world, I wouldn't want to live anywhere else. I love the people of Suffolk.

JOHN NORMAN

Northgate Street (2021)

John Norman is the author of a popular series of weekly articles called Ipswich Icons, *published in the* East Anglian Daily Times.

Unassuming and underused, Northgate Street in Ipswich hides a wealth of history and interest. Running between the Great White Horse and St Margaret's Plain the obvious missing feature is the North Gate, sometimes known as St Margaret's Gate, which was demolished in 1794. The North Gate stood outside the Halberd Inn and allowed access through the town's ramparts for country folk from the farms and villages north and east of the town.

The Halberd provided an extensive range of stables for farmers and travellers who would leave their pony and trap whilst visiting the market. The pub additionally featured a 'steelyard' or weighing machine for horse-drawn wagons (or more particularly their load), which were hoisted a few inches clear of the ground against a counterbalance of known weight. It was advertised as being 'as just and true as any in England'.

The North Gate was clearly a key access into the town, demonstrated by the number of inns and taverns both within, and outside the ramparts. Foremost was the Royal Oak, on the corner of Oak Lane where there is a magnificent carved corner post resplendent with blacksmith and anvil. There are parish records suggesting that there was a building here in 1689, originally a merchant's house which was converted to a public house in the mid nineteenth century. In 1882 the licence was transferred from here, the Northgate Street premises, to the newly built Royal Oak in Felixstowe Road (both Cobbold pubs).

The building, now Oak House, is currently occupied by Jackamans, Solicitors who care for the fine interior including some exquisitely decorated rooms, not all of which are original features of this building. Oak House was substantially rebuilt and restored by Ipswich architect J. A. Sherman in 1913. Sherman was both an architect and developer, buying old Suffolk timber-framed houses, dismantling them, utilising the historical features in his own renovation projects and shipping complete structures to America for re-erection as genuine English vernacular.

In 1906 John Albert Sherman moved into number 9, the property next door. His new house was a late medieval timber-framed building that had been refronted in Georgian times, a common occurrence in Ipswich. It gave older property a fresh brick front without the expense of rebuilding. Lower Brook Street is full of similar examples. Sherman was a prolific architect and his work included the Crematorium in the new cemetery (1928) and Croydon's in Tavern Street

(1930). He also remodelled the Pack Horse Inn in Sloane Street, when St Margaret's Street was widened to take trolley-buses.

In the fifteenth century Suffolk was a part of the Diocese of Norfolk under the leadership of the Bishop of Norwich. The Bishop needed area managers and for Suffolk he appointed William Pykenham as Archdeacon. Both the Bishop and his Archdeacons were Catholics; it was to be another seventy years before Henry VIII split with Rome. Pykenham needed a significant residence to emphasise his new position and he had a large house built in Northgate Street, just inside the ramparts. It was surrounded by a high wall and secured by substantial gates.

The security features were essential given that a fair proportion of Ipswich's population were Protestants and were none too happy with a senior Catholic cleric in their midst. Above the entrance is the Gatehouse (built in 1471), probably one of the oldest buildings in Ipswich. Beyond the gates is the Archdeacon's house, altered and extended to accommodate, since 1885, the Ipswich and Suffolk Club.

Opposite Pykenham's Gatehouse is Ipswich's Central Library, built in 1924 and listed by English Heritage Grade II, it was designed by another Ipswich architect Henry Munro Cautley. The building next door to the library, on the corner of Old Foundry Road was, in the 1960s and 70s, the Mikado Coffee Bar which sold frothy 'expresso' coffee whilst loud music emanated from the juke box, a very different experience from the latest coffee shops which reside at the southern end of Northgate Street.

However the most prominent feature of Northgate Street is not in the street itself, rather the church which provides an end drop to the vista looking north. Bethesda Baptist Church, was built in 1913 for only £7000 of which £3,100, was paid to the United Stone Company of Bristol for all of the stonework including the magnificent Ionic granite columns and the triangular pediment with Bethesda carved bold and large.

Unassuming perhaps, but hiding a wealth of historic features from pargeting, stained glass windows, carved bressumers and polychromic brickwork, Northgate Street is worth a second look.

MAYURI PATEL

A Mutual Understanding (2021)

Mayuri Patel and her husband Chandresh Patel have run the Mac Market convenience shop on a council estate in Ipswich since 1982. Mayuri is also a finance officer at both the Suffolk Law Centre and the Ipswich and Suffolk Council for Racial Equality (ISCRE) and she is Vice Chair / Volunteer for many other Hindu / Indian community initiatives.

I was born and brought up in Mumbai and came to Suffolk when I married my husband. Originally, he came from Uganda to the UK in 1968. After leaving university he came to Suffolk to run his family's shop. We married in 1994 and when I arrived in the UK, I was in my late-twenties. I'm a city girl and my husband had warned me that Ipswich was a quiet town. I think he was surprised that I liked it so much—I really enjoy the quiet. We go out into the countryside when we can, and I can't imagine living anywhere else.

To start with I really struggled with my accent, and I couldn't really understand what people were saying, especially since much of the language is very colloquial. For example, I had never heard of an English roast dinner before! It also took me a while to acclimatise, I always felt the cold even in the summer to the extent that I often had the heating on full blast! Similarly, before moving to Ipswich, I had never been to a pub, I didn't even know what a pub was. I remember the first time I went to a pub with my uncle-in-law—my first drink was tomato juice. Now I go to the pub with my friends and family and I sometimes even get a roast!

When I moved to Suffolk there was no Hindu temple here, we used to go to the temple in Neasden (London) for special celebrations. My daughters always like to go to the temple after their exam results to give thanks. Now we have our own temple in Ipswich; we don't have a full-time priest—the temple is run by the volunteers, and I help with that. As we all are volunteers and work full time, we only manage to open the temple at the weekends and sometimes on weekday evenings when we are celebrating special festivals. Generally, 15-20 people visit the temple during the weekends, up to 100-150 during festivals like Diwali but now it's all online because of Covid.

After coming to the UK, I gained additional finance qualifications and got the job at ISCRE. I have been working at ISCRE for over thirteen years. I love my job. Since the start of the pandemic, I have been working from home—I start work for the Suffolk Law Centre/ISCRE at 6.30 in the morning and finish mid-afternoon. I then help my husband in the shop until we close. Then I cook dinner—traditional Indian food on weekdays and at the weekends we have other cuisines and takeaways. I like to plan my day in advance so I know what I am doing/cooking etc. I love to have all the menus worked out ahead of time.

Long hours are difficult. Corner shops are dying because of the big super-markets. We are now surrounded by various supermarkets all of which compete with our business. Lockdown was a different and difficult time—our shop stayed open and we tried to serve our local community to the best of our ability. We know the locals well and it has become a closely-knit community over time. We often receive phone-calls to ask us to deliver basic food items to the ill or elderly members of the community, and we do that; we truly believe in the importance of working as a community. We're only closed two days a year, Christmas Day and Boxing Day—it's fair to say that we really look forward to those two days!

In the past, we have experienced racism in the shop—sometimes overtly, but mostly it is subtle and hidden. Unfortunately, it still exists.

We have two daughters, one is a qualified doctor and the other will qualify as a doctor next year. My husband is sixty next month and we're thinking of retiring soon.

During quiet time in the shop, I read Indian novels or catch up with friends on the phone. I love to knit scarves for the Suffolk weather! My husband and I chat about our day and love to pass time together. Marriage is a mutual adjustment and understanding, you just have to get on with it!

Our dream is to retire nearby in Suffolk and to have a big garden. Since we live above the shop at the moment, we don't have a garden. I'd love to try to grow Indian vegetables and herbs to remind me of my childhood in India. I'm looking forward to that; it's a lot of hard work at the moment but that's my dream: a Suffolk garden.

CHARLES DICKENS

Mr Pickwick Journeys to Ipswich and Meets with a Romantic Adventure with a Middle-Aged Lady in Yellow Curl-Papers

From *The Pickwick Papers* (1837)

In the main street of Ipswich, on the left-hand side of the way, a short distance after you have passed through the open space fronting the Town Hall, stands an inn known far and wide by the appellation of the 'Great White Horse', rendered the more conspicuous by a stone statue of some rampacious animal with flowing mane and tail, distantly resembling an insane cart-horse, which is elevated above the principal door. The Great White Horse is famous in the neighbourhood, in the same degree as a prize ox, or a county-paper-chronicled turnip, or unwieldy pig—for its enormous size. Never were such labyrinths of uncarpeted passages, such clusters of mouldy, badly-lighted rooms, such huge numbers of small dens for eating or sleeping in, beneath any one roof, as are collected together between the four walls of the Great White Horse at Ipswich.

It was at the door of this overgrown tavern that the London coach stopped, at the same hour every evening; and it was from this same London coach, that Mr Pickwick dismounted.

A corpulent man, with a fortnight's napkin under his arm, and coeval stockings on his legs, slowly desisted from his occupation of staring down the street, and condescended to order the boots to bring in the gentlemen's luggage; and preceding them down a long, dark passage, ushered them into a large, badly-furnished apartment, with a dirty grate, in which a small fire was making a wretched attempt to be cheerful, but was fast sinking beneath the dispiriting influence of the place.

'This is your room, sir,' said the chambermaid.

'Very well,' replied Mr Pickwick, looking round him. It was a tolerably large double-bedded room, with a fire; upon the whole, a more comfortable-looking apartment than Mr Pickwick's short experience of the accommodations of the Great White Horse had led him to expect.

'Nobody sleeps in the other bed, of course,' said Mr Pickwick.

'Oh, no, Sir.'

'Very good. Tell my servant to bring me up some hot water at half-past eight in the morning, and that I shall not want him any more to-night.'

'Yes, Sir,' and bidding Mr Pickwick good-night, the chambermaid retired, and left him alone.

Mr Pickwick began to undress, when he recollected he had left his watch on the table downstairs.

Now this watch was a special favourite with Mr Pickwick, having been carried about, beneath the shadow of his waistcoat, for a greater number of years than we feel called upon to state at present. The possibility of going to sleep, unless it were ticking gently beneath his pillow, or in the watch-pocket over his head, had never entered Mr Pickwick's brain. So as it was pretty late now, and he was unwilling to ring his bell at that hour of the night, he slipped on his coat, of which he had just divested himself, and taking the japanned candlestick in his hand, walked quietly downstairs.

The more stairs Mr Pickwick went down, the more stairs there seemed to be to descend, and again and again, when Mr Pickwick got into some narrow passage, and began to congratulate himself on having gained the ground-floor, did another flight of stairs appear before his astonished eyes. At last he reached a stone hall, which he remembered to have seen when he entered the house. Passage after passage did he explore; room after room did he peep into; at length, as he was on the point of giving up the search in despair, he opened the door of the identical room in which he had spent the evening, and beheld his missing property on the table.

Mr Pickwick seized the watch in triumph, and proceeded to retrace his steps to his bedchamber. If his progress downward had been attended with difficulties and uncertainty, his journey back was infinitely more perplexing. Rows of doors, garnished with boots of every shape, make, and size, branched off in every possible direction. A dozen times did he softly turn the handle of some bedroom door which resembled his own, when a gruff cry from within of 'Who the devil's that?' or 'What do you want here?' caused him to steal away, on tiptoe, with a perfectly marvellous celerity. He was reduced to the verge of despair, when an open door attracted his attention. He peeped in. Right at last! There were the two beds, whose situation he perfectly remembered, and the fire still burning. His candle, not a long one when he first received it, had flickered away in the drafts of air through which he had passed and sank into the socket as he closed the door after him. 'No matter,' said Mr Pickwick, 'I can undress myself just as well by the light of the fire.'

The bedsteads stood one on each side of the door; and on the inner side of each was a little path, terminating in a rush-bottomed chair, just wide enough to admit of a person's getting into or out of bed, on that side, if he or she thought proper. Having carefully drawn the curtains of his bed on the outside, Mr Pickwick sat down on the rush-bottomed chair, and leisurely divested himself of his shoes and gaiters. He then took off and folded up his coat, waistcoat, and neckcloth, and slowly drawing on his tasselled nightcap, secured it firmly on his head, by tying beneath his chin the strings which he always had attached to that article of dress. He was suddenly stopped by a most unexpected interruption: to wit, the entrance into the room of some person with a candle, who, after locking the door, advanced to the dressing-table, and set down the light upon it.

The person, whoever it was, had come in so suddenly and with so little noise, that Mr Pickwick had had no time to call out, or oppose their entrance. Who could it be? A robber? Some evil-minded person who had seen him come upstairs with a handsome watch in his hand, perhaps. What was he to do?

The only way in which Mr Pickwick could catch a glimpse of his mysterious visitor with the least danger of being seen himself, was by creeping on to the bed, and peeping out from between the curtains on the opposite side. To this manœuvre he accordingly resorted. Keeping the curtains carefully closed with his hand, so that nothing more of him could be seen than his face and nightcap, and putting on his spectacles, he mustered up courage and looked out.

Mr Pickwick almost fainted with horror and dismay. Standing before the dressing-glass was a middle-aged lady, in yellow curl-papers, busily engaged in brushing what ladies call their 'back-hair.' However the unconscious middle-aged lady came into that room, it was quite clear that she contemplated remaining there for the night; for she had brought a rushlight and shade with her, which, with praiseworthy precaution against fire, she had stationed in a basin on the floor, where it was glimmering away, like a gigantic lighthouse in a particularly small piece of water.

'Bless my soul!' thought Mr Pickwick, 'what a dreadful thing!'

'Hem!' said the lady; and in went Mr Pickwick's head with automaton-like rapidity.

'I never met with anything so awful as this,' thought poor Mr Pickwick, the cold perspiration starting in drops upon his nightcap. 'Never. This is fearful.'

It was quite impossible to resist the urgent desire to see what was going forward. So out went Mr Pickwick's head again. The prospect was worse than before. The middle-aged lady had finished arranging her hair; had carefully enveloped it in a muslin nightcap with a small plaited border; and was gazing pensively on the fire.

'This matter is growing alarming,' reasoned Mr Pickwick with himself. 'I can't allow things to go on in this way. By the self-possession of that lady, it is clear to me that I must have come into the wrong room. If I call out she'll alarm the house; but if I remain here the consequences will be still more frightful.'

Mr Pickwick, it is quite unnecessary to say, was one of the most modest and delicate-minded of mortals. The very idea of exhibiting his nightcap to a lady overpowered him, but he had tied those confounded strings in a knot, and, do what he would, he couldn't get it off. The disclosure must be made. There was only one other way of doing it. He shrunk behind the curtains, and called out very loudly—

'Ha-hum!'

That the lady started at this unexpected sound was evident, by her falling up against the rushlight shade; that she persuaded herself it must have been the effect of imagination was equally clear, for when Mr Pickwick, under the impression that she had fainted away stone-dead with fright, ventured to peep out again, she was gazing pensively on the fire as before.

'Most extraordinary female this,' thought Mr Pickwick, popping in again. 'Ha-hum!'

These last sounds, so like those in which, as legends inform us, the ferocious giant Blunderbore was in the habit of expressing his opinion that it was time to lay the cloth, were too distinctly audible to be again mistaken for the workings of fancy.

'Gracious Heaven!' said the middle-aged lady, 'what's that?'

'It's—it's—only a gentleman, Ma'am,' said Mr Pickwick, from behind the curtains.

'A gentleman!' said the lady, with a terrific scream.

'It's all over!' thought Mr Pickwick.

'A strange man!' shrieked the lady. Another instant and the house would be alarmed. Her garments rustled as she rushed towards the door.

'Ma'am,' said Mr Pickwick, thrusting out his head in the extremity of his desperation, 'Ma'am!'

Now, although Mr Pickwick was not actuated by any definite object in putting out his head, it was instantaneously productive of a good effect. The lady, as we have already stated, was near the door. She must pass it, to reach the staircase, and she would most undoubtedly have done so by this time, had not the sudden apparition of Mr Pickwick's nightcap driven her back into the remotest corner of the apartment, where she stood staring wildly at Mr Pickwick, while Mr Pickwick in his turn stared wildly at her.

'Wretch,' said the lady, covering her eyes with her hands, 'what do you want here?'

'Nothing, Ma'am; nothing whatever, Ma'am,' said Mr Pickwick earnestly.

'Nothing!' said the lady, looking up.

'Nothing, Ma'am, upon my honour,' said Mr Pickwick, nodding his head so energetically, that the tassel of his nightcap danced again. 'I am almost ready to sink, Ma'am, beneath the confusion of addressing a lady in my nightcap (here the lady hastily snatched off hers), but I can't get it off, Ma'am (here Mr Pickwick gave it a tremendous tug, in proof of the statement). It is evident to me, Ma'am, now, that I have mistaken this bedroom for my own. I had not been here five minutes, Ma'am, when you suddenly entered it.'

'If this improbable story be really true, Sir,' said the lady, sobbing violently, 'you will leave it instantly.'

'I will, Ma'am, with the greatest pleasure,' replied Mr Pickwick.

'Phiz' (Hablot K. Browne), *'Standing before the dressing-glass was a middle-aged lady in yellow curl-papers, busily engaged in brushing what ladies call their "back hair."'* Household Edition (1874) of Dickens's *Pickwick Papers.*

'Instantly, Sir,' said the lady.

'Certainly, Ma'am,' interposed Mr Pickwick, very quickly. 'Certainly, Ma'am. I—I—am very sorry, Ma'am,' said Mr Pickwick, making his appearance at the bottom of the bed, 'to have been the innocent occasion of this alarm and emotion; deeply sorry, Ma'am.'

The lady pointed to the door. One excellent quality of Mr Pickwick's character was beautifully displayed at this moment, under the most trying circumstances. Although he had hastily put on his hat over his nightcap, after the manner of the old patrol; although he carried his shoes and gaiters in his hand, and his coat and waistcoat over his arm; nothing could subdue his native politeness.

'I am exceedingly sorry, Ma'am,' said Mr Pickwick, bowing very low.

'If you are, Sir, you will at once leave the room,' said the lady.

'Immediately, Ma'am; this instant, Ma'am,' said Mr Pickwick, opening the door, and dropping both his shoes with a crash in so doing.

'I trust, Ma'am,' resumed Mr Pickwick, gathering up his shoes, and turning round to bow again—'I trust, Ma'am, that my unblemished character, and the devoted respect I entertain for your sex, will plead as some slight excuse for this—' But before Mr Pickwick could conclude the sentence, the lady had thrust him into the passage, and locked and bolted the door behind him.

Whatever grounds of self-congratulation Mr Pickwick might have for having escaped so quietly from his late awkward situation, his present position was by no means enviable. He was alone, in an open passage, in a strange house in the middle of the night, half dressed; it was not to be supposed that he could find his way in perfect darkness to a room which he had been wholly unable to discover with a light, and if he made the slightest noise in his fruitless attempts to do so, he stood every chance of being shot at, and perhaps killed, by some wakeful traveller. He had no resource but to remain where he was until daylight appeared. So after groping his way a few paces down the passage, and, to his infinite alarm, stumbling over several pairs of boots in so doing, Mr Pickwick crouched into a little recess in the wall, to wait for morning, as philosophically as he might.

PATRICIA HIGHSMITH

Dreaming of Murder

From *A Suspension of Mercy* (1965)

Patricia Highsmith (1921–1995) moved to Britain from America and came to live in Earl Soham in 1964, in Bridge Cottage—formerly two country cottages, knocked together. The following year she began A Suspension of Mercy, *in which an artistic but penurious couple come to live in a Suffolk country cottage. The American husband, an unsuccessful writer, enjoys increasingly vivid fantasises about murdering his English wife. And the threadbare house in the middle of the Suffolk countryside certainly creates an ominous atmosphere of impending madness and violence. As the novel opens, we know that nothing good can ever happen in a house like this.*

The land around Sydney and Alicia Bartleby's two-storey cottage was flat, like most Suffolk country. A road, two-laned and paved, went by the house at a distance of twenty yards. To one side of the front walk, which was of slightly askew flagstones, five young elms gave some privacy, and on the other side a tall, bushy hedge provided a better screen for thirty feet. For this reason, Sydney had never trimmed it. The front lawn was as untended as the hedge. The grass grew in tufts, and where it didn't, fairy rings had eaten circles exposing green-brown earth. The Bartlebys took better care of the ground behind the house, and they had besides a vegetable and flower garden an ornamental pond some five feet across that Sydney had made with a cemented pile of interesting stones in its centre, but they had never succeeded in keeping goldfish alive in it, and two frogs they had put there had decided to go somewhere else.

The road led to Ipswich and London in one direction and towards Framlingham in the other. Behind the house, their property trickled off vaguely, bounded by nothing visible, and beyond lay a field belonging to a farmer whose house was out of sight. The Bartlebys were supposed to live in Blycom Heath, but Blycom Heath proper was two miles away towards Framlingham. It was a lonely neighbourhood from the point of view of people and neighbours, but Sydney and Alicia had their own pursuits—writing and painting—they had each other's company all day, and they had made a few friends who were scattered as far away as Lowestoft. But they had to drive five miles to Framlingham to get so much as a shoe repair or a bottle of Chinese ink. Sometimes Alicia did feel geographically lonely, as if she and Sydney lived at some deserted pole of the earth.

'Darling, the garbage tonight. Don't forget,' Alicia said with such gentleness, Sydney might have laughed if he had been in a better mood or if there had been other people present.

The dustmen came only once a fortnight, so it was a serious matter if they forgot to put all the garbage out at the edge of the road. Their one dustbin of inadequate size was always at the edge of the road, and into this went tins and bottles only. Papers they burnt, and vegetable and fruit parings they threw on their compost heap, but since orange juice and tomatoes and lots of other things came in cans and bottles, this department was always bulging at the end of two weeks, and a couple of cartons stood full in the toolhouse for days before the dustmen arrived. Usually it was raining on the eve of garbage day, so Sydney had to carry the cartons out across muddy ground, drop them by the dustbin, and hope they would not dissolve by morning.

'It's annoying that one has to feel ashamed of having garbage in the English countryside,' Sydney said. 'What's so abnormal about having garbage, I'd like to know? Do they think people don't eat?'

Alicia calmly girded herself for the defence of her country. 'It's not so shameful to have garbage. Who said it was shameful?'

'Perhaps it isn't, but they make it so,' Sydney replied just as calmly. 'By taking so long between collections, they focus people's attention on it—rub it in their faces, practically. Just like the drinking hours. You find a pub door locked in your face, so you want a drink more than ever and drink two or three the next chance you get.'

Alicia defended the pub hours on the grounds that it cut down drinking, and the infrequent garbage disposal on the grounds that more frequent disposal would put up the rates, and so this discussion, which they had had before, went on for about two minutes more and left them both in a rather irritated mood, as neither had convinced the other of his point.

Alicia was less irritated, and in fact her irritation was mostly a pretence. It was her country, she liked it, and often it crossed her mind to say that if Sydney didn't like it, he might leave, but she had never said this. She loved teasing Sydney, even on the delicate subject of his writing, because the answer to his problem seemed so simple to her: Sydney should relax, be more natural, more happy, and write what he pleased, then it would be good and it would sell. She had said this to him many times, and he came back at her with some complex and masculine answer, upholding the virtue of hard thinking and aiming at markets.

'But we decided to live in the country just so we could relax,' she had said to him a few times, but this was like oil on the fire, and Sydney would really flare up then, asking her if she thought living in the country with a million bucolic chores was more conducive to relaxing than a flat in London, however small. Well, rents in London were high and getting higher, and if she pinned Sydney down, he didn't want to live in London really, because he preferred a country landscape and preferred to wear chinos and shirts without a tie and old plimsolls, and he actually liked mending a fence occasionally and pottering around in the garden.

As she washed the dishes, she looked out now and then at Sydney, prowling

Eamonn McCabe, *Suffolk Gateway*, 2018.

Eamonn McCabe (born 1948) is a British professional photographer who began his career as a sports photographer, and then turned his attention to general editorial portraiture for the Observer *and the* Guardian.

about in his plimsolls that he had put on as soon as he got home. He had carried the garbage cartons out, and now he was looking at the garden in the dusk, bending now and then to remove a weed. The lettuce had just come up, but nothing else so far.

A huge blackbird pecked in the grass in front of Sydney. Somewhere else, the bird that attempted to sing 'Blow the Man Down' was trying again. Sydney wondered what kind of bird it was. The sailorbird, perhaps. He shivered under his sweater as the sun went behind a cloud. He was bored to the point of sleepiness.

The very house they lived in with its tricky plumbing, its very real slanting and charming wooden rafters on which he bumped his head nearly every day, the English soil that got under his nails when he gardened, Alicia's very snores that troubled his sleep about one night out of seven, seemed all unreal like a play he himself had cooked up, a not very good play.

TOM HESTER

The Port of Felixstowe: A Busy Morning in May

After a first career as an investment banker spent mostly in the Far East Tom Hester now works as a ship's Master. He has sailed his own boat, Papagena, *round the world, and he is presently running vessels supporting the offshore renewables industry in the North Sea.*

The Port of Felixstowe, originally founded in 1875, is now the first purpose-built and busiest of the United Kingdom's container ports, and deals with 48% of Britain's containerised trade. The Landguard terminal was opened in 1967.

Here is a snapshot of seaborne activity off the Suffolk coast taken early one morning in May 2021. The image is produced by AIS (Automatic Identification System), which is used by vessels and maritime traffic controllers in tandem with Radar to monitor ship movements in their vicinity.

It is busy out there, with about thirty ships in an area roughly twenty miles N/S and ten E/W. Bigger ships (giant container ships in or outbound for Felixstowe) draw up to 16m and there are plenty of patches in the picture with less than 5m over them. To keep the huge vessels from bumping into the sandbanks (or one another) they are routed along deep waters in Traffic Separation Schemes (TSS) monitored here by the officers of the Sunk Vessel Traffic Service (VTS). The VTS will be watching carefully to ensure not only that larger commercial vessels are using the appropriate TSS but also helping coordinate the pilot vessels dropping off and collecting the pilots who guide the ships in for the last few miles and the tugs that help nudge them alongside into their berths for unloading.

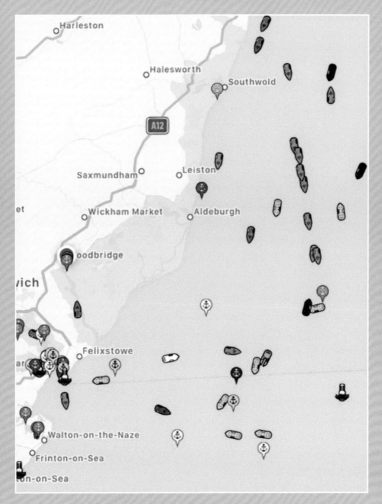

KEY

Big ships. You can see one just approaching Languard Point and two each in the Sunk East TSS and Sunk North TSS all inbound for Felixstowe.

The pilot vessel *St Christopher*.

The stream of boats heading S from Lowestoft are Crew Transfer Vessels (CTV) taking technicians out to work on the Greater Gabbard wind farm which you can see in reasonable visibility, about twelve miles off the coast. The CTV is 'pushed onto' the tower, the technicians climb to the platform and then crane up their gear and attend to the myriad needs of the turbine. Wind farms may be clean and green but they are far from maintenance free. There can be up to twenty vessels in the field on a busy day and the area in our image also includes the Galloper and Gunfleet wind farms.

A dredger called *City of London*, about at the same level as Felixstowe, is engaged in sucking up sand and gravel from the banks off Aldeburgh for use in the building industry.

Two fishing vessels just north of Southwold.

DEAN PARKIN AND JACK ROSE

Growing up on the Beach

From *The Grit: The Story of Lowestoft's Beach Village* (2019)

Dean Parkin is a poet, writer and workshop leader specialising in schools and community projects. He co-wrote The Grit: The Story of Lowestoft's Beach Village *(1997) with Jack Rose—fisherman, lifeboatman, local historian and former resident of the village. The book inspired Dean's first theatre show,* Pearls from the Grit, *which toured Suffolk and Norfolk in 2018 and 2019. A new, revised and illustrated edition of the book was published in 2019.*

Growing up on the Beach in the early part of the twentieth century was very different from children's lives today. With the whole of the Denes to play on, the north beach nearby and freedom to roam the streets, many of the people speak of their childhood happiness in spite of the hardship of the time. When the shops started selling wooden tops and whips every child wanted a top, and a lot of fun we had in seeing who could whip their top and make it spin the longest. Then the time came for wooden hoops with a stick to bowl them along Whapload Road. No problem with traffic in those days, we could see and hear the odd horse and cart coming, and we just let it pass and carried on bowling or whipping. Sometimes if the weather was hot, the tar melted on the road and stuck to your shoes, or your feet if you had no shoes on.

Ronny Wilson was born on The Grit, and lived at 4 East Street, opposite the Rising Sun, his mother running a sweet shop. 'We used to go swimming from the beach and when I was a boy we used to sleep on the beach. We slept down there right through the summer period, we spent four weeks down there and never went home, except to wash our clothes out. My mother used to give us a few spuds and a bit of lard, and we slept down there in an old sack tent behind the gasworks. We used to go down on the market, knock off a couple of herring, light a fire, split them, put them on the fire and roast them for dinner.'

Money was scarce and pocket money for children was mostly unheard of. If you wanted money, even as a child you had to work for it. Billy Keith says, 'We used to sit down near the Coastguard and see the boats come round and say, so and so is on that boat, someone else is on that one, you go to that house, and you go to that one, and we used to run to their house and tell them that their husbands were coming home, and then we'd get treated. And then you'd go and tell the men as they were getting off the boats that we'd let their wives know and they'd treat us as well.'

On May Day, children would roam around together banging tins or saucepans, and chanting a ditty which went, 'Climbing up the walls, Knocking down the spiders, Cabbages and turnips too, Put them in your aluminium saucepan, And we'll have a rare old stew!' Children dressed up in old clothes, blackened their faces with burnt cork and walked round the streets after tea singing this song, which was sung to the tune of a Salvation Army hymn. They knocked on doors, tin can in hand, for any small donations.

The Beach Village gave children freedom and the community gave them great security. But the children of The Grit were poor. 'Most of the children went to school with no boots or shoes,' recalls Mr E.J. Day who was born in 1903, 'but each year before the bad weather the parish used to send boxes of clogs to the school and if our mothers could afford it, we all got a pair for threepence.' They were never far away from hardship at home and many can remember how every Friday afternoon the sons of fishermen would be excused from lessons to go and get their fathers' wages from the company office to save the postage money.

After the Second World War, the over-exploitation of the shoals resulted in dwindling catches and by the mid-1960s the home fishing voyage ceased altogether. The contrast was stark for many Gritsters who vividly recalled how the fishing village came to life every autumn with the arrival of the Scottish fishing fleet and the fisher girls.

The fishermen would purchase provisions and supplies from the local shops and pubs, while the Scots girls and coopers would take board and lodgings on

The Sparrow Nest Barrow Boys.

The Grit, benefitting many families and helping them to make ends meet. 'Every September prior to the herring season,' Ruby Timberley recalls, 'the Scots girls would arrive at lodgings which had already been arranged for them by the firm they worked for. They needed to be as close as possible to the pickling plots, near to Hamilton Dock where the drifters landed the herring. It gave the people who took them into their homes a few pounds to help stock up with coal or buy their children some clothes for the winter. The girls duly arrived with their large wooden boxes with all they would need whilst away from home. These came by lorry from their fishing boats.'

'These 'girls' as we called them—though some were middle-aged—worked very hard in bitter weather, early and late. They worked with their fingers wrapped round with rags to prevent the knives they used so skilfully from cutting them. Some would gut herrings and some would pack the herring in barrels between layers of salt. The coopers put on the lid, knocked in wooden nails and then they were ready for export to Russia. These Scots girls were a jolly lot. They didn't work on Sundays, but went to church or chapel. If during the week, owing to the weather, there was no fish for a couple of hours, they were not idle but got out the jerseys they were knitting for their men folk. They would walk through the town in twos and threes, knitting and talking as they went.'

Many of the children from the Beach Village would visit the curing yards to try to scrounge a few herring and, though the yard foreman sometimes chased them away, one way of getting free fish was to cheek the Scots girls who would then throw one or two herrings at them. The girls would be told off for doing this but they retaliated with a few well-chosen words and the foreman would usually beat a hasty retreat. What he didn't know was that as the Scots girls threw the herrings at the children, they would give them a wink, knowing they would be taking them home to tea!

In October 1936 the Scots girls went on strike over their pay, demanding an extra two pence a barrel, and two and sixpence extra lodging allowance. Meetings were held on Battery Green, which in those days was a stretch of grassland, and it was here that tempers rose and some colourful language was spoken as the girls fought for their rights.

During this strike, some of the girls carried on working and had to be protected by the police, as words flew—along with one or two gutting knives. The strike ended when the drifters were brought almost to a standstill and the Herring Board were forced to relent, although the girls never got the lodging allowance they asked for.

By this time the Scottish fleet had considerably reduced in size, and the following year herring catches on the home voyage were just a third of the 1913 level. Most of the European market for herring had collapsed and the silver shoals had become rarer and unpredictable, all resulting in hardship for the fishermen between the wars. Money had always been scarce in fishing families. Even in the decade before the First World War when the herring industry was at its height, it wasn't the fishermen who made the profit, but the skippers and the boat owners.

Many times fishermen could be away for a week or ten days and when they returned to shore have nothing to show for the journey. With the long periods away fishing, or just chasing work around the country, family life was difficult. Norma Wilson recalls, 'Because my Dad was a fisherman he used to go away for quite a while and when he came home my eldest sister used to cry because she didn't know who he was.'

Fishing or a related job was in many cases all The Grit had to offer. The only way of bettering your lot was to become a skipper, as fishermen tended to leave the Beach Village when they became skippers. The hard life of fishing offered little security and the risks were all too regularly illustrated. 'In 1930 when I was just two years old, my father was lost at sea,' recalls Eric Horne. 'He was on a fishing vessel working the cod ground. My mother was left a widow with three young boys to raise on her own. The widow's pension (known, I recall, as the Lloyd George pension) of just ten shillings a week did not go very far. Whatever work came along had to be taken. Charring (housework for the better off) brought in two shillings a day, while other jobs included making or repairing fishing nets and peeling onions for picking at a house down Old Nelson Street. For this job we all gave a hand at home, washing hundreds of salvaged jam jars which my brothers and I then delivered to the pickling house in a barrow made from a sugar-box and old pram wheels.

The Grit has always been an industrial area, although at one time most of the industries to be found there related to fishing. Herring nets were made at Beeton's Sunrise Net Works in East Street and tanned for strength in the net yards, while the net stores housed the fishing gear between trips. An essential part of each store were the beating chambers where the nets were repaired by a team of beatsters.

At the start of the twentieth century, a beatster's wage was eight or nine shillings a week, although apprentices received nothing for the first year and only two and sixpence a week during their second year. Due to the large amount of nets that needed to be mended, many were repaired at home as well as in the chambers. Women would work in the evening by oil lamp and in every house where a beatster lived you could find a beatster's hook, which was a big staple, driven into the woodwork around the window or into the door-frame for this purpose.

Birds Eye was certainly a modest venture when it first arrived on The Grit. 'I can remember Birds Eye opening in 1949,' says Brian Springer. 'They used to come in the summer for the pea season. Never had no freezers or nothing. They'd hire the freezers from Lowestoft Ice Company, who were opposite the Rising Sun. They used to have blokes walking with an electric barrow backwards and forwards to the factory, taking peas to the freezers.'

The small depot soon grew into a complete production unit by 1952 and that same year the company invested £70,000 to build the plant required for freezing peas. In subsequent decades the Birds Eye factory along Whapload Road went from strength to strength. To meet increasing demand the massive Steakhouse building was added in the mid 1980s, and in 1988 the company's entire vegetable packing operation was transferred here. The development of the factory continued into the 1990s: following an £18 million investment, Denes IV was opened in 1993 with three lines running twenty-four hours a day, seven days a week. The factory had five main production buildings over an area of some thirty-one acres and had around 1,500 employees.

In 2019 the company celebrated the seventieth anniversary of its arrival in Lowestoft and now had a state-of-the-art modern food plant, which was the focus of a behind-the-scenes BBC television documentary, *Inside the Factory*, presented by Greg Wallace. Greg concluded the documentary, 'This is an enormous food processing plant, basically making mountains of mashed potato that they form into waffle shapes. What really astounds me is how few people there are making them. This means that the responsibility for millions of families' waffles are in the hands of just a few workers here in this factory in Lowestoft.'

In this very place over a hundred years earlier on one day—12th October 1913—nearly 8,000 fishermen caught 10 million herring which were processed by thousands of fisher girls in a year when 466 million herring were exported to Germany and Russia. Now, over a century later, just 'a few workers' produce a million waffles every twenty-four hours. It's easy to see what those numbers mean in terms of employment and how in the twenty-first century these very few workers are no longer required to live next door to the factory. Community spirit is no longer the product of people living and working together in the same place.

DONNY COLE

A World of Its Own:
The Lowestoft Fish Market

*Donny Cole's family business, J. T. Cole, is the longest-running fish merchant in Lowestoft.
It was founded by his grandfather in 1935, and Donny himself left Lowestoft Grammar
School and went to work in the Lowestoft fish market when he was seventeen in 1954.
Donny left the family business to do National Service in the Royal Navy in 1956, rising
from the ranks to become a sub-lieutenant. After National Service he returned to the family
firm. In his teens he was a Queen's Scout.*

I started as a barrow-boy, that was the lowest of the low. But it was like a family, all
the boys stuck together and we had some good times, and some bad times—some
fights. It was a world of its own. The Lowestoft fish market was a hundred times
as big as it is now.

First, you're greeted by the sound of the seagulls; we started early, I was up
every morning at half past five or earlier. The market sale started at seven, by
this time all the fish was landed and laid out all round the fish market, two or
three hundred boxes a day. There were hundreds of trawlers in those days, fishing
off the Norwegian coast; and people were on the phone to their best customers
to find what they wanted. It was sent to the inland markets and to Billingsgate.
There were a lot of fights but most of them were controlled; it was almost all men
and there was a lot of competition. It was a bit like the Mafia, it really was! But
friendly rivalry.

Each company had a barrow-boy, so there were about sixty or seventy bar-
row-boys in all. It made a man of you. There was an iron wheel on the barrows,
and you had to wheel it along the granite tiles, and you had to get the weight perfectly balanced—seventy stone on a barrow. And nothing could stop you. And we
wore clogs, and the clogs had irons you nailed onto the soles. Once or twice I lost
control of the barrow, that was a disaster, the fish would spill out. People would
help you then, we always helped each other. I had my first wage packet, after a
hard week's work, and it was jolly hard work, it was £2 17s.

The next step up was to become a filleter and then you could indulge in
what was called casual labour; if one company had a lot more fish than they
could handle you could help them out. Sometimes we were down there filleting
till midnight. And it was dangerous, when you were sharpening the knife, your
hand could slip; I cut myself once or twice but I still have my fingers. And the
conditions in the winter were terrible. It was open to the sea and the wind would
come straight through, and the snow was horrendous. And the water in the fillet-

ing tanks would freeze. We had oilskins but we were always damp and wet. I'm suffering from that now, with arthritis.

I had friends who went to sea, instead of coming on the market. If you were really keen, as a skipper you could be earning more than the Prime Minister at the age of twenty-three. There was a lot of money coming into Lowestoft in those days: everyone was connected with the fishing industry: the net-makers, the box-makers, ship-builders. For everyone who went to sea there were a lot of people on shore connected with them.

After the war, most of the trucks were repossessed American Army trucks, and we had one of them, an old Chevrolet. And we used to get all this fish sorted, graded, packed in ice, and then there was an almighty rush to get it nailed down in wooden boxes and away to the railway sidings. I used to go with my father sometimes, and we got in the queue which ran from the market down to the station square. There was a policeman on duty who stood in a box on the corner, directing traffic. And he would see our lorry way back in the queue, and stop everything and wave us through. As we went through my father would say 'All right, Bert', and give him a bag of fish, we never waited ever. That policeman must have eaten more fish than you can imagine.

I was ambitious to earn money and I started to sell shellfish, because no one was selling shellfish and there was a demand for it: cockles, mussels, whelks and prawns. I had cockle stalls in Lowestoft and Yarmouth and Southwold and Kessingland. So I had my own business but I was still working as a filleter for the family firm. And they decided they wanted me in the business, they could see I was getting edgy and they were frightened I would leave. So the four directors, my grandfather and my father and my uncles, had a meeting and decided to buy me out.

It all started changing when there was a lot of trouble with quotas. And a lot of men went to work on support ships for the oil industry; they were sought after because of their knowledge of the North Sea. Joining the Common Market was the death knell. People were buying and selling quotas who had no idea about fishing. There were less and less boats. Now, there's no fish in Lowestoft. There's skate, you can buy skate for peanuts. But if I went down the fish market this week there's no cod left, it's changed completely. Iceland is catching it and sending it here.

Now and again you get an unusual catch, some fish that would go up to the fish lab here and they'd find out what it was, a ribbon-fish or a balloon-fish or whatever. But one day in the 1960s there was a Royal Sturgeon landed, it was enormous, at least ten feet long. Sturgeons very rarely come into the North Sea. And it was called a Royal Sturgeon because it belongs to the Queen and you have to offer it to the Queen. But this was only a formality. So my uncle in his wisdom rang the Royal Household. And then he got a call back to say that the Queen was delighted and she would accept it! We weren't expecting that. I think in his mind he'd already carved it up and sold it, so that was a bit of a shock. It had to be delivered to Buckingham Palace at a certain time two days later. So the best lorry, which was hardly new, was painted and scrubbed and polished. And a special coffin was made for the sturgeon. And ice. And a brand-new tarpaulin, new ropes, everything. And Tommy Wright who was also a filleter, he drove a lorry and decided he was going to take it to London. And so he took it to London and drove straight through Buckingham Palace gates, and to the Royal Kitchen. Three days later, we got a personal letter from the Queen thanking us and saying it was enjoyed by the Royal Household and it was delicious.

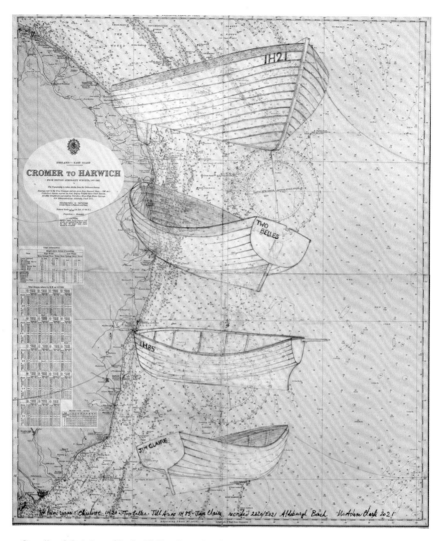

Caroline McAdam Clark, *Fishing Boats in Memoriam*, 2021. Pencil and wash drawing on vintage charts of the East Anglian coast.

Caroline McAdam Clark is a Member of the Royal Watercolour Society. These works were inspired by her early memories of watching the fishing boats setting off for the day from the beach at Aldeburgh, often in a line of ten or fifteen. Some twelve remain today decaying on the shingle, and these three drawings are in memory not only of those twelve (still identifiable by their numbers or names) but of all those long since gone. They swing on their anchors in the sky, ghosts of themselves, recalling the practice of hanging replica model ships and boats from the rafters of sea side churches and chapels—symbols of the safe havens to which the boats will return.

KEVIN CROSSLEY-HOLLAND

A Quiet Mind

From *The Breaking Hour* (2015)

Kevin Crossley-Holland writes poems, translates from the Anglo-Saxon, reworks traditional tales and writes prize-winning historical fiction for children. He has collaborated with artists Norman Ackroyd and James Dodds, and many composers including Nicola LeFanu, Bob Chilcott and Celia McDowell.

A QUIET MIND

Disembarrassed of all obligations,
the little rituals, dozens of chores
I require and even cherish,
well away from that lofty place
where hunks of chalk, knapped flint
and pale pink brick make subtle harmonies,

and light flooding from four quarters
quickens the colours of invigoration,
quietens the tones of contemplation;
where, through the study's double door,
I can hear women's voices dovetailing
in the kitchen, the old kettle shushing,

yet sit at the desk rebuked for knowing all of it
not as it is but for what I'm making of it
– a cell, a shield where I leave
the spirit like mud on the doorstep
and there's always something more pressing
than to sit and dream and wait and write:

I crouch at the hearth of your Suffolk house
well within earshot of the German Ocean
but for the huge throat gulping and roaring
and the howitzer of a north-easterly
hurling pellets of hail and snow,
coldest of corn, across the tiled courtyard.

The other rooms are pantry-chill, cellar-chill,
heavy-curtained inside, snow-curtained outside,
but here the heart is simmering with half-said
and unsaid because there's no need to say,
the cracking of vast, slow-burning plane logs,
laughter, the antiphon of old friendship.

One by one I start to jettison dog–eared files:
CURRENT, ACTION, URGENT, HERE AND NOW.
I call to postpone long-arranged meetings,
then make an appointment for a heart
out of tune. I write postcards to bright teenagers,
and order mulch for the wakening beds.

George Crabbe crabbed here, Quilter composed,
Boyd hoisted his canvas, Hill located a peacock.
Here on this cusp of a sandy peninsula
lay gold and garnets in the graves of Wuffings,
and the scop sang: Relish every thing!
Make good use of each and every thing!

The lion on your sooty fire-back
opens his jaws; lying flat, the shining bellows sigh.
John Ogilby's on his way from London to Yarmouth
(122 miles, 5 furlongs). Even Guinevere escapes
her unending, stricken dream… What's the point
of memory if not to help resolve us?

Until once again I begin to link words
and discover a story—very far from certain
which way forward, knowing only the gift
is mine to fashion and give what's due back:
come the bright morning when I purr north,
unhurrying, quick to myself again.

Alex Curry, *Barn Interior*, 2020.

Alexander Curry is a multidisciplinary artist living in Suffolk. His work includes detailed constructional and architectural drawings which reflect on the rural environment. He is also an experienced timber frame designer and builder.

RICHARD BARBER

Jocelin of Brakelond

Richard Barber is a medieval historian and publisher who has lived in Suffolk for the last fifty years. His own books are mainly on Arthurian literature and on later medieval history, particularly chivalry. He is also a publisher, and helped to found Boydell & Brewer Ltd in 1969.

The great abbeys built in England in the century after the Norman conquest survive only as ruins or as the core of monumental churches transfigured by later generations. Even less survives of their culture and organisation: powerhouses of religion and state with their loyalties divided between king and pope, their sudden fall as a result of Henry VIII's quarrel with Rome left little trace of an extraordinary way of life. St Edmund, king of the East Angles, martyred in 869 by Danish invaders, was revered almost as a patron saint of England by Anglo-Saxons, Danes and Normans as one dynasty succeeded another in the eleventh century. Canute ordered the building of a stone church at Bury St Edmunds in 1020; Edward the Confessor gave it wide lands, roughly the extent of modern West Suffolk, in 1044; and William I gave the abbey its independence from the local bishop.

The abbots of such a place were important figures in the world of the Benedictine order to which they belonged. But the lands which they held as tenants of the crown also made them important vassals of the king, with the duty of providing troops for his army. High ranking clergy might go further: William I's half-brother, Odo bishop of Bayeux, is shown on the Bayeux tapestry in the thick of the fight at the battle of Hastings. And abbots were also at the head of a major organisation which ran not only the abbey itself, but its substantial landholdings, and had to deal with its neighbours in the town, a town which owed its very existence to the abbey. The abbot of Bury St Edmunds needed many skills in order to deal with these wildly varied tasks.

Jocelin of Brakelond began his chronicle in 1173, the year he entered the monastery. This was during the rebellion of Henry II's sons against their father. A decisive battle had been fought just outside the town, when Flemish mercenaries hired by Henry's eldest son had been defeated. Jocelin's concern, however, is within the abbey, and particularly with the abbots under whom he served. The abbey's affairs were in a sorry state, and Hugh, the abbot, 'was grown old and his eyes waxed somewhat dim'. The debts of the abbey mounted year by year, increasing by a hundred or two hundred pounds annually, often covered by unauthorised borrowing. Eight years later, in 1181, Hugh died, and the central figure of Jocelin's history became abbot. This was his mentor Samson.

Jocelin's account of Samson and his doings is one of a number of vivid auto-biographies and biographies written in the twelfth century, and ranks with the best of them. Let us begin with the portrait of Samson at the time of his election. Visual portraits were unknown in the twelfth century: failing an artist, Jocelin creates in words the figure of someone whom we would instantly recognise, and goes on to depict his character in a series of telling episodes.

Abbot Samson was of middle height, and almost entirely bald; his face was neither round nor long, his nose prominent, his lips thick, his eyes clear as crystal and of penetrating glance; his hearing of the sharpest; his eyebrows grew long and were often clipped; a slight cold made him soon grow hoarse. On the day of his election he was forty-seven years old, and had been a monk for seventeen. He had a few white hairs in a red beard and a very few in the hair of his head, which was black and rather curly; but within fourteen years of his election he was white as snow. He was a man of extreme sobriety, never given to sloth, extremely strong and ever ready to go either on horseback or on foot, until old age prevailed and tempered his eagerness. When he heard of the capture of the Cross and the fall of Jerusalem, he began to wear drawers of haircloth, and a shirt of hair instead of wool, and to abstain from flesh and meat; none the less he desired that meat should be placed before him when he sat at table, that so our alms might be increased. He preferred fresh milk and honey and the like to any other food. He hated liars and drunkards and wordy fellows, since virtue loves itself and hates its opposite. He condemned those who murmur at their food and drink, especially if they were monks, and preserved the old way of life that he had followed as a cloister monk.

He was eloquent both in French and Latin, having regard rather to the sense of what he had to say than to ornaments of speech. He read English perfectly, and used to preach in English to the people, but in the speech of Norfolk, where he was born and bred, and to this end he ordered a pulpit to be set up in the church for the benefit of his hearers and as an ornament to the church. The Abbot seemed also to love the active life better than the contemplative; he had more praise for good obedientiaries than for good cloister monks; and rarely did he approve of any man solely for his knowledge of literature, unless he were also wise in worldly affairs. And when he heard of any prelate that he grew faint beneath the burden of his pastoral cares and turned anchorite, he did not praise him for so doing. He was loth to bestow much praise on kindly men, for he said, 'He that seeks to please everyone, ought to please nobody.' So in the first year of his abbacy he regarded all flatterers with hatred, especially if they were monks. But in process of time he seemed more ready to give ear to them and to be more friendly toward them. Wherefore it came to pass that, when a certain brother skilled in this art kneeled before him, and under pretence of giving him some advice had poured the oil of flattery into his ears, I laughed softly as I stood afar off: but when the monk retired, he called me and asked me why I laughed, and I replied that it was because the world was full of flatterers. To which the Abbot made answer, 'My son, it is long since I have been acquainted with flatterers, and it is therefore that I cannot help listening to them. In many things I must feign, and in many I must dissemble, to maintain peace in the Convent. I shall not cease to listen to their words, but they will not deceive me, as they deceived my predecessor who was so foolish as to put faith in their counsels, so that long before his death neither he nor his household had aught to eat save what was borrowed from their creditors; nor on the day of his burial was there anything that could be given to the poor save only fifty shillings, which were received from Richard the tenant of Palgrave because it was that very day when he entered on his tenancy at Palgrave.' I was comforted by these words. And in truth the Abbot was at pains to have his house well-disciplined and a household that, although large, was all of it necessary, and every week he heard the account of his expenditure, not by deputy, but in person, which had never been the custom of his predecessor. As for the monks who had been his comrades before he succeeded to the abbacy, and had stood high in his love and regard, he rarely promoted them to office on the strength of his former affection, unless they were fit; wherefore some of our brethren, who had favoured his election as Abbot, said that he showed less regard than was seemly toward those who had loved him before he was Abbot, and that he loved those better who had both openly and in secret disparaged him, and had publicly and even in the hearing of many called him an angry and unsociable man, a haughty fellow and a vexatious litigant from Norfolk. But as after his succession to the abbacy he vouchsafed no indiscreet affection or honour to those who had once been his friends, even so he showed no sign of ran-cour or hatred to others, such as their conduct might seem to deserve, sometimes rendering good for evil and doing good to those who had persecuted him. He also had a habit, which I have never marked in any other man, namely, that he warmly loved many towards whom he never or rarely showed a loving countenance, nor conformed to the proverb 'where your love is, there your eye is also.' And he had another characteristic that calls for wonder, namely, that he wittingly put up with losses in temporal matters at the hands of his servants, and acknowledged that he did so; but to my thinking the reason was this, that he might wait for a suitable occasion to set matters right with greater prudence or that by shutting his eyes to the offence he might avoid great loss.

He loved his kin in moderation, and not over tenderly, as others are wont to do. For he had no kin within the third degree or at any rate pretended that this was so. But he desired to treat those as being of his blood, who had treated him as their kinsman when he was a poor cloister monk. To the son of Elias, the butler of Abbot Hugh, when he did homage to him for his father's land, he said in full court; 'For seven years have I put off your homage for the land which Abbot Hugh gave your father, because the gift of that land was to the detriment of the hall of Elmswell, but now I give way, for I remember the kindness which your father showed me when I was in chains ; for he sent me a portion of that very same wine which his lord was used to drink, bidding me to be comforted in God.' To Master Walter, the son of Master William of Diss, when he besought him of his charity that he might have the vicarage of the church of Chevington, he replied; ' Your father was master of the schools : and when I was a poor clerk, he, out of pure charity and making no conditions, gave me admission to his school and the opportunity of learning; and I now for God's sake grant your desire.' When it chanced that two knights of, William and Norman were amerced in his court, he thus addressed them in the presence of all,

'When I was a cloister monk and having been sent to Durham on business of our Church, I was returning home by Risby, I was benighted and asked Lord Norman to give me lodging; but he utterly refused to take me in; but when I approached the house of Lord William and asked for lodging, I was received by him with honour. Wherefore from Norman I will recover twenty shillings, to wit, the full amerciment without mercy. But to William I offer my thanks and gratefully remit the amerciment of twenty shillings which he owes me.'

Jocelin was particularly well placed to describe Samson and his deeds, as he became chaplain to the abbot four months after his election. At this election, the monks had the right to choose their preferred candidates, who had to be presented to the king, who had the final say. Henry II had fought a bitter battle with Thomas Becket, archbishop of Canterbury, over the king's right in such matters. When the monks declared their two choices, their prior and Samson, and were asked whom they wanted, they answered unanimously in favour of Samson.

> ... the king said, 'You have presented Samson to me: I do not know him. If you had presented your Prior, I should have accepted him; for I have seen him and know him. But, as it is, I will do what you desire. But have a care; for by the very eyes of God, if you do ill, I will be at you!' Samson fell at the king's feet and kissed them then rose in haste, and in haste went to the altar with the brethren, singing 'Miserere mei, Deus', his head held high and his countenance unchanged. And when the king saw this, he said to those who stood by, 'By God's eyes, this elect thinks himself worthy to be the guardian of his Abbey'.

By the time that Jocelin came to write his chronicle, probably around 1198, this side of Samson's character had come to the fore. Samson had inherited a disastrous situation—there was talk of bonds for over three thousand pounds which had been borrowed (and partly repaid)—and the abbot had needed all his energy and skill to retrieve the situation. But in so doing, he had become increasingly autocratic. His repeated attempts to bring the abbey's finances in order led him to encroach on the rights of the convent. The property of the abbey was divided between the abbot and the monks, who formed the convent, and elected their own officials. After a devastating fire in the very heart of the abbey, in the shrine of St Edmund, in 1198, Samson blamed the monks for their negligence; he had already come to regard the monks as too fond of luxuries, particularly good food and wine.

The key official in all this was the cellarer. Now it may well be that Jocelin himself was the cellarer; there is a sharp disagreement between scholars on this, as there were at least two other monks of the same name at this time. Even if Jocelin was not the direct target of Samson's wrath, the ending of the chronicle is very different from its opening. In 1201, embroiled in quarrels not only with the convent but with the bishop of Ely, Samson was summoned by king John, then in Normandy. He was 'somewhat trouble by his bodily weakness', but was determined to go in order to defend his rights. This is what Jocelin has to say:

> Meanwhile we heard certain persons murmuring and saying that the Abbot was zealous and anxious about the liberties of his barony, but never said a word about the liberties of the Convent which we had lost in his time—to wit, the loss of the court and liberties of the Cellarer—nor about the liberties of the Sacrist as regards

the appointing of the town reeves with the assent of the Convent. And so the Lord stirred up the spirit of three brethren of moderate understanding, who, calling in a number of others, spoke to the Prior, counselling him to speak with the Abbot upon the matter and to ask him on our behalf that, on his departure, he would make provision that his Church should suffer no loss in respect of his liberties. ·When the Abbot heard this, be said things which he ought not to have said, swearing that he would be master as long as he lived. But as evening drew near, he spoke more gently with the Prior, and on the morrow, when he was about to depart and take his leave, he said as he sat in Chapter that he had satisfied all his servants and had made his will, as though he were near his end ; and then beginning to speak of those liberties, he excused himself saying that he had changed ancient customs to prevent default of the King's justice; and he threw the blame on the Sacrist, and said that if Durand the town-reeve, who was then ill, should die, the Sacrist should have the reeveship in his hands and should propose a name in the presence of the Chapter according to the ancient custom, yet that this should none the less be done by the Abbot's counsel. But he said that he would in no wise remit the gifts and presents which were due every year from the reeve. But when we asked what was to be done concerning the loss of the Cellarer's court and more especially of the halfpence which he used to receive for the renewal of pledges, he was moved thereat and asked us by what authority we demanded a royal right and things pertaining to royal customs: and the answer was given him that we had possessed that right ever since the foundation of our Church, and even during the first three years of his own abbacy, and that we still possessed this liberty of renewing pledges in all our manors. And we said that we ought not to lose our right for the sake of a hundred shillings which he privily received from the reeve every year; and we boldly demanded such seizin as we had even in his own time. But the Abbot finding himself in a strait how to reply and wishing to leave us in quiet and depart in peace, gave orders that those halfpence and the other dues exacted by the Cellarer should be sequestrated until his return ; and he promised that on his homecoming he would in all things work with our counsel and would make just disposition and restore to every man that which was his own. This done, there was a calm, but not a great calm, since in promises there's none but may be rich.

The last years of Samson's rule, before his death in 1211, were far from calm, as Jocelin seems to anticipate. On his death, however, he was remembered as a great abbot, even allowing for the laudatory tone of the entries in another contemporary abbey chronicle:

> He had ruled the abbey committed to him successfully for thirty years, less two months, and freed it from all kinds of debts and extended its very extensive privileges, liberties, possessions and buildings, and he had renewed religious observance both inside and outside the abbey very sufficiently.

Fair enough. But Jocelin has the real story which, with all its contrast and contradictions is both more real and much more dramatic.

MEG ROSOFF

Heading for the Beach

From *The Great Godden* (2020)

Meg Rosoff grew up in a suburb of Boston and moved to Britain in 1989. Her first novel, How I Live Now, *has sold more than a million copies; it won the Guardian Children's Prize and the Printz Award in the US and was made into a film. Her subsequent eight novels have been awarded or shortlisted for, among others, the Carnegie Medal and the National Book Award. She is the winner of the Astrid Lindgren Memorial Award for Children's Literature. Her latest book is* The Great Godden. *She lives between London and Shingle Street in Suffolk.*

Every year when school ends we jam the car full of indispensable junk and head for the beach. By the time six people have crammed their bare essentials into the car, Dad says he can't see out of the windows and there's no room for any of us, so half of everything is removed but it doesn't seem to help; I always end up sitting on a tennis racket or a bag of shoes. By the time we set off, everyone's in a foul mood.

The drive is a nightmare of shoving and arguing and Mum shouting that if we don't all pipe down she's going to have a breakdown and once a year Dad actually pulls over the side of the road and says he'll just sit there till everyone shuts the fuck up.

We've been coming to the beach since we were born, and on the theory that life existed even before that, Dad's been coming since he was a child, and Mum since she met Dad and gave birth to us four.

The drive takes hours but eventually we come off the motorway and that's when the mood changes. The familiarity of the route does something to our brains and we start to whine silently, like dogs approaching a park. It's half an hour precisely from the roundabout to the house and we know every inch of landscape on the way. Bonus points are earned for deer or horses glimpsed from car windows or an owl sitting on a fence post or Harry the Hare hopping down the road. Harry frequently appears in the middle of the road on the day we arrive and then again on the day we leave; incontrovertible proof that our world is a sophisticated computer simulation.

There's no such thing as a casual arrival. We pull into the grass drive, scramble out of the car, and then shout and shove our way into the house, which smells of ancient upholstery, salt, and musty stale air till we open all the windows and let the sea breeze pour through in waves.

Our house is picturesque and annoying in equal measure. For one thing it's smaller than it looks, which is funny because most houses are the opposite. My great-great-grandfather built it for his wife as a wedding present in 1913, constructed in what Mum calls Post-Victorian-Mad-Wife-in-the-Attic style. It stayed in the family till the 1930s, when my ancestor had to sell it to pay off gambling debts. His son (my great-grandfather) bought it back twenty years later, restored the original periwinkle blue, and thereafter everyone refrained from mentioning the time it left the family.

Our house was built as a summer place, a kind of folly, not to be lived in year round, so we don't. It's draughty, has no insulation, and the pipes freeze if you don't drain them and fill the toilets with anti-freeze in November, but we love every tower and turret and odd-shaped window and the event the short staircase that ends in a cupboard. My great-great grandfather must have had a great-great sense of humour because everything in the house is pointlessly idiosyncratic. But you can see the sea from nearly every window.

My bedroom is the watchtower. Most people wouldn't want it because it is ridiculously small, no room to swing a rat. Someone tall enough could touch all four walls at once by lying flat with arms and legs outstretched. The tower comes with a built-in captain's bed and a ladder, and the ladder goes up to a tiny widow's walk, so-named because women needed a place to walk while gazing out to sea through the telescope, waiting for their husbands to come back. Or not. Hence widow.

I am the possessor of the brass telescope that belonged to my great-grandfather. He was in the Navy and in his later years spent a lot of time doing what I do—standing in the square tower with his telescope trained outwards. I have no idea what he saw—probably the same things I do: Jupiter, owls, hares, foxes and the occasional naked swimmer. It's kind of an unwritten rule that the telescope goes with the room. No one takes a vote, it just gets handed to the right person. Theoretically, the telescope and the room might have gone to Mattie, Tamsin or Alex, but it didn't.

There are lots of traditions in my family, like the passing down of this house and the passing down of the telescope. On the other hand, we're distinctly lacking in the kind of traditions grand families have, like naming every oldest son Alfred or being feeble-minded, and there's no sign of the gambling gene re-emerging so that's kind of a relief. But, wobble aside, when it comes to keeping property in the family from one generation to the next we're practically on a par with the Queen.

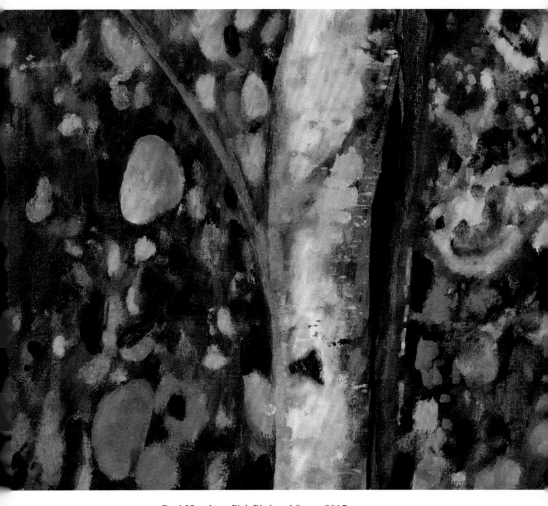

Paul Hamlyn, *Pink Birch and Stones*, 2017.

Paul Hamlyn was born in Stockport. He studied Fine Arts at St Martins School of Art in 1983 and received an MA from Goldsmiths in 1988. He has lived and worked in Nepal and worked as an illustrator in Europe and the America. He lives between London and Shingle Street. 'I spend a lot of time on the Suffolk coast near Ipswich, where long shingle beaches turn to saltwater marsh and then to scrubby woodland interspersed with farmland. I enjoy the blurred lines between land and water, hazy grey sea and grey sky.'

INDIA KNIGHT

At Home in Suffolk (2021)

India Knight is a journalist and novelist. She writes a regular column in the Sunday Times *and her novels have been translated into twenty-eight languages.*

I'd always felt weirdly at home in Suffolk, years before we moved here. I'd come on holiday when the children were small—once, on the way to Southwold twenty-odd years ago, the hours-long bickering in the back of the car reached such a dementing intensity that their father pulled up just beyond Reydon, by the boarding school there, and told the boys to get out and behold their new school, and that we'd drop off their uniform in a few days. Extremely mean trick, and our parenting skills have improved a bit since, but it did stun them into blissful silence for at least three minutes.

Anyway: I felt at home, even with children bashing each other on the head with buckets on the beach and constantly trying to cuddle/steal other people's dogs, or crying because we couldn't take crabs back to London as pets. We all really liked the fields of pigs—we'd shout 'PIGS!' at the top of our voices whenever we passed some, a habit that has stuck (my younger son, strapped into his car seat, once quietly said 'and tiny little piggerinos' to himself in a satisfied way).

I liked the landscape and I liked the sky, obviously—the sky continues to be responsible for dozens if not hundreds of almost out-of-body experiences—and the bleak North Sea, and the reed beds and the boats, and I liked that I could make nice food out of honesty stalls and fishermen's huts, in contrast to other holiday locations, where we'd arrive and immediately start looking for a giant ugly supermarket.

The coast was the gateway drug during all those half terms and long weekends over the years. Eventually we ventured inland, away from tourists, and I liked it even more. I loved the market towns, quietly going about their business and seeming so self-reliant and contented. I liked how everywhere felt slightly empty and under-populated, so that people were always secondary to landscape, like little dots on an enormous canvas, and how often you'd turn a corner into what felt like another century, not just fleetingly but for hours on end. I liked the water that wasn't the sea—the horse ponds you'd come across, and the rivers, with dragonflies and sometimes a frayed old rope dangling from a tree halfway down some overgrown track, to help you jump in. I liked how it was all so artless—how nothing was for show, or twee, or contrived, and how you could lose yourself completely and not see a single other human being if you didn't want to. I liked how everyone worked all the time—it's not an indolent county, Suffolk. At certain times of the year my neighbours are in their fields all night. All the young people I know have at least three jobs.

It was only when we moved here six years ago that the penny dropped: one of the reasons I felt so at home was that Suffolk reminded me of the Belgium of my childhood. More than reminded: it is a sort of mirror image. The Belgian coast, where I spent half of all my summer holidays between the ages of 0 and 18, is about seventy nautical miles from the beach at Southwold. When we drive to Norwich, Holland and Belgium appear on the right of the sat nav screen. The B&B I like in Bruges is, it turns out, exactly 3.5 hours away by car from my front door, about an hour more than it takes to get to London, which still seems extraordinary and great. We nip to Bruges a lot. And to Ghent. And to an incredible fish shack in an unattractive part of Zeebrugge port. And we say hello to my late grandmother's small white beach cabin in the dunes at Knokke Le Zoute. I love being able to do these things. Growing up, I was embarrassed of being Belgian—so ploddy and unglamorous, so flat and dull, so grey and green and full of water, with too much sky and endless yellow fields. And, it turns out, so absolutely in my bones that moving to Suffolk felt, and feels, like coming home. It took about another three years to figure out that the remote, rambling farmhouse I live in is not unlike my aunt's house in the Belgian countryside.

So I took to Suffolk. I loved it and that was that. People said 'Just wait until the bleak winters that never end, just wait until you're stuck in your field and it's pitch black at 4pm with nary a streetlight for comfort, just wait, just wait, just wait.' But I love the bleak winters and look forward to them, to battening in with a fire and a pile of books (bookshops! That's another thing. You can really get the measure of a place by its independent bookshops). I love how dark it gets, because what could be nicer than being all cosy inside in the yellow light, making a stew? I don't even mind trudging out to the animals when the rain has turned our heavy clay to glue. And now I've been here a while, I love so many other things, too: the grey horses that appear every Easter near Cratfield, bumbling about on the road, penned in only by cattle grids and always glad of an apple, the stepdancing competitions and the faces of the old men who take part in them, my friends' secret monthly pub, where the punters spontaneously sing or dance or recite something in between pints, and the not-secret but still magical Low House at Laxfield. And the food! There is just such good food being grown or raised hyper-locally. And the people, of course, but that's less surprising because people who move to Suffolk are already self-selecting: you know that you like a lot of the same things. Mind you I once sat next to a local vicar and politely asked him about dwindling numbers of punters, and he matter-of-factly said 'Well, it's partly because of the covens, of course.' Once I'd finished coughing, I thought about it and realised I wasn't that surprised. It's Suffolk. There's magic everywhere.

Corder shooting Maria Marten.

P. 147.

RUTH RENDELL

The Molecatcher's Daughter

From *Ruth Rendell's Suffolk* (1989)

Novelist Ruth Rendell (1930–2015) lived in Polstead from 1970 until 1983. Although clearly a lovely place, it's striking that it's the story of a murder which attracted her as a crime writer.

The church of St Mary is small and lovely. It would be a nice place to be married in. It is Norman, yet very light inside, with a white gleam about it. It may have the earliest surviving English bricks and, alone among Suffolk's medieval church towers, has a stone spire. William Dowsing, the Reformation iconoclast, broke up the old glass, forty-five pictures, no less.

Pond House, on the other side of the pond—Polstead means 'a place of pools'—was built in 1760. Its dovecote is said to hold the curious record of being the largest in the county. Corder's House, once called Street Farm, then Corders, now Street Farm again, is older, timber-framed, a big house at the foot of the hill which leads up to Polstead Green. I used to live in the thatched cottage near the top on the left hand side. When they thatched the roof in the late sixties they found among the rotting straw a wasp nest as tall as a man.

In Street Farm once lived William Corder. He was hanged for murder in 1829 and the horrid detail of that event is that they bound an account of his crime in his own skin. 'He suffered at Bury,' M.R. James says laconically of him. In fact, he was the last man to be hanged there in public.

Later opinions have varied as to the chances of his guilt. Certainly he had been the lover among many others, of Maria Marten. He had promised to marry her and run off with her from her father the molecatcher's house. Maria disappeared. The interest of her story and the undoubted reason for its survival as 'case' and melodrama, lies in her stepmother's dream. The second Mrs Marten dreamed that she saw Maria's grave in the Red Barn. This was a barn, now gone, not in itself red but turned to that colour by the rays of the setting sun. They dug in the Red Barn and found poor Maria's body. By this time William Corder was living in London, running a school and married to a respectable woman, who no doubt knew nothing about any of it. They arrested him and he spent his last night of liberty in an upper room at Cock Farm. This house which faces Polstead

'Corder shooting Maria Marten': William Corder's murder of Maria Marten in the Red Barn in 1827.

Green has been said by some to be haunted by Corder whose footsteps can be heard overhead.

In the week Corder was executed, two of his brothers, while drunk, drove their horse and cart into Polstead Pond and were drowned. What must that have been like for old Mrs Corder? It hardly bears thinking of, even at this distance of time.

There is a plaque by the side of the church that says Maria is buried close at hand. The two brothers in their horse and cart haunt the environs of the pond. The Rector of that time, no one knows why, drives down Rectory Hill in a carriage drawn by a headless horse. A band of ghostly friars inexplicably walks through the air where there was once a path before the road was cut. Well, maybe.

Kathleen Hale, *Orlando the Marmalade Cat, a Seaside Holiday*, 1952.

In the 1920s artist Kathleen Hale met Cedric Morris and Arthur Lett Haines in Paris, later frequenting their Benton End community. Both Cecil Morris and Arthur Lett Haines had a huge impact on Hale's life, both appearing in the backgrounds of her illustrated Orlando the Marmalade Cat *books for children. In this book Orlando and his wife Grace come on holiday to the seaside town of Owlbarrow (Aldeburgh).*

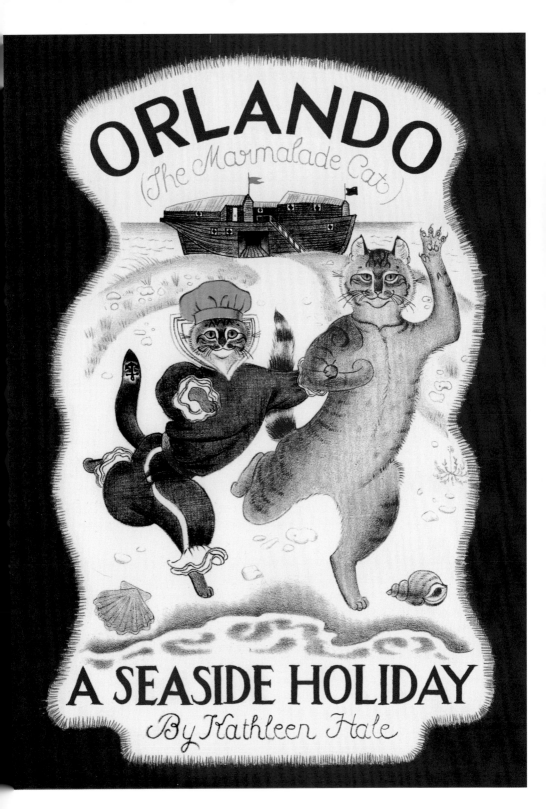

MAGGI HAMBLING

Remembering Benton End

From *Benton End Remembered* (2002)

Maggi Hambling CBE is one of Britain's most celebrated artists. Though principally a painter, her best-known public works are the sculptures A Conversation with Oscar Wilde *and A* Sculpture for Mary Wollstonecraft *in London, and the 4-metre-high steel* Scallop *on Aldeburgh beach. She was born, lives and works in Suffolk.*

I first realised that I could possibly become an artist when I was fourteen and at Amberfield School in Nacton, near Ipswich. I managed to do a painting in the last ten minutes of an art exam during which I had otherwise done nothing but flick paint at other girls and eye the teacher with whom I was madly in love. Without even trying I had come top in art, whereas my experience of maths was the opposite. I had failed to pass the entrance exam to Ipswich High School.

I was given a lot of encouragement by Yvonne Drewry, the art teacher, but my parents needed some reassurance that becoming an artist was a good idea, so in 1960 I took my first two oil paintings to what was known in Hadleigh as the 'Artists' House'. Lett [Haines] answered the door and replied to my request to see Sir Cedric [Morris] that he was having his dinner. I asked if I could wait and was amazed to see Lett bringing dish after dish to the long kitchen table. Cedric was friendly and charming. I propped up my paintings and received encouraging, though completely contradictory, criticisms from each of them. I finally left what in Hadleigh was considered a notorious house at nine-thirty in the evening. My mother thought I had been sold into the white slave trade.

I was still at school but Lett asked me if I would like to come and paint during the holiday so I arrived on the first morning after the end of term. I was too shy to knock so I sat in the ditch outside the gates and painted there. Lucy Harwood called me in for elevenses and that was the beginning. Alan Brooks, known as 'China', was the regular helper in the kitchen but when he was not there I helped Lett. He was a harsh critic, especially of my ways in the kitchen, and I was often reduced to tears by the end of the week, but his excuse was, 'You don't pick holes in a rotten apple.' I sometimes had to scrape maggots off the meat as there were lots of flies in the kitchen and the fridge, placed next to the Aga, was less than efficient. Still, I was accepted; I found a card on the seat of my donkey which said, 'This seat is still hot from the seat of Maggi Soop,' and I have been known as Maggi rather than Margaret ever since.

Lett was my mentor and he it was who taught me the importance of imagination. He told me that I should get my work into the relationship of being my

Maggi Hambling, *Lett Laughing*, 1975–6.

best friend and that art had to be the absolute priority of one's life. These are the most important things anyone has ever said to me and I have lived by them.

Cedric encouraged me to draw, but I felt that Cedric's students often had a tendency to paint as he did, whereas Lett could address himself to a new person and bring out what you were. He encouraged one's spirit of independence as an artist. The art world can be pretty frightful so it is essential to do what you have to do and bugger other people! Lett had an enormous personality and capacity as a teacher so I learned a lot of about art in our conversations in the kitchen. Nothing was trotted out as a formula and if he couldn't answer a question he was quite prepared to say that he didn't know. He was constantly experimenting in his own work, always responding to everything that was going on and never throwing a

Maggi Hambling, *The Ghost of Cedric Morris*, 1983.

thing away in case he could use it in a sculpture. He encouraged experiment too, advising me to try my idea in another medium whenever I got stuck.

Cedric was more hermetic as a teacher. He had certain ideas which he would pass on, as when he criticised my painting of a neck, 'Remember, it is always a column,' but Lett wouldn't do this. Cedric would sometimes take me into his bedroom and ask me to go through his paintings to decide which to destroy. We would take half a dozen but he never got rid of any of them and back they would go.

Lett had put Cedric in the position of Master Artist and himself as his impresario, cosseting him in such a way that he could live in his own world and not have to look after himself at all.

Cedric resented it if Lett sat down to eat with everyone because he was often drunk and, when drunk, could be very entertaining, taking all the attention away from Cedric. Lett, however, was socially vulnerable. He devoted lots of time to bed and the bottle. He would grumble, when preparing one of his extravagant meals, 'The buggers don't know what they are eating. They might as well have ham sandwiches.' His conversation was highly sophisticated, well laced with sex which he brought into almost everything. He 'communed with God' in the afternoons and I would draw him as he lay in bed. He loved to go out in his 'best frock' (a dark blue suit) and was a very good dancer. There were some wonderful moments, like the time when Elizabeth David visited and Lett took her on a grand tour of the larder and butler's pantry. He took off the silver lid from a tray of 'cold collations' and out flew a moth. Then there was the time when Lucy [Harwood] introduced Lett to someone at The Minories as, 'This is Cedric Morris's um ... er ...,' which he strongly objected to.

I had seven years of art training in the glorious sixties when there were grants for students. I went to Ipswich School of Art, Camberwell and the Slade, all of which gave me the time to work, but nothing was ever like Benton End. Lett was a second father to me and Benton End made me who I am. My mother once said, 'I wish to goodness you'd never set foot in Benton End,' but it was too late.

LAVINIA GREENLAW

Slow Passage, Low Prospect

From *The Casual Perfect* (2011)

Lavinia Greenlaw is a poet and novelist. Her poetry has been shortlisted for the T. S. Eliot Prize, the Forward Prize and the Whitbread Poetry Prize. She won the Costa Poetry Award in 2014 for A Double Sorrow.

AH –

Cloud low on the low land,
such squeezed light
is more than we ask for,
no world but white.

I need the green shadows,
grey water, blue meadows.
How can I be here
when here is so bright?

SPILL

Full moon. September.
Overcast. Light wind.
Five whiting, an eel.
Slight sea with a bit of colour.

No thousand boats.
No particle writhe of the shoal.
The herring is a silver purse,
no longer a purse of silver.

We breathe the fissured air
and walk where we are left to.
The empty sea agrees with the empty harbour:
a silver cloud is not a cloud of silver.

HAZE

We walk the golden way, my love,
where bitter waters run.
We gaze into the overloaded view
and soften.

Like the fields, give up your shape,
become uncertain.
Be neither his nor hers, my love,
be mine, unbutton.

The yellow heat of marigold,
saxifrage and celandine
is not what burns your throat, my love,
just what fills your mind.

BLUES (THAT'S ANOTHER SUNDAY OVER)

Two minutes to five, turn it up.
Fire, food and comfort? Never enough.
What little opened has long since shut.

Coal burns back down into earth
taking with it whatever worlds
might have been seen in its embers.

Scenes from a novel. Dust falls.
The page won't turn, the stranger won't call.
A town that's sinking sinks us all.

The one road out heads towards sunset.
The young drive as if overtaking death
and the old as if following the dead.

The sky bog-black by now
and my mind black by now
and the rain by now, the rain.

OTOLITH

A bear waking in Siberia
breathes out the last of winter
and the wind rolls west:
pine bend, reed sway,
sea plunge, sea fray,
sluice dribble, crab snap,
a merchant's Flemish beaver hat,
tooth rattle, jet boom,
curlew splash, cathedral tone,
dog confusion, jackdaw bluff,
the passing bells, the plunge and fray,
sea bend and sea sway,
the passing birds, the Flemish bluff,
a bear's loose tooth, sea breath,
corncrake, godwit, stonechat,
which of them is coming back,
the last of winter, gasp of spring,
and earth, and air, and rain.

RICHARD COBBOLD

A Bareback Ride for the Doctor

From *The History of Margaret Catchpole, a Suffolk Girl* (1845)

The Reverend Richard Cobbold's colourful account of the servant girl who turned horse thief and gaol breaker was intended as a cautionary tale to his Victorian contemporaries but he clearly admired her pluck. Daughter of a ploughman in Nacton, Margaret worked in service for several households, including that of Cobbold's mother. Her life took a different path when she stole the Cobbolds' strawberry roan to follow her lover, the smuggler and fugitive William Laud, to London, riding seventy miles in ten hours dressed as a boy. She was detected, arrested and held in Ipswich Gaol, from which she escaped using a clothes line to scale a twenty-two foot wall. Recaptured on the beach—Laud was shot in the skirmish with the militia—Margaret was sentenced to death, but her punishment was commuted and she was tranported to Australia in 1801. She landed in Botany Bay and went on to be a respected livestock manager and the first female convict chronicler of Australia's early frontier history and, in January 1814, she was officially pardoned by the British government. She became one of her colony's most respected midwives and frequently acted as a nurse.

Here she steals her first horse, but in a worthy cause.

Margaret grew up to her thirteenth year, a fine, active, intelligent girl. She had a brother younger than herself by five or six years, of whom she was very fond, from having nursed him during the occasional absence of her mother. Her elder sister was always, as we have stated, of a sickly constitution, and very delicate: she had very little bodily strength, but she had learned to knit and to sew, and in these things she excelled, and was the sempstress of the whole family. She was of a sweet temper, so gentle, so affectionate, and so quiet, that, though a complete contrast to her sister, she nevertheless maintained a just ascendancy over the high spirit of Margaret, which was always curbed by any quiet reproof from the calm wisdom of the invalid.

We have seen something of Margaret's infant spirit: we must now record a simple fact of her childhood, which exhibits a singular instance of intrepidity and presence of mind in a child not yet fourteen years old.

It chanced that her mother one day sent her down to the farm-house to ask for a little broth, which had been promised by Mrs. Denton, her mistress, for poor Susan. Her father and her brothers were all at work on a distant part of the farm; and, being harvest-time, master and man were every one engaged. When Margaret arrived at the gate, she heard a shriek from a female in the house, and in another minute she was in the kitchen, where the mistress of the house had suddenly fallen down in a fit. In one moment the girl of fourteen exhibited a character which showed the powerful impetus of a strong mind. The two girls in the house were shrieking with fright over their fallen mistress, and were incapable of rendering the least assistance. They stood wringing their hands and stamping their feet, and exclaiming, 'Oh, my mistress is dead!—Oh, my mistress is dead!'

'She is not dead!' said Margaret; 'she is not dead! Don't stand blubbering there, but get some cold water; lift up her head, untie her cap, loose her gown, and raise her into the chair.' Not waiting to see how her words were taken, she did the work herself, and caused the others to help her. She used the water freely, and gave the chest full play, dragged the chair toward the door, sent one of the girls for some vinegar, and made the other rub her hands and feet; and did not slacken her attention until she saw some symptoms of returning animation. When the breathing became more composed, and the extremities more sensitive, she sent off one of the girls to the harvest-field for help; and telling the servant-girl that she was going for Dr. Stebbing, she went to the stable, unslipped the knot by which the pony was tied to the rack; and, with only the halter in her hand, without saddle or bridle, she sprang upon the fiery little Suffolk Punch, snapped her fingers instead of a whip, and was up the sandy lane, and on to the high road to Ipswich, before the other girl was fairly across the first field towards her master. She did not stop even to tell her mother where she was going, but dashed past the cottage.

On she went, and well had she her own wishes answered by the fiery little animal she bestrode. Her heart was up, and so was the pony's, who, feeling a light weight upon his back, and a tight seat over his ribs, gave full play to his lungs and legs, and answered to her heart's content the snap of the finger for expedition. Those who beheld the animal would be astonished, and ask where all the speed could be. But speed there was in his strong and well-knit limbs. So close was he put together, that his action was almost like a ball bounding down the side of Malvern hills. Nothing seemed to check the speed of Margaret or her steed. She passed every cart jogging on to Ipswich market, without taking any notice of the drivers, though she knew many of them well. Her mistress and the doctor were the only things in her mind's eye at this time, and they were four miles asunder, and the sooner she could bring them together the better. She even met Admiral Vernon's carriage just as she turned on to the Ipswich race-course, at the part now called Nacton Corner. The Admiral's attention was called to the extraordinary sight of a female child astride a pony at full speed, with nothing but a halter over his head, and that held as loosely as if the rider wished to go at full speed. The servants called to the child, even the Admiral was sufficiently excited to do the same; but he might as well have attempted to stop a vessel in full sail, with a strong and favourable wind.

Away she dashed, regardless of any impediment. She passed one young farmer from Stratton Hall, who rode what might be termed a high-bred horse. It was a noble turf, and an open course; and the young man, as much astonished as if it were an apparition before him, though convinced that it was flesh and blood, stuck his spurs into his charger's side, and gave him his rein with the full determination to overtake her. But this was not so easy a task as he anticipated. The little nag, hearing the clank of heels behind him, turned his head first on one side, then on the other; and, lifting up his nose like a stag, darted onward with redoubled speed. Not Mazeppa with more sudden bound could have sprung forward with more spirit than this wild little home-bred nag did down the wide turf of the race-course. The youth called aloud to know what was the matter, but Margaret heeded him not; and long before she reached the stewards' stand, she had fairly distanced the young squire of Stratton Hall. At length she reached the end of the race-course, and came on to the common of Bishop's Hill. It is a very deep descent down that hill to the town of Ipswich, which from its summit seems to lie at the very bottom of an extensive pit. But it is a noble expanse that lies before the spectator upon that eminence. The beautiful river flowing to the left, and forming an expanded semicircle bordering the town, and the distant country rising with amphitheatric grandeur beyond the barracks, and above the towers of twelve churches, might induce even a hasty traveller to pause and look upon that sight. But Margaret did not pause. Down she dashed from the verge of the hill into the very thickest part of the back hamlet of St. Clement's. It was market-day, and scores of pig-carts, and carriers' vans, and waggons, stood on one side of the road, taking up nearly half the street. But on through them all at full speed dashed the intrepid girl. From every house people rushed to see the sight—a girl, with her bonnet hanging down behind her, and going like lightning through the crowded thoroughfare, was an extraordinary sight.

People gave way as she rode fearlessly on, and followed her up St. Clement's Fore Street, over the stone pavement across the wash into Orwell Place, where lived the ever humane though eccentric surgeon, Mr. George Stebbing. But not until she reached his very door did Margaret give the first check to the pony.

A passing spectator, who was at the moment opposite the surgeon's door, with an instinctive thought of her errand, gave a violent ring at the surgery-bell, and received such a joyous 'Thank you, sir,' from the child, that he stopped to see the result.

By this time the street was full of spectators, all anxious to know what was the matter; but Margaret's eye was fixed upon the door, and the very moment it was opened and the doctor himself appeared, she exclaimed, 'Oh, come to my mistress, sir, directly!—come to my mistress!'

PETER SAGER

Wool Churches, Tudor Mansions

From *East Anglia* (1994)

The five great wool towns of Suffolk—Sudbury, Lavenham, Long Melford, Clare and Hadleigh—were at the centre of the medieval wool trade. The Flemish weavers, or 'Flemings' whom Edward III invited to England in 1334 brought the knowledge of how to produce woollens rather than the traditional worsteds. By the fifteenth and sixteenth centuries the Stour valley was the scene of what was the most intensive and efficient industrial activity in England. The seventeenth century, however, saw the dominance of Suffolk woollens yielding to the 'new draperies', produced in Holland and then Yorkshire.

The streets of Lavenham are like timber-framed avenues, and the village itself might almost be a petrified forest, with windows and doors between the rows of silvery oak trunks. Walk downhill from the church, along the elegant curve of Church Street, and up the High Street to the market: it's like walking through a medieval world that is better preserved than any other in England.

Lavenham is one of the old drapery towns, those Suffolk centres that used to export their materials in the Middle Ages via Ipswich to Holland and Spain. This hill town in the fields, which today seems more like a farming village, enjoyed its peak during the reign of Henry VIII, when it was the fourteenth richest town in England. For almost six hundred years the weavers flourished in Lavenham: first it was their famous blue cloth, then fine yarn, damask and flannel, serge and shalloon, and finally coconut matting, crinoline and horsehair mattresses. The last weaving mill closed in 1930. What remained were the houses of the clothiers and weavers, their old workshops, inns and guildhalls, all making up a town that goes back to the War of the Roses.

Stalls go up in the triangular Market Place as they have since the market cross was built in 1502; you can picture the farmers selling their wares every Thursday, year after year, century after century; you can hear the cheers and the clattering hooves as Queen Elizabeth I comes to Lavenham, in 1578, escorted by five hundred squires in black and white silk and 1,500 servants on horseback; you can shudder at the bull baiting that marked Guy Fawkes Day until 1842—the last such show on British soil. In this nation of animal lovers, public executions (viewed no doubt as a more humane spectacle) continued for a good deal longer.

It's in the market place that you'll find Lavenham's most spectacular timber-framed house, the Guildhall, built c. 1520 by the Guild of Corpus Christi, one of the town's four medieval guilds. This was where the clothiers met, fixed prices and wages, settled disputes and, on 3 February—St Blaise's Day—held a banquet in honour of their patron saint. In their heyday, during the fifteenth century, the weavers of Lavenham produced up to half a million square feet of finest cloth per year.

Beneath Water Street there still flows the stream whose waters were once used by the clothiers to full their materials in the yards behind their houses. The latter reflect the whole range of Lavenham's development, from the fourteenth-century cottages of the hand-weavers to Roper & Sons' Victorian horsehair factory of 1891.

There was once a time when timber-framed houses were out. Everyone thought they were old-fashioned—relics of rustic, medieval architecture. The good citizens of seventeenth-century Lavenham dutifully covered up all their timbering with a thick coat of plaster. The few who could afford it even put a Georgian brick mask in front of their old wooden façade, for example 'The Willows' in Church Street. Even the timbers of 'The Swan' were covered in bricks until 1933. But after the war, people began to restore these houses, many of which were in a sorry state, and then the pendulum swung the other way: the threat of decay and demolition was replaced by a positive orgy of timbering—so much so that the Suffolk Preservation Society complained that there was far more timbering in Lavenham now than had ever been intended.

Little Hall, in the Market Place, is a beautifully restored timber-framed building (fourteenth to fifteenth century), and it is the headquarters of the Suffolk Preservation Society, which was founded in 1929. This is the largest association of its kind at county level in all England, and has some 2,200 members. 'Lots of dukes and lords, old soldiers and writers,' the director Paul Edwards told me. When he gets up from his desk, he bumps his head on the ceiling of Little Hall. 'In Suffolk we've probably got the richest collection of historic buildings and,' he adds tendentiously, 'the sorriest amount of state support.' There are about 12,000 listed buildings in Suffolk and three hundred of them in Lavenham alone.

Lavenham remains a model for all restorers. Even the Postmaster General made his contribution to the preservation of Lavenham's historical image: in 1967 he agreed to take down all the telegraph poles in the High Street and lay his cables underground. Another historical feature still to be seen on many houses is Suffolk Pink, a sort of pink whitewash that develops a patina of its own, much better than the normal shiny housepaint.

One of the great sights that the tourists come to see stands triumphantly on a hill just outside the town: there, majestically, the soaring tower of St Peter and St Paul gazes down divinely over town and country. This is one of the great wool churches of Suffolk, built between 1485 and 1525, at the peak of the cloth industry's prosperity. The building material alone is clear evidence of Lavenham's wealth: imported Barnack limestone, set off by the homely local flint. The work of the stonemasons and woodcarvers is masterly: the ornate crenellations of the nave and side aisles, the porch with its fan vault, the exquisite wooden screen in the Spring Chantry (1525) with its carved foliage, columns and grotesques. For his chantry chapel and the completion of the tower, the clothier Thomas Spring paid £200, which at that time was a considerable sum. His coat of arms appears thirty-two times on the parapet, more even than the star emblem of the 13th Earl of Oxford, the other great patron of the church. Another well-loved feature is the sound of Lavenham's eight bells, while fans of gravestone poetry will admire the following: 'Hurrah! My boys, at the Parson's fall, / For if he lived he'd buried us all.'

LIZ TRENOW

From Spitalfields to Sudbury

Adapted from *The Silk Family* (2020)

Liz Trenow is a bestselling author of historical fiction, including Under a Wartime Sky *and* The Silk Weaver. *Her family have been silk weavers for nearly three hundred years, and she was brought up in Little Cornard in the Stour Valley in Suffolk.*

Silk worms have never been grown in any quantities in these chilly latitudes, yet Britain has for centuries been one of the premier producers of the finest woven silk. Today only a few silk weaving companies remain in this country, and these are almost exclusively based in the market town of Sudbury: Stephen Walters & Sons, Humphries Weaving, Gainsborough Silk Weaving Company and Vanners Silk.

The oldest firm, Stephen Walters & Sons, has been weaving silk for more than three hundred years, in continuous ownership by the same family. It was founded in 1720 by Benjamin Walters in Spitalfields, London where immigrant French Calvinists, known as Huguenots, had settled, bringing with them the art of fine silk design and weaving, and passing on their skills to apprentices including early generations of the Walters family.

But by the end of the eighteenth century trade was becoming difficult. Weaving rates were fixed by Parliament in a series of laws called the Spitalfields Acts, and a movement towards free trade meant greater competition from imported silks and cottons. At the same time, fashion was moving towards a simpler, more natural look, as reflected by the Romantic Movement. As a result the demand for elaborate patterned fabric was much reduced. Journeymen organised trade unions—then illegal—to fight for better piece rates. Riots became frequent and in the streets a lady thought to be wearing imported fabrics might even have her dress cut away.

These industrial disputes led many companies to seek manufacturing premises outside the city. Towns in East Anglia offered water mills to power the new twisting frames, as well as a supply of (cheaper) workers with residual weaving skills from the once-thriving wool industry. The development of a railway network made transport of silk to and from London much easier and quicker. The newly-opened Liverpool Street Station was conveniently close to the Walters' London offices and at the end of the line was Sudbury, already an established silk weaving centre. By 1844 there were said to be more than 600 hand loom silk weavers working in the town. Their houses, with large first floor windows, can still be seen today in Melford Road, North Street and Gainsborough Street.

William Folliott, hand-painted Rose and Thistle design, woven in silk by Daniel Walters and Sons for the Buckingham Palace ballroom in 1859.

Of Huguenot descent, Folliott was a talented textile designer and created many royal commissions, including the crimson velvets and the imperial 'cloth of gold' mantle for the coronation of King Edward VII and later, the coronation robes for King George V, as well as Queen Mary's dresses.

In 1860 Stephen Walters & Sons built a new factory at Acton Square in the centre of town, although much of the weaving continued to be undertaken by home-workers. In 1900 they moved to a much larger two-storey silk mill, the first factory in the town specifically designed for power looms, which is where they are still based today.

In the 1940s, after surviving the Second World War by weaving parachute silk, the company added an innovative product to their range: custom-woven Jacquard designs for club ties. The then-proprietor Peter Walters was awarded the MBE for Service to Exports but he turned it down, commending his factory manager instead. He did not reveal this to any of his family until 2010, when he was ninety-five.

The firm continues to keep royal company, having woven silk for the lining for Queen Elizabeth's Coronation Robe, the gown for Prince Charles' investiture, and the wedding dresses of both Princess Anne and Diana, Princess of Wales. Walters' silk fabric adorns many prestigious interiors including Buckingham Palace, 10 Downing Street, Chatsworth House and The White House.

RICHARD NEGUS

A Love Letter to the Hedge

From his blog *Words From the Hedge* (2020)

Richard Negus is a hedge-layer, photographer and writer. 'I lay hedges on farms, shoots and estates throughout East Anglia, predominately for landowners who are as passionate about conservation as I am. East Anglia has no unique hedge laying style of its own, therefore I have adapted a number of traditional styles to suit our own unique landscape and the game and wildlife that calls it home.'

My chainsaw requires an elaborate series of pumping, priming and lever twisting. Only then, followed by repeated pulls on its cord, can I coax the engine into sputtering life. It hates me stopping for a tea break. A fifteen-minute rest leaves it like a dozing soldier, reluctant to perform its duties. I turn back to the hedge, glancing at the stems I cut and laid before I stopped to sip a cup of sweet black tea, scalding hot from my battered flask. They lay one over the next like a thorny row of toppled dominoes. Long scars stare out where I have chopped through the stems, or pleachers as they are called in our strange language of the hedge. So pale when first cut, they have now started to change colour. The maple turns a satsuma orange, the spindle ivory-like, hazel and hawthorn a cookie brown. I make some upward cuts with my saw, taking away the side growth from a hawthorn pleacher. It is January and no leaves adorn this gnarled and curlicued limb; a handful of berries, unclaimed by blackbird or thrush still gamely cling on. The little saw roars once more and I make a diagonal cut downwards from right to left.

I watch with an attentive eye through the mesh of my visor, looking for the base of the thorn to slightly give. This indicates I have made my cut sufficiently deep and reduced the rigidity of the growing plant. The top of my wrist flips the saw's safety bar forward and my thumb depresses the stop button. The thunder clap shift from anarchic roar to silence is dizzying, yet there is never real silence here. Rooks caw raucously and the chittering and squabbling of the long-tailed tits is both endless and amusing. One of the cock pheasants crows a challenge over at the wood some four score yards away. He quits his row and I hear him ruffle his mantle when he hears no rival's reply.

Placing my saw down to my right, with gloved hands I bend the thorny pleacher gently over. Using my bill hook to make a final cut, I lay the clean limb to nestle and intertwine with its neighbour. The hinge does its job. Thick enough to support the pleacher in its new position of 40 degrees or so, but sufficiently flexible to allow me to alter nature. I flick the chainsaw back into life. Warmed up now it is speedily responsive. I trim off the heel of the stool and take a sideways step to my right to repeat the process with the next branch, then the next, then the next. I will stake and bind my hedge before I go home when the sun sets, this will guard my work from the pestiferous wind that loves to pluck at a hedge and undo hours of work. When I drive away, I survey my work in the gleam of my truck's headlights. It is a sight I never grow tired of; it also pays my bills.

The stylised image of a hedge-layer is that of a leather jerkined rustic, pipe smoke curling about his cap, cutting away in a towering line of thorn and branch with a viciously sharp and curiously shaped bill hook. The bill hook is indeed an ancient tool, first found trimming Mesopotamian vines or Israelite briars. Bronze examples, thought to be over 1,000 years old, have been found in Egypt. At various points in history the humble bill lost its role as a tool for making good. It was instead called upon to become a thing of hate and destruction. This ergonomic tool of regeneration was downgraded to cut through muscle, bone and sinew, serving as the makeshift weapon for serfs and bondsmen, dragooned into leaving their land-based toil to become soldiers in some war or other for some lord, king or other. I own three billhooks. The youngest, a Yorkshire-style hook, was made in 1941 and is stamped with a military crow's foot. My oldest, and favourite—a Midland style bill—was crafted by a long-forgotten Leicestershire smith in the 1920s. As the decades have rolled by its handle has been replaced numerous times but the cutting blade is as sharp as a razor and takes an edge as only old hand-forged steel can. Purists sneer at my using a chainsaw to lay hedges, claiming that an axe should be used if a pleacher is too thick to be cut with a billhook. Many of these purists are amateurs, extremely talented amateurs it must be said, competing in hedge-laying competitions throughout the land. But I have a job to do at Flea Barn and the niceties and purities of craft are as relevant to me as a traction engine is to the tractor driver discing a field in his behemoth John Deere. I have a mile of hedge to lay and I don't have time to dwell upon tradition for the sake of tradition.

Hedges, unlike woodland, are and always will be a construct of man. Romano Britons cut and laid small trees to form livestock-retaining enclosures. Gaps were filled by transplanting thorny shrubs. The traces of these early hedges can still be seen today. After harvest, when the summer sun bakes the stubbles dusty yellow, the land reveals her ancient secrets to the questing camera of the drone. Dark lines, the memories of hedgerows long gone, spread out like the veins on the back of my father's hand.

As crop production increased, so hedges proliferated; they kept browsing wildlife out and gifted tender plants protection from the elements. Hedges acted as near-permanent boundaries, their permanency led to the fields being given names. What would Sheffield, Huddersfield or Enfield be without the hedge? Hedges became walls, delineating the ownership of land. When hedges grew too large and shaded out growing crops they were cut. If gaps appeared, enabling cattle or sheep to escape, they were filled by laid lengths. When the hedge got in

Andrew Smiley, *New thatch by Master Thatcher David Rackham at Grove Farm Barn, Bramfield,* 2012.

the way they were coppiced and hacked. But these hedgerow battlements were too massive by now to be removed by mere hand-tools. Trees were left behind and grew from saplings into towering elm or curlicued oak. The blackthorn suckers merely waited for a back to be turned to spring up and become a bank of scrub.

These ancients had no thought that their hedge planting and management was providing habitat for wildlife. The idea that our forebears were somehow more at one with nature is a nonsense. It is the fantasy of earnest middle-class, middle Englanders; those who turn to Extinction Rebellion and carve their own wooden spoons which they use to sup soya mush imported from halfway round the globe. The hedge is merely another example of man harnessing and mastering nature for his own ends. Plants such as hawthorn, blackthorn, field maple, hazel, dogwood and rose all happily grow cheek by jowl with one another. They are also precocious and forgiving enough to allow man to cut and trim them to his whim, growing and regrowing with a speed and thickness that suits our needs. It was mere happenstance that man's creation of the hedge suited wildlife, not due to any Anglo Saxon proto-conservationists. A mixed hedge plays nursery to tree and house sparrows, yellowhammers, linnets, robins, blackbirds, thrushes, wrens and tits both blue and great. Finches, be they green, chaf, gold or bull also rear their young in the crosswork of limbs.

The grey partridge and pheasant escape from raptors in its thorny understory and weave their ground nests in the hedgerow's lee. Shrews, mice and voles scurry and feed here. The hedgehog's very name screams its preferred habitat. Rabbits and rats tunnel amongst the roots, the stoats and weasels follow them to dance then feast on the squealing subterranean inhabitants. Deer shelter from the elements here and badgers build their cavernous setts, foxes take up residence when brock decides to evacuate. Invertebrates—beetles, aphids, bees, flies, wasps and mites—call the hedge home. All-comers may feast upon the fruits borne by the hedge in autumn. This man-made thing, created to keep cows and sheep in and wind and rain out is so much more than a barrier. If the woods are the lungs of the land, the hedgerows are the arteries. I love hedges.

Since 1945 landowners had been cajoled and funded, encouraged and primed to remove hedgerows. The livestock farmers had duly grubbed out the bullfinch and replaced it with barbed wire. In arable country, the hedges that remained were sad affairs. Filled with gaps, sparse remnants of old. Cut and smashed to sticks in the ground, barely clinging onto life, unloved and of little ecological value. However, in the early 1990s Whitehall called an about-turn. The value of the hedge was once more realised. Not now as a barrier, but as a priceless wildlife habitat. Government grants were now made available for planting kilometre upon kilometre of new hedges, frequently in the very places where the previous government's grants had paid to rip out miles upon miles of old hedgerows. The landscape of Suffolk has, over the past twenty-five years or so, become lined with hedging whips, guarded with hare and deer proof plastic spirals. The new plantings grew, their trunks restricted by their plastic tubes and bare of growth. What should have been hedges became linear rows of lollipops. The upper boughs gave security to some of the birdlife that had so long missed the hedgerows. Yet these replacement hedgerows were of no use to the grey partridges or wild pheasants. The small mammals, the voles and dormice, hedgehogs and wood-mice found no shelter here, exposed as they were to predators. The wind and rain could whip through these new havens, that were in truth no haven at all, an umbrella frame with no canvas. To remedy these failings is my lot. The hedge-layer was once the man who renovated the old. Today I am the man who makes good the new. Ninety per cent of the hedges I lay or coppice have been planted within the past twenty years. This is to be celebrated; the hedge has become a thing of veneration once more, a good hedge is as much of a mark of a good farmer as is his yield per hectare.

FRANCIS YOUNG

Royal Bury St Edmunds *(2021)*

Dr Francis Young, who was born in Bury St Edmunds, is a historian specializing in the history of religion and belief. He is the author, editor or co-author of eighteen books. He is interested in how history illuminates the nature of belief and in the intersections between religion, folklore, magic and other forms of supernatural belief.

The question 'Where did they bury St Edmund?' is an old pub quiz joke—the answer being, of course, virtually the same as the question: Bury St Edmunds. As Beodericsworth, the town of Bury St Edmunds pre-dates the cult of St Edmund, but in the tenth century the shrine gave the town a new identity—and, most importantly, a royal identity. From the moment the body of St Edmund was taken from the location of the king's martyrdom and placed in the old wooden church of St Mary, Bury became important to the self-image of England's kings. The House of Wessex sought to unify England under the same title Edmund had claimed for himself, *Rex Anglorum*. King Æthelstan named one of his sons Edmund; and that Edmund, when he himself succeeded as king of England, made a crucial grant of privileges to St Edmund's shrine in 945. Yet while St Edmund consistently attracted the favour of England's kings, Bury's saint also acquired a reputation for holding monarchs to account. It was this characteristic of the saint that played an important role in the early development of ideas of constitutional government.

King Edmund I's grant of the *banleuca* (the traditional boundary of the town) was the first of many royal benefactions to Bury St Edmunds, the greatest of which was the foundation of a Benedictine monastery to staff St Edmund's shrine in around 1020. Yet the abbey's royal founder, the Anglo-Danish King Cnut, may have acted as much from fear as from magnanimity. Four years earlier Cnut's father, Swein, had suffered a sudden death when he threatened to tax the people of Bury—killed, it was rumoured, by the lance of a spectral St Edmund executing judgement on the presumptuous Swein. The killing of Swein would go on to become Edmund's best-known miracle, ensuring that royal patronage of the great abbey was always tinged with threat. Virtually every medieval monarch, from Edward the Confessor to Henry VII, made at least one pilgrimage to Bury St Edmunds (and often several), but St Edmund was no mute patron of English royalty. Edmund demanded recognition of his rights. From the beginning he was viewed not only as a royal saint but as a patron and protector of the English people, as the antiphon for his feast proclaimed: *Ave rex gentis Anglorum*, 'Hail, king of the English people!'

The Norman monarchs displayed conspicuous veneration for St Edmund, compensating for their lack of Englishness by seeking to recruit the support of England's patron saint. Indeed, Bury was the only English abbey in the reign of William the Conqueror to own lands in Normandy, rather than vice versa. But one English king, John, failed to show the proper honour due to the saint. On his first visit to Bury, John failed to bring an offering for St Edmund; instead, he presented an embroidered cloth borrowed from the monks. John then refused to ratify the election of Hugh of Northwold as abbot. Hugh, determined to hold John to account, hosted a gathering of barons at the abbey in October 1214. According to the chronicler Roger of Wendover, the barons swore an oath at the high altar to compel King John to confirm a great charter of liberties for the barons and commons of England. On 10 June 1215 the barons fulfilled their oath when John affixed his seal to Magna Carta at Runnymede—and that very day, Abbot Hugh cornered the king in the meadow to secure royal confirmation of his election; a final humiliation for a king who had failed to respect the liberties of St Edmund.

Other monarchs proved wiser than John. In 1290 the fearsome Edward I awoke from a terrifying dream in which St Edmund threatened to make him a second Swein if he failed to restore Bury's privileges. Accordingly, Edward sent his banner to touch the shrine of St Edmund and went to war against the Scots under Edmund's patronage. In 1296 Edward declared his final victory over the Welsh at a Parliament in Bury. Yet no king was more devoted to St Edmund than the unfortunate Henry VI, who stayed at the abbey between Christmas 1433 and Easter 1434. The monk-poet John Lydgate presented Henry with a splendid memento of his visit, an illuminated copy of *The Lives of Saints Edmund and Fremund*, which still survives in the British Library and shows the young king praying at the shrine of St Edmund.

In 1486 Henry VII became the last monarch to visit the shrine of St Edmund, giving thanks for his victory over Richard III at Bosworth Field. But the abbey's royal history was not yet quite over. In 1533 the abbey church witnessed the royal funeral of Henry VIII's youngest sister Mary, dowager queen of France. It is said that Mary's burial in the abbey church almost tempted her brother to spare it, and that he contemplated erecting Bury as a cathedral like the abbeys of Peterborough and Gloucester. In the event, the dissolution proceeded and Queen Mary was reinterred in St Mary's Church. But whereas other monastic houses were quickly sold off to local landowners, Bury remained a royal possession for some time. The stone from the abbey was taken to be used in the construction of a series of new forts, designed to withstand artillery, which Henry VIII was building on the south coast.

The dissolution brought an end to royal pilgrimages to St Edmund's shrine. But the idea that monarchs could and should be held to account by the people endured—an idea that arguably had its germ in St Edmund's slaying of the

MS illumination of Henry VI praying at the shrine of St Edmund in 1433 from John Lydgate's *Lives of Saints Edmund and Fremund*, British Library MS Harley 2278, fol. 4v.

presumptuous Swein and found its earliest formal expression in Magna Carta, which was the fulfilment of the oath sworn by the barons at St Edmund's high altar. In 1970 a pageant performed in the Abbey Gardens for the 1100th anniversary of Edmund's martyrdom linked St Edmund and Magna Carta with Thomas Paine's *Rights of Man*, with the American Revolution, and even with the struggle against Communism. While these connections may be tenuous and remote, it is nevertheless true that St Edmund was a saint with an unusually complex relationship with royalty; distinctive features of his cult helped preserve and foster ideas of royal accountability that ultimately ushered in modern Britain's constitutional monarchy.

The Other Side of Suffolk (2021)

Born in Mississippi, USA, Carla Cooper Carlisle has been a political activist, teacher, journalist, restaurateur and writer. For many years she wrote a regular 'Spectator' column in Country Life *magazine.*

When I came to Wyken as a bride I did not look out onto the vast landscape and big skies and say to myself 'Halleluja! Home on the Range!'

I did not gaze up at the chimneys of the sugar-beet factory in Bury St Edmunds, the sky-high landmark nine miles north of the farm, and feel the awe that pilgrims felt as they saw cathedrals in the distance. I took my time. I did what Southern women are taught by their grandmothers: I practised an 'intelligent silence'.

Although I lived in Putney I had visited Suffolk lots of times. That is to say: one side of Suffolk. I went to operas at Snape, walked the shingle beach at Aldeburgh, braved the cold water in the grey North Sea. I attended concerts in the church in Blythburgh, I knew Walberswick and Thorpeness and Southwold. I ate Dover sole at the Butley Oysterage in Orford and I met people who had known Benjamin Britten and Peter Pears and told such good stories that I felt like I'd known them too. I had an early edition of *Suffolk Scene*, Julian Tennyson's one book, and hummed at the words 'Everyone wants to lie in his own country: this is mine, I shall feel safe if I have the scream of the birds and the moan of the wind and the lapping of the water all round me, and the lonely woods and marshes I love so well.'

What I didn't understand: Tennyson's 'own' country was another country—East Suffolk, known for its beauty and wildness. Once upon a time, it was the poorer cousin of West Suffolk, home of the barley barons and wheat farmers, grand estates and stately homes: Ickworth, Euston Hall, the quirky and magnificent Elveden. In its isolation, wildness and poverty East Suffolk was another world: composers, actors, artists and writers. People who lived on the edge were drawn to the sea's edge. Bohemian, beautiful and brave.

It took a while to understand the divide. Of course I knew divided lands: I was born and raised at the dead end of the Mason-Dixon line, the North-South divide that was as alive in 1965 as it was in 1865. On a summer day I could survey the acres of sugar beet, shade my eyes and swear I was looking out at rows of cotton. Even the land was as flat as the Delta. I knew I wasn't living in the Sahara of the Bozart but I hankered after the vision of the Henry Moore sculpture in the distance between the acts of *Peter Grimes*.

Slowly I began to accept the divide. Even the land on the farm was two countries. There's the boulder clay, known in these parts as Man's Land: heavy, unyielding, able to defeat the blades of a plough in dry spells, rutted as swampland in wet winters.

Then there is Boy's Land: light, sandy, an ecological world apart. In hot summers every crop that is planted on these light fields bakes and dies. In this small country of 1,000 acres, the soils are as territorial as Israelis and Palestinians. Nowhere do they merge to form a neutral patch of earth but remain as emphatic as old enemies.

Over time I learned how to reach down and stick my fingers in the earth, checking the moisture beneath the dry crumbled surface. And over time I began to love this side of Suffolk. Looking out onto a field of barley blowing in the wind, seeing the seagulls behind the plough, is like owning a canvas by Harry Becker. Watching the combines gliding across fields into the night, machines the size of North Sea oil platforms, stops me in my tracks as if I was witnessing a Christo installation.

This side of Suffolk would now struggle to claim its identity as the more 'authentic' Suffolk, the land of Becker and *Akenfield*. 'Farming community' is a wistful memory since almost no one tills the soil in this machine age, but look inside a village church on the day of a funeral and every pew is filled. There is a sense of place and it is timeless. For now.

As for the inferiority complex of West Suffolk harboured during the Culture versus Agriculture days, I reckon we are over that now. Maybe it started when a cottage on west side became half the price of a cottage on the east side, but now the artists and writers have begun to settle here. We don't have Snape and the lapping of water but each summer there is a country music festival at Euston that I love. It's more B.B. King and Elvis than Britten and Pears but I love it. As they say on this side of Suffolk: *you can take a donkey travellin' but it won't come back a horse.*

ROD THOMSON

Master Hugh and the Bury Bible *(2021)*

Rod Thomson is Emeritus Professor of Medieval History at the University of Tasmania. He has written on the libraries of Bury St Edmunds and St Albans abbeys, on the Benedictine scholar-historian William of Malmesbury, and has made descriptive catalogues of the manuscripts at Lincoln, Hereford and Worcester Cathedrals, and at Merton College, Oxford.

Around the year 1130 the great Benedictine abbey at Bury St Edmunds was in a state of healthy turmoil. The rebuilding of the ancient church on a huge scale must have turned it largely into a building-site. Its ambitious, cosmopolitan abbot, the Italian Anselm (1121–48), together with the abbey's most senior monks, spear-headed a project which, as well as the gigantic building, involved new bronze doors, bells for the crossing tower, and the provision of many books and smaller but precious ornaments.

Most of this was swept away by Henry VIII, if not earlier, and now there exist only the ruins of the main building (like a group of large sand-castles, as a friend once told me), some of the books and a seal-matrix. But among the books is one of the greatest artistic objects from the romanesque period: a mammoth bible now known as the Bury Bible. Measuring 525 × 350 mm, this is not the largest surviving medieval book—the Winchester Bible for one is a good deal larger—but it is among the comparatively small number of which each opening (i.e. double-page) must have comprised one single, trimmed calf-skin. Even this is not complete. Only the first volume, containing the Old Testament books less the Psalter, remains, the second volume having been cut up, apparently in the sixteenth century, for use in the bindings of printed books. And within the surviving volume, six framed miniatures, in bright, rich colours and gold, survive of an original twelve, plus forty-two initials in colours and gold, of an original forty-four.

All this was the work of a single outstanding artist, named Master Hugh. He is the only artist before the Italian renaissance who was commemorated for the quality of his work. At the abbey, a late thirteenth-century chronicle, known as the *Gesta Sacristarum* ('The Deeds of the Sacrists') tells us that Hervey, sacrist under Abbot Anselm and brother of Prior Talbot, 'underwrote the cost of writing a great bible for his brother the prior and arranged for it to be incomparably decorated by the hand of Master Hugh. As Hugh was unable to find any suitable vellum in these parts, he bought parchment in Scotland.' In a fifteenth-century register from the abbey a list of benefactors mentions the bible commissioned by Talbot and Hervey: '[Ringing of the bells] for sacrist Hervey ... who met all the expenses of his brother Talbot, then prior, for the great Bible copied for the refec-

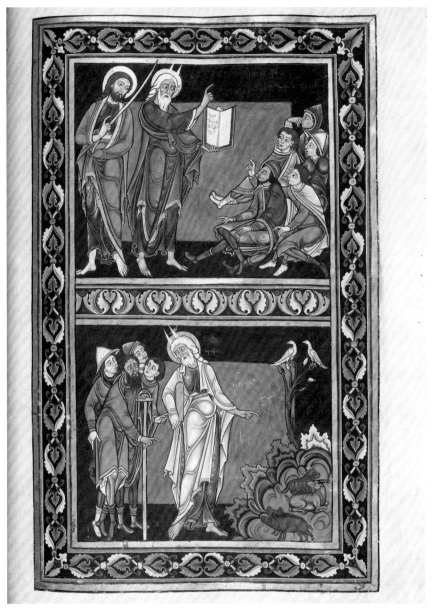

Frontispiece to *Deuteronomy*. Folio 94 from the Bury Bible St Edmundsbury Cathedral,
Bury St Edmunds.

tory in two volumes.' The refectory was where the monks ate, their meals accompanied by readings from sacred texts. Other references to Master Hugh credit him
with other works. Again in the *Gesta*, a project instituted by the sacrists Hervey and
Ralph is named: 'Also the double doors at the front of the church, carved by the

hands of Master Hugh, who as he surpassed all others in his other works, in this wondrous work surpassed himself.' And Abbot Anselm is said to have been the patron of this work. In the *Gesta* once more, of Ralph's sucessor sacrist Helyas, nephew of Abbot Anselm's successor Ording (1148–56): 'He had the cross in the choir with Mary and John carved incomparably by the hand of Master Hugh'. Finally, another manuscript from the abbey preserves verses from one of the bells in the church's crossing tower: 'On the bell called Hugh's: This glorious object commissioned by the Martyr Edmund / This gift paid for by Anselm, Hugh's hand prepares for founding.'

There are two remarkable features of this material: firstly, that the abbey held the artist in such esteem centuries after his lifetime, and secondly, that he is shown to have been a versatile professional, capable of metalwork on both larger and smaller scale, cast and carved, as well as of painting in books. And there is more: his style connects him with work done in Canterbury Cathedral: the mural of St Paul being bitten by a viper, in the chapel of St Anselm, probably by his own hand.

But where did he come from, and what were the main influences upon him? These questions have so far proved impossible to answer, but now some clues move us forward. He was obviously strongly influenced by Byzantine painting, at first hand rather than through other western 'Byzantinizing' works such as had already appeared in Burgundy and southern Italy. In both colours, style and iconography, the murals in the little Cyprus church of Asinou, done by a great artist doubtless from Constantinople are, as another friend put it to me, 'like being inside the Bury Bible'. And recently, scientific examination has revealed alphabetical letters underneath the Bible's paintings, there to guide the painter in the colours to be used: A, P, B, X and Φ. The last two, the meaning of which is unclear, have been held to show Greek influence. That said, the materials used by Hugh for the colours, and the method of applying them, are thoroughly western. Incidentally, the guide-letters probably show that Master Hugh allowed members of his atelier to paint in the ground colours, while he himself added the shading and other surface detail. Certainly the doors and bell would have needed a team of workmen to make them.

The Bible's monumental script was done by a single scribe who may or may not have been Hugh himself. The lesser painted initials, in the style of Bury's own scriptorium, may have been executed by two men. They are the only features of the book that show the influence of the locality in and for which it was made. Previous famous books made at the abbey, decorated by the 'Alexis Master' who also worked at St Albans, do not seem to have influenced Master Hugh. Equally, his subsequent influence was profound and widespread, but it was not particularly felt at the abbey itself. He was, after all, just passing through.

AMICIA DE MOUBRAY

Ickworth (2021)

Amicia de Moubray is a journalist and editor specialising in architecture, heritage and interiors. She is co-author with David Black of Carpets for the Home *and author of* Twentieth Century Castles in Britain.

'The House, the House, the House!' wrote Frederick Hervey, Bishop of Derry and 4th Earl of Bristol, to his daughter, from his sick bed in Naples in 1796. Ickworth, Suffolk, is surely one of the most eccentric of all English country houses.

In a county that rejoices in a wealth of venerable medieval houses, many of them romantically moated and built of mellow red brick, the imposing neo-classical stuccoed, pillared and domed rotunda flanked by two extensive quadrant wings is an extraordinary sight.

Sadly, the Earl-Bishop, who spent much of his life away from Suffolk, did not see the first stone being laid, and nor did he live to see his house completed. When he died, just the lower tier and part of the upper tier were completed and the wings had not risen above three or four feet.

A highly individual character, hailing from notoriously wacky stock, the Earl-Bishop (1730-1803) was described by his contemporary and political rival Lord Charlemont as 'more brilliant than solid. His family was indeed famous for talents, equally so for eccentricity, and the eccentricity of the whole race shone out and seemed to be concentrated in him.'

He lived a life of remarkable contrasts. He lived from time to time in Ireland, as Bishop firstly of Cloyne (1767), a remote area of Co. Cork, and subsequently of Derry (1768). Both appointments were procured by his elder brother, the 2nd Earl, Lord Lieutenant of Ireland. During extensive sojourns in Ireland and also in Germany he collected works of art as he travelled. The many Bristol hotels are named after him. He visited Italy six times between 1765 and his death in 1803. But he never spent very long in Suffolk, the county where his family had resided since the fifteenth century.

However, in 1792 he came to Ickworth, which he had not visited for ten years, to choose a site to build a new house. Ten years before, he had brought in Capability Brown to produce 'Plans and elevations for an Intire New House'. Sadly, these plans have not survived. He chose a site at Acworth, northwards of the old manor house near the church, before departing for the Continent, never to return.

Like that other great eighteenth-century eccentric, William Beckford, the Earl-Bishop poured money into grandiose building projects and collecting. He derived his wealth by shrewdly increasing the renewal fines on the leases of the

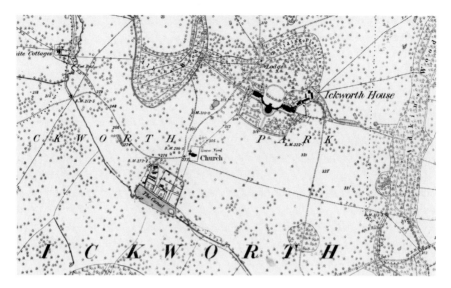

diocesan estate of Derry from £7,000 to £20,000 a year from the staggering 70,000 acres of land attached to the bishopric.

The Earl-Bishop had already built a substantial mansion at Downhill in Co. Londonderry in 1775 and another at Ballyscullion in 1787, a house similar to Ickworth with a central oval and flanking wings. Ballyscullion was dismantled in 1813. The ruins were known as the 'Bishop's Folly'.

His love of oval buildings might have been linked with the preponderance of round towered churches to be found in Suffolk. But the truth is that he was influenced by Belle Isle, an elegant round house designed by John Plaw on an island in Lake Windermere in 1776.

The Irish architect Francis Sandys exhibited plans for Ickworth at the Royal Academy in 1797, drawing on designs executed earlier in Italy by Mario Asprucci. Sandys with his brother, Joseph, had already worked for the Earl-Bishop at Ballyscullion.

Settled in Suffolk, Sandys subsequently had several commissions in and around Bury St Edmunds, including the façade and vestibule of the Athenaeum, Finborough Hall, and is also believed to have designed Worlingham Hall, near Beccles.

Work on Ickworth started in 1795. It must have been extraordinarily difficult to work for such an opinionated patron as the distant Earl-Bishop. Francis's brother, Joseph, constructed a papier-mâché model of the house on the scale of one inch to twelve feet, which was sent out to Italy.

Ickworth was to be a museum and art gallery on a truly megalomaniac scale—600ft long, the central oval 120ft × 106ft, and the library 78ft × 30ft. Each wing was to consist of a vestibule opening into a gallery 100ft long and occupying the full height, some 30ft. The whole ensemble was to be nearly twice the size of

Ballyscullion. There was a practical element to the vast scale. 'My lungs always played more freely, my spirit spontaneously rose much higher in lofty rooms than in low ones when the atmosphere is too much tainted with … our own bodies, & also for the sake of throwing my attick-storey (is possible) into St. Paul's 3rd Heaven,' the Earl-Bishop wrote to his friend John Symonds.

He intended to live in the rotunda and use the wings as galleries for his works of art. Again to Symonds he wrote: 'I wish to unite magnificence with convenience and simplicity with dignity—no redundancy—no superfluity—no one unnecessary room.'

During his prodigious Continental travels he had accrued an impressive collection of paintings. Dismissive of contemporary galleries—'in general both confused and uninstructive'—his striking vision was for 'my galleries to exhibit an historical progress of the art of Painting both in Germany and Italy. Mine by classing the authors under the different schools, will show the characteristic Excellence of each, instruct the young mind and edify the old.

Venice – Coloring, Titian
Bologna – Composition, Guido
Roman – Sentiment, Rafael
Florence – Drawing M. Angelo
Naples – Extravagance, Salvator Rosa, Polimea …?'

Alas, it was never to be. His collection was confiscated by Napoleonic troops in Rome in 1798. He was then imprisoned in Milan for nine months. In vain the Earl-Bishop spent the last few years of his life trying to retrieve his possessions. A petition was signed by 323 artists living in Rome calling for the release of the collections but it came to nothing.

'He is one of the greatest curiosities alive,' writes the Irish Catherine Wilmot in a letter home from Rome in 1803. Shortly after the Earl-Bishop met a sorry end—dying of gout on the road to Albano in the outhouse of a cottage of an Italian farmer who would not admit the heretic prelate into his house.

The final twist in the curious tale of this larger than life character is that when his coffin was being shipped back to the family vault at Ickworth it had to be disguised as the packing case for an antique statue.

In 1804 a fifty-foot tall obelisk in memory of the Earl-Bishop was erected by the inhabitants of Londonderry. Ickworth is now a property of the National Trust.

Reading Gardner's History (2021)

Simon Loftus (former President of Southwold Museum) is the author of several books on social history.

T H E Study of *Antiquity* being generally agreeable to the Difpofition of many ingenious People, I have prefumed to publifh this fmall Tract of fome Places, efpecially the once famous CITY of D U N W I C H, which will afford Speculation fufficient to ruminate on the Viciffitude, and Inftability of fublunary Things.

That wonderful sentence, reminiscent of the seventeenth-century Norfolk polymath Sir Thomas Browne, opens the Preface to Thomas Gardner's *Historical Account of Dunwich, Blithburgh, Southwold*, published in 1754. This masterpiece of local history quotes from numerous documents that have long since vanished and explores byways of social history that are recorded nowhere else. It prompts the 'Speculation' that Gardner loved.

I speculate, first of all, on Gardner himself. Who was this extraordinary man? Born in 1690, he first appears in the records in 1729, when he was appointed Town Constable. The municipal offices followed in swift succession—Deputy Controller of the Port of Southwold, Sergeant at Arms, Fen Reeve, Member of the Assembly, Inspector of the Work-House and Salt Tax Officer. In 1756 he was elected Churchwarden and the following year was one of the Bailiffs of Southwold. Two years later he was appointed Chamberlain, responsible for keeping the town accounts. So this was a capable and highly respected man, trusted by his fellow townsmen, or at least by those who controlled the affairs of the Borough.

Gardner was also a down-to-earth person, with fingers in many pies, as was typical of the time. Described as a 'joiner' for much of his life, he supplied building materials for the church, repaired the town windmill and seems to have acted in some respects as an undertaker. On several occasions there were payments to Gardner for making coffins and to his second wife Molly for making shifts—probably shrouds. Like most who could afford it, he also owned a share in a boat—the sloop *John & Sarah*.

These glimpses suggest a practical man, perhaps the equivalent of a local builder, but there was another side to him, the scholar and historian. In 1745, he exhibited 'A true and exact plate, containing the boundaries of the town of Dunwich, and the entries of certain records and evidences' at the Society of Antiquar-

The Salt Tax Office, in a drawing by Hamlet
Watling, 1848, and photographed in 1903.

ies in London. This was the first public evidence of what became his consuming
passion—a history of his town and locality.

It must have been about this time that Gardner was appointed the Salt Tax
Officer. It was a position of some importance when the tax on salt was a significant stream of government revenue, and it demanded rigorous integrity. Salt des-
tined for the fishing fleet was exempt from the tax, so Gardner needed a watchful
eye to ensure that John May, owner of the Southwold salt works, wasn't fiddling
his books and selling tax-free salt for domestic use.

The Salt Tax office was in a building on South Green—originally constructed
as a small hospital for sick and wounded seamen in the aftermath of the Battle
of Sole Bay. A drawing by Hamlet Watling, dated 1848, depicts the building as it
originally appeared, and a photo of 1903 shows the truncated remnant, shortly
before it was demolished and the seventeenth-century coats of arms were incor-
porated in its replacement, The Cottage.

Gardner's role became increasingly important after 1750, when Southwold
was chosen as the headquarters of the Free British Fishery, established by Act of
Parliament. The object was to revive the nation's fishing industry and compete
with the Dutch, our long-standing rivals for dominance of the European herring
markets. £500,000 was voted for the endeavour, equivalent to almost £100 million in modern money.

Wharves and warehouses, a net house, tan office, cooper's workshop and a
row of cottages in Church Street were built for this new venture, and the entrance
to Southwold's harbour was improved by the completion of two piers. Fifty large
busses (broad-beamed herring boats) were constructed and fitted out, and the Salt
Works vastly increased its production.

We can guess that the increased responsibilities of his role may have allowed

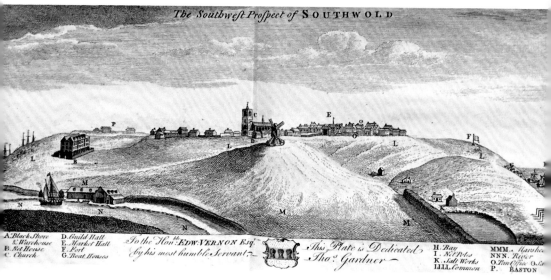

The Southwest Prospect of SOUTHWOLD

A. Black Shore   D. Guild Hall
&. Warehouse   E. Market Hall
B. Net House   F. Fort
C. Church   G. Boat Houses

To the Hon.ble EDW. VERNON Esq.
by his most humble Servant

This Plate is Dedicated
Tho.s Gardner

H. Bay   MMM. Marshes
I. Net Polls   NNN. River
K. Salt Works   O. Pan Office O. &c
LLLL. Common   P.   BASTON

Thomas Gardner, 'The Southwest Prospect of Southwold', 1754.

Gardner to employ a clerk to undertake much of the work, leaving him time to pursue his researches as an historian, because the project that he had embarked on required an extraordinary amount of research—transcribing and summarising documents, examining buildings and ruins for traces of their past, collecting coins and curiosities and fossils, many of which he engraved as illustrations. It was a stupendous labour and Gardner was duly grateful to those who had made it possible.

He published his masterpiece in 1754 and dedicated it to the Harbour Commissioners. It was financed by a long list of subscribers, headed by the 'His late Highness, Frederick Prince of Wales'—the first Governor of the Free British Fishery. Gardner's engraving of 'The Southwest Prospect of Southwold', which accompanied his history, showed all the new developments that the Fishery had brought to the town.

The book itself is elegantly printed (with occasionally erratic pagination) but it is clear that Gardner expected his readers to make notes in it, amplifying the text, because blank pages were bound in at frequent intervals, right from the start. In my own copy, those pages remain empty, as published, but in each of the four copies owned by Southwold Museum they have been annotated by later owners with additional information and two of these copies have been rebound, with numerous extra leaves inserted, together with engraved illustrations, printed handbills and other ephemera. The result is a fascinating resource for local historians.

Perhaps our most interesting copy is that which was formerly owned by Francis Henry Vertue (1822–1894) and Dudley Collings (1870–1955), both of whom were Southwold surgeons and antiquaries. Vertue was also a Borough Magistrate, 'well known for his convictions regarding justice and right', and Dudley Collings was the founding Curator of Southwold Museum.

Vertue extended Gardner's story into the nineteenth century, preserving ephemera that ranged from fierce polemics surrounding the reform of the Borough in 1835 to a newspaper cutting from March 1890, recording the death at ninety-three of the diarist James Maggs—and a bill for some bacon that Maggs bought a few years before his death. Maggs's *Southwold Diaries* (subsequently published by the Suffolk Records Society) are among our greatest treasures, but his own copy of Gardner's *History* (with 'numerous manuscript additions and annotations' and 'additional printed and manuscript tracts bound in') escaped our grasp. It came up for auction twenty years ago and fetched four times the high estimate. I should love to know where it can now be found.

As you can see, Gardner's own habit of digressions has rubbed off onto me as I write this article, but at the back of my mind, all the time, is the mystery of the man himself, a question that remains unanswered. We know that he lived in a house in Park Lane, we know that he worked in the Salt Tax office on South Green, and we know that he died at the age of seventy-nine, on 30 March 1769, and was buried in Southwold churchyard between his two wives, Rachel and Mary. *Betwixt honour and virtue here doth lie, The remains of old antiquity.* But that beautiful phrase which I quoted at the beginning—that his book 'will inform Speculation sufficient to ruminate on the Vicissitude, and Instability of sublunary things'— continues to haunt me. Who was this man—on the one hand so practical and competent, on the other so buried in dusty documents and past history—yet capable of writing those words—words which seem to echo Thomas Browne and anticipate W.G. Sebald?

That sense of a thread through time is embodied in the tale of a strange discovery (an echo of Browne's *Urne-Buriall*) with which Gardner ends his account of Dunwich.

'Within the walls of the Grey Friars at Dunwich, a Labourer discovered a small earthen Vessel, which he thinking contained Treasure, broke into Shreds. On the Top of it was a flat Piece of Brass, with the dimension of and Inscription on this Figure.' The 'figure' is an engraving by Gardner of a medieval ring brooch, with an undecipherable inscription on one side and, on the other, the words *Ave Maria Gracia Plena* (Hail Mary full of Grace). And he adds an intriguing note, without explanation, that 'The heart of Dame *Hawise Poynings* was reposited at this Place.'

It reads like a mystery, a brief glimpse of an unrecoverable past, but in 2004 this same bronze brooch reappeared at auction, together with a copy of Gardner's History. It had been handed down from one Suffolk antiquary to another, lovingly cherished, until it was sold for £3,000.

IAN COLLINS

From the Punjab to Elveden:
the Poignant Story of Duleep Singh (2021)

Ian Collins is a writer and curator. His books include three surveys of East Anglian art which, together with many cultural features in the Eastern Daily Press, *led to his landmark exhibitions* Masterpieces: Art and East Anglia *and* Fabergé from St Petersburg to Sandringham *at the Sainsbury Centre in Norwich. He lives in Southwold.*

Improvements to the A11 have meant an end to the once-common snarl-ups at the Elveden staggered crossroads. But, rather than hurrying by on the bypass, take the Elveden turning and pause in a perfectly preserved English feudal village where all is not what it seems.

The estate wedged against the Suffolk-Norfolk border near Thetford has been owned by the Earls of Iveagh since 1894. They made their fortune brewing Guinness in Ireland but their portion of East Anglia is much closer to India.

Today the churchyard may contain carloads or even coach parties of Asian families, the men in turbans and beards denoting the Sikh religion. For this is a place of pilgrimage for people from all over the world with roots in the Punjab.

A portrait painted in London, in 1854, shows a handsome mahajarah in fine silks and carrying a ceremonial sword. Amid ropes of pearls around his neck there is a miniature likeness of Queen Victoria, on her way to becoming Empress of India. It still hangs in her beloved Osborne House—a holiday palace on the Isle of Wight.

Born in 1838, Duleep Singh was the last Sikh ruler of the Punjab. The youngest son of Rani Jindan, 16th wife of Ranjit Singh, he had come to the throne aged five after a series of bloody coups eliminated every other contender.

He was promptly welcomed into Victoria's family circle, to the dismay of certain British grandees. (Much later, this colour-blind monarch would condemn as racist diplomatic protests over high-placed Indian staff in her household.)

In a symbolic gesture, Duleep Singh then presented the Koh-i-noor to Victoria. The fist-sized diamond had actually been surrendered after effective British annexation of the Sikh kingdom. Maybe he was well shot of it, for the great gem—now in the crown of the late Queen Mother and displayed in the Tower of London—is said to cast a curse on male owners.

Franz Xaver Winterhalter, *The Maharajah Duleep Singh*, 1854.
The portrait hangs in the Durbar Corridor at Osborne House.

Anyway, with a splendid pension from the India Office, the ousted king settled in style on the 17,000-acre Elveden Estate in 1863 (having viewed and rejected Sandringham). He married Bamba Müller, a part-German, part-Ethiopian who spoke only Arabic.

The Black Prince of Elveden spent wildly—creating a marble-clad, semi-oriental palace for his growing family, hosting splendid shooting parties for the Prince of Wales and rebuilding the village church, school and estate cottages until the money ran out. Victoria was forced to distance herself from her friend when the India Office refused her requests to bail him out.

An aggrieved Duleep Singh then renounced Christianity and tried to reclaim his kingdom. He was stopped at Aden (today's Yemen), where the Indian administration's authority then began. He sent his family back to Elveden (his wife dying soon afterwards) but chose exile for himself in Paris.

Here the royal refugee entered a world of labyrinthine intrigue. At one point he went to Russia, having had his pocket picked en route by a British agent. He envisaged a Russo-Afghan force invading India, sparking a Sikh revolt and supported by a Fenian rebellion in Ireland. Bengalis were to sabotage the railways and Egyptian nationalists to cut off the Suez Canal.

The elaborate conspiracy unravelled. Broke and broken, Duleep Singh returned to Paris, where he suffered a massive stroke. He had planned to marry his companion Ada Weatherill, who had borne him two children but may also have been a British spy.

Loyal friends in Britain, blaming all the plotting on a bout of madness, arranged a final meeting with Victoria, who was holidaying in Nice. According to the queen, a highly emotional encounter saw the dying Duleep Singh collapsing in tears and begging forgiveness.

His son, Prince Frederick, brought his body back to Elveden, for burial in 1893. Victoria and the Prince of Wales sent wreaths to the funeral.

Prince Freddy was a noted archaeologist and antiquarian, and also an unswerving monarchist. He lived at the moated Blo Norton Hall, near Thetford, where a portrait of Oliver Cromwell was hung upside down in the lavatory.

LUKE WRIGHT

A12

From *The Toll* (2017)

Luke Wright is a poet and broadcaster. His poetry stage shows have toured the world and played sold-out runs in London and Edinburgh. He is a regular contributor to BBC Radio and his verse documentary on Channel 4 was nominated for a Grierson Award. His first collection, Mondeo Man, *was published in 2013. His first play,* What I Learned from Johnny Bevan, *won a Fringe First Award, The Stage Award for Acting Excellence and the Saboteur Award for Best Spoken Word Show. He lives in Suffolk.*

A12

England's crude appendix scar,
The Essex/Suffolk artery,
salt-baked, potholed, chocked with cars
across the Orwell, Colne and Lea,
The Romans' great, paved Inter V.

From Blackwall mouth to Breydon Water,
worlds away from London noise,
the Orbital's delinquent daughter,
friend to suits in souped-up toys
and woodchip-larynxed good ol' boys.

Where Witham trees are linocuts
against an endless swirl of blues,
where rat-faced booners slice you up
and eighteen-wheelers rumble-snooze
en route to Brussels, Bonn or Bruges.

Worst road in Britain, so they say,
a dim-lit strip of late-night truth.
You'll never be a motorway;
your tar tattoos are too uncouth,
ground down for years by tyre and hoof.

But I will have you, ruts and all;
your grey macadam's in my bone.
You take me from the fug and sprawl
to Suffolk's icy brine and foam:
you take me home.

Charlie Mackesy, *Suffolk*, 2021.

Charlie Mackesy is an artist, cartoonist, book illustrator and author of The Boy, The Mole, The Fox and The Horse. *He lives in Walberswick.*

ACKNOWLEDGEMENTS

Every effort has been made to trace or contact copyright holders. The editors would like to thank all the contributors who have given their work so generously.

'Navigating Home', © Karin Altenberg 2021.

Maxwell Armfield, *Double Concerto at Snape*, 1969, © The Bridgeman Art Library / the artist's estate. Reproduced by permission of Britten Pears Arts.

'Jocelin of Brakelond', © Richard Barber 2021.

The Muck Cart, c. 1913 by Harry Becker. Reproduced by permission of the Victoria and Albert Museum, London.

'The Christmas Market' from *Corduroy*, 1930, © the Estate of Adrian Bell. Reproduced by permission of Faber & Faber Ltd.

The Famous Dyed Sheep at the 2019 Latitude Festival. Photo credit: Guy Bell / Alamy Stock Photo.

'The Thornham Parva Retable' from *A Guide to the Thornham Parva Retable*, 2003, © Paul Binski. Reproduced by permission of Parochial Church Council for St Mary Magdalene, Thornham Magna and St Mary's, Thornham Parva.

Black Shuck, The Picture Art Collection / Alamy Stock Photo.

'Searching for Doggerland', extract from *Time Song* by Julia Blackburn. © Julia Blackburn, 2019. Extract reproduced by permission of The Random House Group Ltd.

'The Cricket Match' from *The Easternmost House*, 2019, © Juliet Blaxland. Reproduced by permission of Sandstone Press.

'Staverton Thicks' from *The Time by the Sea*, 2013, © Ronald Blythe. Reproduced by permission of Faber & Faber Ltd.

'One Shell Wide' from *The Shingle Street Shell Line*, 2018, © Els Bottema and Lida Kindersley. Reproduced by permission of the Cardozo Kindersley Workshop.

Introduction and 'Thorpeness Scrapbook', © Craig Brown 2021.

Frontispiece to *Deuteronomy*. Folio 94 from the Bury Bible, St Edmundsbury Cathedral, Bury St Edmunds. Reproduced by permission of the Parker Library, Corpus Christi College, Cambridge.

Photograph of James Cable, reproduced by permission of Aldeburgh Museum Charitable Trust.

Extract 'New Neighbours' from *Worth* by Jon Canter. © Jon Canter, 2011, published by Vintage. Extract reproduced by permission of The Random House Group Ltd.

'The Other Side of Suffolk', © Carla Carlisle 2021.

Staverton Oaks, monoprint drypoint etching, © Derek Chambers 2021.

Fishing Boats in Memoriam, 2021, pencil and wash drawing by Caroline McAdam Clark, © Caroline McAdam Clark. Reproduced by permission of the artist.

Snooks, pen and watercolour illustration from *Another Year of Plumdog* by Emma Chichester Clark. © Emma Chichester Clark, 2014, published by Jonathan Cape. Extract reproduced by permission of The Random House Group Ltd.

'The Other Side of the Alde' from *Tribute to Benjamin Britten on his Fiftieth Birthday*, 1963, © the Estate of Kenneth Clark. Reproduced by permission of Faber & Faber Ltd and the Estate of Kenneth Clark c/o The Hanbury Agency Ltd, 27 Walcot Square, London SE11 4UB. All rights reserved.

Acknowledgements

'A World of its Own, the Lowestoft Fish Market', © Donny Cole 2021.

'From the Punjab to Elveden', © Ian Collins 2021.

Boat-Building near Flatford, 1815, by John Constable. Reproduced by permission of the Victoria and Albert Museum, London.

'Corder shooting Maria Marten', reproduced by permission of Stewart Evans.

Town Fox at his Favourite Puddle, photograph, © Frances Crickmore 2021.

'A Quiet Mind' from *The Breaking Hour*, 2015, © Kevin Crossley Holland. Reproduced by permission of Enitharmon Press.

Barn Interior, 2020, Indian ink on lining paper, © Alex Curry. Reproduced by permission of the artist.

'Ed Sheeran Drops Round', extract from the film screenplay *Yesterday* (2018) written by Jack Barth & Richard Curtis. Script editor Emma Freud © 2018 Working Title Films Limited. Reproduced by permission of Richard Curtis and Emma Freud.

Extract 'Swimming with Otters' from *Waterlog* by Roger Deakin. © Roger Deakin, 1999, published by Vintage. Extract reproduced by permission of The Random House Group Ltd.

Woodcut illustration *The Wild Man* from *The Wild Man of Orford*, 1995, © James Dodds. Reproduced by permission of Jardine Press Ltd.

The Creek Men, 2009, photograph, © Laurence Edwards. Reproduced by permission of the sculptor.

'The Martyrdom of St Edmund' from *Life, Passion, and Miracles of St Edmund, King and Martyr*. Purchased by J.P. Morgan (1867–1943) in 1927. Photographic credit: The Morgan Library & Museum, New York. Reproduced by permission of The Morgan Library & Museum. MS M.736, fol. 14r.

Foreword © Clare, Countess of Euston 2021.

'The Wisdom of the Bees' from *The Pattern under the Plough*, 1966, © the Estate of George Ewart Evans. Reproduced by permission of Faber & Faber Ltd.

'The Weighing of Souls: Saint Michael and the Devil', from the Wenhaston Doom, c.1500–1520. English School, (16th century). Photo credit: © Mark Fiennes Archive / Bridgeman Images.

'My Father's Arms', © Ralph Fiennes 2021.

Suffolk Estuary, dust-jacket illustration, © Jeff Fisher 2021.

'Not an Everyday Experience' from *The Bookshop*, © the Estate of Penelope Fitzgerald 1978. Reproduced by permission of HarperCollins Publishers Ltd.

Rose and Thistle, design for silk, 1859. Reproduced from *The Silk Family* by Liz Trenow by permission of Stephen Walters & Sons Ltd.

Frankel's name and pedigree reproduced by permission of Juddmonte Farms Ltd.

'A Summer Fête' from *The Sea House*, 2003, © Esther Freud. Reproduced by permission of Penguin Books Ltd.

Thomas Gainsborough, *Wooded Landscape with a Cottage and Shepherd*, 1748. Reproduced by permission of Yale Center for British Art, Paul Mellon Collection.

Winter Garden, 2006, © Annabel Gault.

'Nightscape' from *Under the Stars, a Journey into Light*, 2020, © Matt Gaw. Reproduced by permission of Elliott and Thompson.

Mr Thompson's Bees, ink drawing, © David Gentleman 2013. *Pagodas, Orford Ness*, lithograph, © David Gentleman 2007. Reproduced by permission of the artist. *The Yellow Digger from In the Country*, 2014, © David Gentleman. Reproduced by permission of Full Circle Editions.

Endpapers: Kessingland Footpath Map, © Wilfrid George. Reproduced by permission of Wilfrid George.

Burrow Hill, Towards Gedgrave Marshes, August 2008, oil on linen, © Kate Giles 2008.

'An Adventure', © Albert Grant 2021.

'Slow Passage, Low Prospect' from *The Casual Perfect*, 2011, © Lavinia Greenlaw. Reproduced by permission of Faber & Faber Ltd.

'Butley Creek' from *The Oyster Isles*, 2019, © Bobby Groves. Reproduced by permission of Hachette UK.

Image from *Orlando the Marmalade Cat, A Seaside Holiday by Kathleen Hale* © Kathleen Hale 1991, published by Frederick Warne.

Maggi Hambling, 'Remembering Benton End', from *Benton End Remembered*, compiled and edited by Gwynneth Reynolds and Diana Grace and first published by Unicorn Press in 2002. © 2002 The Cedric Morris Estate; the Lett Haines Estate; the compilers and contributors.

Lett Laughing, 1975–6, oil on board, and *The Ghost of Cedric Morris*, 1983, oil on canvas, © Maggi Hambling. Reproduced by permission of the artist.

'In Suffolk', from *Collected Poems*, 1998, © estate of Michael Hamburger. Reproduced by permission of Carcanet Press.

'Freedom is the only manner' from *Gainsborough*, 2017, © James Hamilton. Reproduced by permission of Weidenfeld & Nicolson.

Pink Birch and Stones, 2017, acrylic and oil on canvas, © Paul Hamlyn. Reproduced by permission of the artist.

Watching the Bidding and Taking Bids – Poultry and Game Auction, pencil drawings, © Jason Gathorne-Hardy 2004.

'Winter in Suffolk' from *The Stubborn Light of Things*, 2020, © Melissa Harrison. Reproduced by permission of Faber & Faber Ltd.

'A Suffolk Glossary' from *Sloightly on th' Huh!*, 2004, © Charlie Haylock. Reproduced by permission of Countryside Books.

'A Political Crisis for the Suffolk Punch', © Paul Heiney 1990.

'A Busy Morning in May', © Tom Hester 2021. Image screenshot, © Ship Finder. Reproduced by permission of Pink Froot.

'Dreaming of Murder' from *A Suspension of Mercy*, 1965, © the Estate of Patricia Highsmith. Reproduced by permission of Little, Brown Book Group Ltd, UK.

Illustration from *The Pillbox*, © David Hughes 2015. Reproduced by permission of The Random House Group Ltd.

'Sciapod', © Lucy Hughes-Hallett 2021.

The Human Fruit Machine, photo credit and © Mary James 2021.

Covehithe, photo credit and © Bill Jackson 2021.

'Superintendent Adam Dalgliesh in Suffolk' from *Unnatural Causes*, 1967, © the Estate of P.D. James. Reproduced by permission of Faber & Faber Ltd.

'A More Gentle Country', © Josephine 2021.

'Lady Eve Balfour', © William Kendall 2021.

'At Home in Suffolk', © India Knight 2021.

'A Late Frost', © Olivia Laing 2021.

Maidens on Marigolds, oil on canvas, © Ffiona Lewis 2020.

'Reading Gardner's History', © Simon Loftus 2021.

Installation view, Sarah Lucas, *Perceval*, Aldeburgh Festival, Suffolk, 2011, © Sarah Lucas, courtesy Sadie Coles HQ, London. Photo: © Philip Vile.

'The Suffolk Nightingale' from *The Barley Bird*, 2010, © Richard Mabey. Reproduced by permission of Full Circle Editions.

'A Government Inspector in Henry VIII's Suffolk' adapted from *Thomas Cromwell: a Life*, 2018, © Diarmaid MacCulloch. Reproduced by permission of the author.

Essay (adapted by author) entitled 'Sun Birds and Cashmere Spheres' taken from *Vesper Flights*, 2020, by Helen Macdonald. © Helen Macdonald, 2020, first published by Jonathan Cape. Extract reproduced by permission of The Random House Group Ltd.

'Orfordness' from *The Wild Places*, 2007, © Robert Macfarlane. Reproduced by permission of Granta Books.

'Sutton Hoo Helmet' from *A History of the World in 100 Objects* by Neil MacGregor, © the Trustees of the British Museum and the BBC, 2010, published by Allen Lane, 2010. Reproduced by permission of Penguin Books Ltd. ©

Suffolk, ink drawing, © Charlie Mackesy 2021.

Suffolk Gateway, photograph, © Eamonn McCabe 2018. Reproduced by permission of the photographer.

Poem 'Covehithe' taken from *Shingle Street* by Blake Morrison. © Blake Morrison 2015, published by Chatto & Windus. Extract reproduced by permission of The Random House Group Ltd.

'Ickworth', © Amicia de Moubray 2021.

Moving Up to the Start: Under Starter's Orders, Newmarket, c. 1937. Reproduced by permission the estate of Sir Alfred Munnings. © courtesy of the British Sporting Art Trust.

Waxing Moon, 2020, oil on linen, © Helen Napper.

Sketch of Framlingham Castle 1956 by John Nash, © the Estate of John Nash. Reproduced by permission of the owner Dr Stephen Lock CBE.

'A Love Letter to the Hedge' from *Words From the Hedge*, 2020, © Richard Negus. Reproduced by permission of the author.

Sweffling Church, 2019, oil on board, © Tessa Newcomb.

'Northgate Street', © John Norman 2021.

Extract 'The Saints' from *Warlight* by Michael Ondaatje. © Michael Ondaatje, 2018, published by Vintage. Extract reproduced by permission of The Random House Group Ltd.

'The Newmarket Sales' from *Tattersalls 250*, 2016, © Bill Oppenheim. Reproduced by permission of Tattersalls.

'On Constable' reproduced from *Spirit of Place: Artists, Writers and the British Landscape*, by Susan Owens, © 2020 Thames and Hudson Ltd.

Extract from *The Grit*, 1997, revised and updated 2019, © Dean Parkin and Jack Rose. Reproduced by permission of Corner Street.

'A Mutual Understanding', © Mayuri Patel 2021.

Walberswick Marshes, oil on canvas, © Sarah Muir Poland 2016.

Extract from *The Dig*, 2008, © John Preston 2007, published by Viking 2007, Penguin Books 2008, 2021. Reproduced by permission of Penguin Books Ltd.

Frontispiece, *Coronation Tickets* © Matt Pritchett 2021.

'Full Circle to Walberswick' © Libby Purves 2021.

'The Molecatcher's Daughter' from *Ruth Rendell's Suffolk*, 1989, © Kingsmarkham Enterprises Ltd. Reproduced by permission of Kingsmarkham Enterprises Ltd.

'Windsong' from *Semi-Detached*, 2006, © Griff Rhys Jones. Reproduced by permission of Penguin Random House UK.

'Blythburgh Angel' photograph from *The Angel Roofs of East Anglia*, 2015, © Michael Rimmer. Reproduced by permission of The Lutterworth Press.

'Spring' and 'On Time', © Robin Robertson 2021. Reproduced by permission of the author.

The Sparrow Nest Barrow Boys, photograph reproduced by permission of The Jack Rose Collection.

'Heading for the Beach' from *The Great Godden* 2020, © Meg Rosoff. Reproduced by permission of Bloomsbury Books.

'Wool Churches, Tudor Houses', from *East Anglia*, 1994, translated from the German, © Peter Sager. Reproduced by permission of Pallas Athene Books.

'Islands' from *Suffolk in the Middle Ages*, 1986, by Norman Scarfe, © Scarfe Charitable Trust. Reproduced by permission of Boydell and Brewer.

Sciapod, photo credit John James.

'Suffolk's Greatest Treasure', © Brough Scott 2021.

Extract 'The Sailors' Reading Room' from *The Rings of Saturn* by W.S. Sebald translated by Michael Hulse. © Vito von Eichborn Verlag GmbH & Co. Verlag, Frankfurt am Main, 1995. English translation © Michael Hulse, 1998. Published by Vintage. Extract reproduced by permission of The Random House Group Ltd.

'The Tractor Boys', © David Sheepshanks 2021.

'Castle on the Hill' lyrics by Ed Sheeran and Benjamin Levin, © 2017 Please Don't Forget To Pay Me Music/Sony/ATV Music/Publishing/ Universal/MCA Music Limited. Reproduced by permission of Ed Sheeran MBE.

New Thatch at Grove Farm Barn, photograph, © Andrew Smiley 2012.

'The Wolf Pits', revised retelling from *The Last Woodwose*, © Thea Smiley 2021.

'Eliza Acton's Hot Punch Sauce', © Delia Smith 2021. *For Delia's steamed puddings, further recipes and Cookery School videos visit deliaonline.com.*

A Game of Cards, photograph reproduced with the permission of Southwold Sailors' Reading Room.

The Sutton Hoo helmet, photograph © The Trustees of the British Museum.

'Everything about Suffolk is Unexpected' from *Suffolk Scene*, Blackie and Son Ltd, 1939, © the Estate of Julian Tennyson. Reproduced by permission of Penelope Tennyson.

'Master Hugh and the Bury Bible', © Rod Thomson 2021.

Extract 'Lady Muck of the Vegetable World' from *The Road Home* by Rose Tremain. © Rose Tremain, 2007, published by Vintage. Extract reproduced by permission of The Random House Group Ltd.

'From Spitalfields to Sudbury', from *The Silk Family*, 2020, © Liz Trenow. Reproduced by
permission of Stephen Walters & Sons Ltd.

'A Safe Retreat', © Lucy Walker (a version of this chapter appeared originally on
brittenpearsarts.org)

Shingle Street, linocut, © Janet Watson 2021.

The Maharajah Duleep Singh, 1854, by Franz Xaver Winterhalter. Oil on canvas.
Reproduced by permission of the Royal Collection Trust / © Her Majesty Queen
Elizabeth II 2021.

The Warren Hill, c.1715 by John Wootton. Credit: Private Collection. Photo © Christie's
Images / Bridgeman Images.

'A12' from *The Toll*, 2017, © Luke Wright. Reproduced by permission of Penned in the
Margins.

'Royal Bury St Edmunds' © Francis Young 2021. Illustration 'Henry VI as a boy kneeling
at the tomb of St Edmund' from Harley MS 2278 f.4v English School, (15th century).
© British Library Board. All Rights Reserved / Bridgeman Images.

Thanks also go to:

Daphne Astor	Harriet Bailey	Louis Baum
Liz Calder	Christopher Edwards	Freddie Gage
Clare Greenwell	Nathan Hamilton	Tom Hester
Sam Denny Hodson	Gulshan Kayembe	Jonathan Marsden
Celandine Mitchell Cotts	Daniel Partridge	Hugh Pierce
Geoffrey Probert	Robert Rous	Henry Rowan Robinson
David Sheepshanks	Emma Shercliff	Enid Stephenson
Sesi Turnbull	Julius Walters	Frances Welch

A NOTE ON THE EDITORS

Elizabeth Burke read English at Cambridge and worked as a non-fiction editor in
publishing before moving to the BBC, where she won numerous awards for
her radio documentaries and became a Commissioning Editor for Radio 4.
She now runs *Private Passions* on BBC Radio 3 and adapts and produces new
books for Radio 4. She lives near Halesworth.

Dan Franklin read English and American Literature and History at UEA,
graduating in 1970. He held various jobs in publishing until appointed
Publishing Director of Jonathan Cape in 1993. He retired in 2019.
Dan Franklin was elected as an Honorary Fellow of the Royal Society of
Literature in 2019. He lives near Halesworth.

John and Mary James have run The Aldeburgh Bookshop since 2000 and the
Aldeburgh Literary Festival since 2002. Before then Mary was an antiquarian
bookseller with Bernard Quaritch and John was a chartered surveyor. They
live in Snape.

FESTIVAL
OF SUFFOLK
2022
RECOVER · RESET · RECHARGE

A NOTE FROM THE FESTIVAL OF SUFFOLK

All proceeds from the sale of this book will be directed to The Festival of Suffolk Legacy Fund administered by Suffolk Community Foundation.

SUFFOLK
Community
Foundation

Through the delivery of strategic grant-making programmes, the partnership between Festival and Foundation aims to support local voluntary sector organisations to engage their teams and communities with the Festival's aims and objectives.

It is hoped that support will be provided both in the lead up to the Festival and as an ongoing positive legacy for the people of Suffolk.

To find out more please visit www.suffolkcf.org.uk.